FIRST
DO NO HARM

FIRST
DO NO HARM

REFLECTIONS
ON BECOMING A NEUROSURGEON

J. Kenyon Rainer, M.D.

VILLARD BOOKS  *NEW YORK 1987*

All rights reserved under International and Pan-
American Copyright Conventions. Published in the
United States by Villard Books, a division of Random
House, Inc., New York, and simultaneously in Canada
by Random House of Canada Limited, Toronto.

Library of Congress Cataloging-in-Publication Data
Rainer, J. Kenyon, 1952–
First do no harm.
1. Rainer, J. Kenyon, 1952–
2. Neurosurgeons—United States—Biography.
3. Residents (Medicine)—United States—Biography.
I. Title.
RD592.9.R35A3 1987 617'.481'0924 [B] 87-2045
ISBN 0-394-55669-0

Manufactured in United States of America
9 8 7 6 5 4 3 2
First Edition

Book Design: Marie-Hélène Fredericks

For
LAURA AND JOHN
—I'll see you Saturday.

All names of doctors and patients have been changed. In addition, many of the identifying details have been altered in order to disguise identities.

If love is unspoken,
the heart lies listless,
paralyzed, and dying.

If love is only spoken,
the heart stirs
but remains feeble.

But with deeds,
the heart is healed
and arises from its litter.

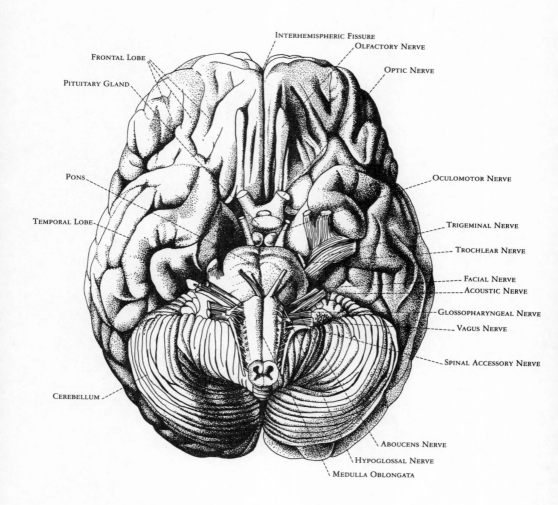

INTERHEMISPHERIC FISSURE
OLFACTORY NERVE
OPTIC NERVE
FRONTAL LOBE
PITUITARY GLAND
OCULOMOTOR NERVE
PONS
TRIGEMINAL NERVE
TEMPORAL LOBE
TROCHLEAR NERVE
FACIAL NERVE
ACOUSTIC NERVE
GLOSSOPHARYNGEAL NERVE
VAGUS NERVE
SPINAL ACCESSORY NERVE
CEREBELLUM
ABOUCENS NERVE
HYPOGLOSSAL NERVE
MEDULLA OBLONGATA

CONTENTS

BEGINNINGS

PART I

CHAPTER 1

I DO SOLEMNLY SWEAR

YELLOW BRAIN oozed like toothpaste from the right ear. Warm blood dripped from the left ear down the earlobe and puddled onto a sheet under the patient's head. Both his eyes were black and swollen shut, and his fractured, disfigured face wiggled and crunched when I touched it. A deep laceration extending from ear to ear across the top of his head was partially hidden by thick brown hair matted with dried blood. His torn blue denim work shirt was blood soaked and littered with chipped teeth. His chest barely moved with each weak breath, and his heart fluttered, paused, and then continued with irregular beats. Nurses cut his overalls away, inserted an IV into each arm, and passed a Foley catheter into his bladder. Emergency room interns searched for additional injuries, but except for the head injury they found none. From the neck down there wasn't a single cut, bruise, or broken bone.

"What happened to this guy?" asked Bill Walker, the chief resident in neurosurgery at the University of Alabama Medical Center.

3

"Fell off a tractor," a nurse answered. "The paramedics said the bush hog he was clearing fields with ran over his head."

"Better trach him, he's about to quit breathing," Walker said to the intern. "Might as well learn how to do one. I'll help you through it."

Walker tilted the man's head back, exposing his neck, and pointed just below the Adam's apple. "Make a three-inch incision here, split the muscle, stay out of the thyroid, and make a one-inch cut through a tracheal ring."

Forty-five seconds later the intern had opened a dime-sized hole in the trachea and inserted a plastic tube. Oxygen flowed into the patient's lungs and changed his blue, cyanotic color to pink. His heart reverted to its normal rhythm and again contracted steadily, pumping blood throughout his body and raising his blood pressure from shock to a safe 130/80. The oxygen sweeping through his body brightened the blood dripping from his ear. He was now stable, out of shock, and receiving sufficient oxygen from a respirator.

"What's his name?" asked Walker.

"O. E. Jenkins," answered the paramedic. "He farms two thousand acres of cotton south of Birmingham."

"How do you fall off a tractor?" Walker asked as he shaved the farmer's head, trying to discover the extent of the laceration.

"His wife said a screw supporting the seat popped loose and threw him backwards off the tractor and under the bush hog blade. Think he'll live, Doc?" asked the paramedic.

"Don't know yet," answered Walker. "He's got a depressed skull fracture across the top of his head, blood clots compressing both sides of the brain, facial fractures, and dirt, hay, hair, and pieces of his hat in his brain. I'll know more after

4

surgery. Ask his wife to step back to the nurses' station so I can talk to her."

Dr. Walker turned his attention to the patient while he waited for Mrs. Jenkins. He instructed the interns to type and cross-match four units of blood for surgery and ordered antibiotics, a tetanus shot, a chest X ray, a complete blood count including hematocrit and hemoglobin, a blood chemistry profile, and arterial blood gases to monitor the oxygen concentration in the blood. Next he ordered Decadron, a steroid used to reduce brain swelling, and started mannitol intravenously to shrink the patient's brain so permanent damage wouldn't result from the pressure building inside his head from the blood clots pressing on the brain. In fifteen minutes the preoperative checklist of blood studies, X rays, and drugs had been completed and Mr. Jenkins was ready to be taken to the operating room. An intern reminded Dr. Walker that an EKG hadn't been done. They saw me standing in the corner of the trauma room.

"We need an EKG stat," the intern said. I stayed in the corner with my hands folded in front of me. I was reluctant to assist since I was so inexperienced. "We need an EKG," the intern repeated. "Are you an EKG technician?"

"No," I said. "I'm a senior medical student on an emergency room elective."

"Can you do EKGs?" he asked.

"Yes."

"Then do one on this patient," the intern said.

"And when you finish it," Dr. Walker added, "tell me what it says. I've forgotten how to read those things."

"Yes, sir," I answered as I pasted electrodes on Mr. Jenkins' chest. Three minutes later I took the completed EKG out to

5

the nurses' station to show Dr. Walker. He was standing outside the trauma room talking to Mrs. Jenkins as an intern and two nurses listened.

"He has a fractured skull," Dr. Walker told her. "There are blood clots and debris in the brain that must be removed. His facial bones are fractured and we did a tracheostomy to keep him breathing. We have to operate, clean up the wound, and remove the blood clots from the brain. It's a terrible injury, Mrs. Jenkins. He may not make it."

"May I please see him before you take him to surgery?" Mrs. Jenkins asked.

"Of course," Dr. Walker answered and guided her to the stretcher in the trauma room where her husband lay naked and unconscious. She leaned over and kissed his cheek, but he didn't respond. The nurses took her out of the room and Dr. Walker motioned the intern to take Mr. Jenkins to the operating room.

"The EKG's normal," I told Dr. Walker.

"Thanks," he said. "Interested in scrubbing in on the surgery?"

"Sure!" I answered quickly, excited by the prospect of helping on a brain operation instead of just watching one.

I helped the intern push Mr. Jenkins' stretcher into the elevator, banging the IV poles and bottles against the walls. A minute later the elevator doors opened outside the operating room on the seventh floor of University Hospital. The intern and I were already dressed in green scrub suits, so we only needed to put on surgical caps, masks, and shoe covers before wheeling Mr. Jenkins back to operating room 8, the neurosurgical suite. Room 8 was cold. The thermostat was set at fifty-five degrees.

"Dr. Walker likes it chilly," the intern said when he saw me look at the thermostat. "It's harder to concentrate when it's hot."

The anesthesiologist and nurses mumbled hello and helped us slide Mr. Jenkins from the stretcher onto the narrow operating table. Nurses stripped the bloody sheets off the stretcher and pushed it back out into the hall. Since Mr. Jenkins was already comatose, an anesthetic wasn't necessary and we didn't have to wait for the anesthesiologist to put the patient to sleep. The anesthesiologist checked the tracheostomy tube, the Foley catheter, and the IV lines and then said, "Have at it, boys."

"Boys" was the slang term applied to the house staff at University Hospital. It was used for interns and residents to remind them they weren't fully trained doctors. Medical students weren't addressed at all. Chief residents, by contrast, were called by their first names, indicating acceptance as a peer by the staff attending physicians.

Bill Walker entered the operating room as the intern and I positioned Mr. Jenkins' head in the Mayfield headrest, a large metal C clamp. We then tightened three steel pins through the scalp and firmly into the skull to hold the head steady. I shuddered as the pins ground into the head, reminding me of a horror movie torture chamber in the depths of a castle. Mr. Jenkins lay flat on his back, his head immobile in the headrest, eyes taped shut, six bright spotlights overhead. Bill Walker pulled a Polaroid camera from the shelf and snapped three close-up pictures of the injured head.

"For the lawyers," Walker said.

"What do you mean?" I asked.

"Someone will get sued for this," he answered. "Either the company that makes the steel screw that popped out of the seat or the manufacturer of the tractor."

"Or you, Bill," the anesthesiologist said.

"That's why I'm taking the pictures," Walker answered. "To protect myself, so if there are any complications the lawyers will know what a mess I was operating on."

"Well, quit taking pictures and get on with the operation," the anesthesiologist said. "I'm planning on taking my family out for dinner tonight. I don't want to spend the whole night passing gas on a dead head."

"Dammit! Don't give up on this man!" Walker snapped at the anesthesiologist. "He may do better than you think."

The intern left for the emergency room to see another accident victim. Bill Walker and I scrubbed our hands for ten minutes at the stainless steel scrub sink, from where we could see O.R. 8 through a glass wall. Nurses washed Mr. Jenkins' shaved head with Betadine, leaving it coated brown and resembling a bowling ball. We entered the room with our wet hands up, allowing the water to drip down to our elbows and away from our clean hands. After we dried our hands with sterile towels, the nurses dressed us in green surgical gowns tied in back and stretched rubber gloves over our sleeves. Walker covered Mr. Jenkins' entire body with blue surgical sheets, leaving only his head exposed. The operation began at 4:30 P.M.

The ear-to-ear laceration was opened to the skull. The scalp was pulled down over his eyes and held with sterile fishhooks attached to rubber bands. As he punched eight quarter-sized burr holes through the skull with an air drill, Bill Walker was careful not to plunge through the bone and into the brain. Next, he passed a Gigli saw wire underneath the skull but above the brain and pulled each end of the wire out of a burr hole. With the wire held stiff between his outstretched hands, he sawed back and forth, cutting the bone between the burr

8

holes. Heat from the saw burned the bone, and wisps of smoke drifted up from the head.

After all eight holes were connected, the entire beveled skull of the forehead was lifted free from the rest of the head, like taking the top off a teapot. Bill Walker dropped the bone flap into a basin of Betadine, which he put onto a Mayo stand away from the operating field. With the skull removed, the covering of the brain, the dura mater, was visible. The dura was discolored from its normal gray to deep blue because of the blood clot beneath it. Stretched tight from the pressure of the blood clot in the brain, the dura looked like the belly of a tick swollen with blood.

"Why don't you open the dura?" Walker asked me.

"No, thanks. I don't want to cut the brain by accident," I answered.

"Don't worry, you won't," he assured me. "The clot has the brain pushed away. You won't hit it."

"Okay," I said. The nurse handed me a clean knife. I cut the dura, and immediately hematoma poured out of the brain. The black clot looked like grape jelly. Walker held a sucker in his right hand and a syringe full of saline in his left. The blood clot, three inches thick and extending over both frontal lobes of the brain, broke into pieces as he irrigated it with water and sucked it away from the brain. The normally pale yellow convolutions of the brain were irritated and red. However, once the subdural hematoma was evacuated and the pressure in the head was relieved, the brain began to pulsate rhythmically with each heart beat.

"Pulsations are a good sign," Walker explained. "Means we've got the pressure in the head back to normal."

Bill Walker continued cleaning the brain, removing the dirt and hair that had been driven by the bush hog blade through

9

the open skull fracture into the brain. He retracted the left frontal lobe and found pieces of the baseball cap Mr. Jenkins had been wearing. He pulled out pieces of hay, twigs, and bits of cow manure from the brain.

"Think this wound will get infected?" I asked.

"It might," Walker answered. "But usually they don't. We'll irrigate it with antibiotics, and if we get all the debris out, he probably won't develop a brain abscess."

"Are you about through, Bill?" the anesthesiologist asked. "It's seven-thirty and I can still make dinner if you'll hurry."

"I'm more concerned about this patient than your dinner," Walker said.

"Some of us don't want the glory of being a brain surgeon. We want to have some free time for other things," the anesthesiologist said.

"I know; I like to do other things too," Walker said. "But we're here working on a Friday night; let's just make the best of it and give this man a good operation."

By 8 P.M. Walker had finished removing all the debris from the brain, which was now relaxed and pulsating, glistening in the foamy antibiotic solution he poured onto it.

"That's where he talks," Walker told me as he pointed to the inferior frontal gyrus in the left hemisphere of the brain. "That's where he laughs and cries," pointing to the left frontal lobe, which he explained controlled emotion. "And that," Walker said, pointing to an area of brain deep between the two cerebral hemispheres, "is where he lives. That's the hypothalamus. Mess that up and your patient remains in a coma or dies." I noticed Bill Walker's hands were steady as he pointed to the hypothalamus, but he wouldn't touch it. He respected the brain and touched only those areas he had to to complete the operation.

10

"Okay, we're through. Let's close his head," Walker said.

First he closed the dura, which felt like construction paper, with fifty black silk sutures. He retrieved the bone flap from the back Mayo stand and tied it into the skull with steel wire. He then closed the scalp with two layers of stitches, and by 9 P.M. the operation was over. Walker wrapped the head with sponges and a brown Ace bandage. We rolled Mr. Jenkins to the recovery room, sat down with the nurses, and drank coffee while we waited for him to wake up. The anesthesiologist left to meet his family for dinner. He didn't stop by the recovery room to check on the patient on his way out of the hospital.

"Incredible injury," a nurse remarked. "It's amazing anyone can survive that kind of head trauma."

"It sure is, but you never know with head injuries," Bill said. "You have to give every patient a try. Sometimes you get somebody back that would have died if you had given up."

By 10 P.M. Mr. Jenkins was restless, thrashing about in bed and beginning to wake up. I returned to the emergency room, where I was on duty, while Bill Walker remained in the recovery room to monitor Mr. Jenkins' condition. The next morning, about 6 A.M., I walked up to the recovery room to check on Mr. Jenkins.

"How's he doing?" I asked Bill Walker, who was standing at the nurses' desk, looking over Mr. Jenkins' chart.

"See for yourself," he answered.

I pulled the curtain back and saw Mr. Jenkins propped up in bed sipping orange juice.

"Son of a bitch!" I whispered.

"Surprised?" Bill Walker asked.

"I sure am," I mumbled. I continued staring at Mr. Jenkins, who was alert, not paralyzed, and talking to the nurse, who had already removed his tracheostomy tube.

11

"It's easy to tell you're not a surgeon," Bill Walker said to me.

"What do you mean?" I asked.

"Swearing, when you were surprised at how well Mr. Jenkins was doing," Bill explained. "A surgeon might curse a complication or death, but never a good result. Surgeons expect success."

I was off duty for twelve hours before my next E.R. shift, so I walked over to the Veterans Administration hospital to pick up my roommate, Chuck Barber, who needed a ride back to our apartment. I found him on Ward 7-A grilling Sharon Tucker, a third-year medical student. Sharon was dressed smartly in a navy blue dress and white lab coat, and her shoulder-length brown hair was pulled back into a ponytail. She was cleaning the lenses of her glasses with a corner of a bed sheet as she listened patiently to Chuck's criticism.

"You have to be more thorough with your histories and physical examinations," he was telling Sharon as I approached. "You should take the patient's blood pressure in both arms, standing up and lying down. You must record all scars on the patient, particularly those relating to previous operations, and you have to check the thyroid gland on everyone." Chuck stopped talking to Sharon when the staff attending physician, chief resident, junior residents, and interns appeared for teaching rounds.

"What patient are you presenting this morning?" the attending physician asked Chuck.

"Sharon Tucker is presenting Mr. Miglaccio," Chuck answered.

I glanced at Sharon. She was caught off guard and nervously fumbled for some notes in her coat pocket. She had just finished her second year of medical school and had been working in the hospital only two weeks. She grabbed the patient's chart as the other doctors walked to Mr. Miglaccio's bedside. Chuck pulled back the curtain, allowing the ten of us to circle the bed. Chuck introduced the patient to the attending physician and chief resident, and then nodded to Sharon to begin.

"Mr. Miglaccio is a forty-eight-year-old Italian," Sharon began, "originally from New York and now a steel worker in Birmingham. His illness began with cough, shortness of breath, and a 104-degree fever. He smokes two packs of Camels a day and has hypertension and diabetes." Sharon touched his shoulder and instructed him to sit up in bed. She pointed to his right lower rib cage, where the lungs showed decreased breath sounds, suggesting a diagnosis of pneumonia. It was obvious that Sharon had been thorough with her examination, and her presentation was excellent. Knowing Chuck was looking for weaknesses in her presentation, she was sure to include the facts that the rectal examination was normal and that the patient had normal male genitalia. She noted a well-healed hernia incision on the right lower abdomen, confirming to all the doctors at the bedside that she had examined Mr. Miglaccio completely.

Chuck looked across the bed at Sharon and said, "You should be more complete in describing the physical examination. You didn't tell us how long Mr. Miglaccio's penis is." All the doctors smiled. They had seen other students caught on this joke before, particularly female students, who were embarrassed to unroll a tape measure and check the length of a man's penis. None of the doctors offered Sharon assistance; it was part of being a medical student.

"Mr. Miglaccio's penis is fourteen inches long," Sharon

answered without hesitation. The patient chuckled. The doctors looked surprised, doubting Sharon had measured it. Chuck called her bluff.

"I measured his penis myself," Chuck asserted. "It's only four inches long!"

The attending physician frowned, disappointed Sharon had bluffed instead of simply admitting she hadn't checked the length of the patient's penis.

"Well, I'm sorry, Dr. Barber, but you're wrong," Sharon argued. "I guess you just don't know how to hold it right!"

The uproar of laughter from doctors and patients echoed throughout the ward and brought nurses running from the nurses' station. Chuck's red face lasted only a few minutes, but Sharon's broad smile persisted all afternoon.

Even though I was tired after being awake for thirty-six hours in the E.R. and operating room, I was unable to sleep as I stretched out on the bed in my efficiency apartment on Birmingham's south side. The seventy-five-dollar-a-month room had a bathroom, kitchenette, and enough space for one double bed and a chest of drawers. I stored my books under the bed and balanced my portable TV on the window sill. I had plenty of room to myself, but some of the married students complained of the cramped quarters. The apartment's main advantage was that it was within walking distance of the hospital, which occasionally allowed students to eat dinner at home when there were no emergencies on the wards.

I continued to think about last night's operation. With only three weeks left in medical school, I would soon be an intern responsible for critically injured patients like Mr. Jenkins. The last four years had given me volumes of medical knowledge but little medical training; facts, but few skills.

14

In our first year of medical school, 124 other freshman students and I had memorized reams of trivia in biochemistry, histology, and gross anatomy. In biochemistry we sat in an ampitheater for two hours each morning from 8 to 10 A.M., copying complex chemical reactions from the chalkboard as Professor Kenzie explained the intricacies of the metabolism of nutrients, such as the breakdown of glycogen into glucose, which supplied the fuel to run the body's machinery. After a ten-minute break, we huddled for two hours over a microscope as we studied histology, the body's architecture on a cellular level. Then, an hour for lunch, usually eaten in the anatomy lab, as we reviewed the organs of the cadaver we had dissected the previous day. In our first year our afternoons, from 1 to 5 P.M., were spent dissecting cadavers—rows of men and women pickled in formalin, lying naked on stainless-steel tables with white neon light flooding their bodies—exposing their open chests, abdomens, and heads in various stages of exploration. Four medical students were assigned to each cadaver. Dressed in white coats to protect our clothes from the formalin, we enjoyed the afternoons feeling the slippery intestines in our fingers; the firm, muscular heart in our palms; the hard, fist-like uterus; and the soft, mushy brain quivering in our hands.

But no amount of study fully prepared us for the anatomy tests. We were required, by feel alone, to name bones hidden inside paper sacks and identify arteries and nerves that had been distorted from operations. Sometimes graduate teaching assistants, standing ten feet apart, flipped bones back and forth between themselves while we sat dutifully in our chairs trying to identify the bones as they sailed through the air. On one examination Professor Martin placed a pelvic bone on the laboratory table and asked if it was a male or female pelvis.

Chuck Barber climbed up on the table during the examination and lay down on top of the bone, pressing his hips firmly against the pelvis. He proclaimed it female, and was right.

The second year required more book work: physiology, pathology, microbiology, and pharmacology. Finally the clinical years arrived, with rotations on internal medicine, surgery, pediatrics, obstetrics and gynecology, psychiatry, and nine months of electives. Internal medicine doctors taught us how to diagnose disease and surgeons how to treat it, confirming the adage, internists know everything and do nothing, surgeons know nothing and do everything, pathologists know everything and do everything, but it's too late. Psychiatrists taught us nothing (except that frequent masturbation improves self-esteem) and confirmed my impression that all psychiatrists were either crazy or becoming crazy. And in four weeks I learned the entire dermatology specialty: if the rash is wet, put something dry on it; if the rash is dry, put something wet on it; if you don't know what the rash is, biopsy it.

After four years of medical education, I could name every bone in the body, every artery and nerve. I understood cellular metabolism and the use of glucose to provide energy for the body. I had memorized the side effects of a hundred drugs and could diagram the architecture of the kidney. I knew the immunizations required by children, the risk factors for stroke and heart attacks, and how to do an autopsy. I had passed dozens of medical examinations and two examinations by the National Board of Medical Examiners. I was a thoroughly programmed medical textbook, but I also knew that soon I would be a doctor, and no one had yet taught me how to take care of a man run over by a tractor.

When I awoke, it was 6 A.M. and time to return to the

emergency room. I had been off duty for twelve hours—six hours of free time to read, watch TV, or play tennis and six hours to sleep. Then, back to the hospital for another thirty-six hours of work. By 6:30 I was wandering through the blue-tiled halls bathed in artificial light, dodging the nurses and interns who moved about with purpose. I began my shift by glancing into each of the twenty examining rooms and returning to the patient who was bleeding most and seemed closest to dying. While standing in the corner, I listened carefully to the residents and interns as they discussed the care of the patient with the nurses. When they said someone needed to sew up the laceration and set the fractured arm, I volunteered. The interns knew I would say yes to anything, whether it was giving an enema or performing a tracheostomy, so it didn't surprise me when Bill Hardy, the E.R. intern, motioned me to come talk to him.

"I want you to cover my calls for an hour while I get new tires put on my car. Everything's closed when I get off at night."

"Sure," I answered. "What do I do?"

"Just hang around the admissions desk. Jill Lawrence, the head nurse, will tell you how to handle the emergencies," Bill explained. "I'll be back in about an hour."

The first three patients were not complicated. One man had been in a car wreck, was in shock, and had a broken pelvis. Jill called the admitting general surgery team, who arrived before I had finished putting an IV into his arm. Immediately they whisked him to surgery and I moved on to the next patient, a young boy who was short of breath and had a swollen foot from a bee sting reaction. Jill drew up a syringe of epinephrine, asked me if it was okay, I nodded yes, and she gave the injection. Minutes later the child was breathing normally. The third patient was a teenaged girl complaining of abdominal pain.

I pressed on her stomach with the palm of my hand, listened with my stethoscope, and then told Jill, "It's either appendicitis or a pelvic infection."

"It's gonorrhea," Jill answered.

"How do you know?" I asked.

"She comes in about every two weeks with the same thing," Jill explained. "Her boyfriend refuses to be treated with penicillin shots, so he keeps infecting her."

"Damn shame," I mumbled. "Who's next?"

"Room ten," Jill answered. "It's a patient with a brain tumor who's just arrived. He's having trouble breathing."

I walked down the hall to Room 10, wondering why Jill would put a critically ill patient so far from the nurses' station and main elevators. It was normally used for victims dead on arrival to the E.R. The small, windowless room was stuffy and poorly lit and felt cramped like a closet. There were no oxygen connections, no emergency drugs or equipment; just a stretcher and one pole light.

The patient lay unconscious on the stretcher, still dressed in his pajamas and bathrobe. He was fat and bald, and his pale, white skin was splotched with blue discolorations because his shallow breathing was providing insufficient oxygen for his body. The sheet beside his head was soiled from vomit, and underneath him it was stained from the loss of bowel control following a seizure. His urine, collecting in a bag attached to his leg, was brown and smelled infected. He was unshaven, his teeth were yellow, and his lips were cracked and covered with small, white sores.

"This is Mr. Turnham," Jill said from the doorway behind me. "He's fifty-eight and taught high school chemistry before the malignant brain tumor was diagnosed. He had a craniotomy eleven months ago. I watched Bill Walker do the operation. The malignancy had spread throughout the brain and he couldn't remove all of the tumor."

"Quick, get him some oxygen," I interrupted.

"There's no oxygen in this room," Jill answered.

"Then get some, dammit! He's about to quit breathing."

I scooped the vomit out of Mr. Turnham's mouth with the corner of the sheet and then pulled his jaw forward to help him breathe more deeply. I felt the pulse in his wrist. It was weak and irregular. His pupils didn't react to light, his skin was becoming cold, and saliva began bubbling out of his nostrils. I rushed over to the door, yanked it open, and yelled down the hall: "I need help; this man's dying!"

Immediately an intern and nurse ran down the hall. Halfway toward me they stopped abruptly. Bill Walker had just come in a back door and told them he would take care of it.

"Bill," I grabbed him by the sleeve and pulled him toward the room, "I'm glad to see you. This man's about to die and Jill won't even bring me some oxygen."

Bill stepped up to the head of the stretcher, pushed the hair back from Mr. Turnham's forehead, glanced at his eyes, and then squeezed his hand. Jill returned with a cart full of emergency equipment. Quickly I placed an oxygen mask over Mr. Turnham's face, pasted EKG electrodes on his chest, and turned on the cardiac monitor. It beeped irregularly as the heartbeats skipped wildly. And then there was one continuous noise and the monitor signaled a straight line, indicating Mr. Turnham's heart had stopped.

"Jill, give me a tube to breathe him, and intracardiac epinephrine, quickly!" I said.

Jill didn't move to help me and I looked up at Bill for help. "Let him go," Bill said quietly.

"I can get him back," I said. "Help me!"

"No," Bill answered. "Let him die."

"Our job is to help people live, not help them die," I pleaded. Now Mr. Turnham was cold and blue all over. The carotid arteries in his neck were no longer pulsating, and his chest had stopped moving.

"Our job is to prolong useful life," Bill said. "His life ended two months ago when he became comatose."

"Maybe his family doesn't agree," I argued.

"Why don't you ask them?" Bill suggested.

"I will."

Jill turned off the oxygen, unplugged the EKG wires, and turned off the cardiac monitor. While Bill wrote on the chart, she put fresh sheets on the stretcher. She removed the tube from Mr. Turnham's bladder, washed his face, cleaned his mouth, and combed his hair, then pulled the sheet up to his neck.

"Ask the family to come back to Room ten," Jill said into the intercom.

Bill met Mr. Turnham's wife and daughter in the hallway, greeted them warmly, and said, "We gave him nine good months, but I know the last two months were hard on you. I got to the room as his breathing and heart were giving out. I decided not to resuscitate him, and he passed away a few moments ago."

"I'm so thankful for the nine months you gave him," Mrs. Turnham said. "But when he went into a coma, and we couldn't feed him or keep him clean . . . he wouldn't have wanted to live like that."

Bill Walker put his arm around Mrs. Turnham as her daugh-

20

ter stepped into the examining room to say good-bye to her father. As I stood there uncomfortably, a nurse ran up and whispered to Jill: "Stab wound to the heart; unconscious."

"Go ahead and get started," Bill said to me. "I'll be there in a few minutes to help you."

The young black boy in Room 1 looked about twelve years old. He lay naked on the stretcher, a thin trickle of blood running down the left side of his chest. The cardiac monitor showed a straight line. His skin was cold, and his pupils were dilated and did not react to light. Jill put an IV into his arm as the other nurse took his blood pressure.

"No blood pressure," she reported.

I stood beside the boy, feeling for a pulse. He wasn't breathing, he had no blood pressure, he was cold, and his pupils didn't react to light, indicating there was no brain function.

"He's dead," I said.

Bill Walker came in as I told Jill to turn off the monitor. He glanced at the blood trickling down the boy's chest, felt the stab wound over the heart, and, without saying a word, took a needle and syringe from a shelf and stuck it into the boy's chest, immediately striking blood in the pericardial sac surrounding the heart. He withdrew the blood, and, with the pressure from the blood around the heart relieved, the heart began beating again. After injecting epinephrine into the boy's heart to strengthen its contractions, he took a knife, cut a twelve-inch incision in the boy's chest, cracked the ribs apart with a steel retractor, and exposed the heart as the boy lay on the stretcher. With the heart in sight and beating again, Bill found the hole the knife had left in the heart wall. He held the hole in the heart with his left hand, squeezed the heart with his right hand, and kept the heart pumping until cardiac surgeons moved the boy to the operating room to repair the damage. Within ten minutes, before he left the emergency room, the boy was moving his arms and legs and mumbling. It was obvious he would live and make a full recovery since there had not been any brain damage during the period of his cardiac arrest.

I left the examining room and wandered down the hall, discouraged that I had just proclaimed a boy dead who had been saved seconds later while I watched. Bill Walker caught up with me at the end of the hall and put his arm on my shoulder.

"Dammit, Bill," I mumbled, "I'll be a doctor in a few days, and I don't even know who to let die."

"Don't worry about it," he replied, "but from now on don't ever hesitate, or be afraid to act."

Graduation day, May 18, 1975, was hot and muggy. Four hundred people gathered in the municipal auditorium to attend the commencement exercises. The coolness inside was a welcome relief from the one-hundred-degree midday sun and smog. One hundred eighteen seniors paraded into the auditorium to the spontaneous applause of proud parents and spouses seated on each side of the center seats reserved for the graduates. My fiancée, Julie DeLoach, was sitting with my parents and brother. She looked the same as when I'd met her in college, five years before: slender, dark shoulder-length hair, light brown eyes, and a smiling, suntanned, freckled face with a dimple in her right cheek. She beamed and winked at me as I walked by.

Following the presentation of awards, the speeches, and a processional across the stage to receive our diplomas, the ceremony concluded with the recitation of the Hippocratic Oath.

"I would like all physicians to stand and repeat the oath after me," Dean Jacobs instructed.

The graduates stood together in a block in the center of the auditorium, and then thirty or forty parents who were also doctors stood up throughout the audience.

"I do solemnly swear by that which I hold most sacred:

"That I will be loyal to the profession of medicine and just and generous to its members;

"That I will lead my life and practice my art in uprightness and honor;

"That into whatsoever house I shall enter, it shall be for the good of the sick to the utmost of my power, I holding myself aloof from wrong, from corruption, and from the temptations of others to vice;

"That I will exercise my art solely for the cure of my patients, and will give no drug, perform no operation for a criminal purpose, even if solicited, for less suggest;

"That whatsoever I shall see or hear of the lives of men which is not fitting to be spoken, I will keep inviolably secret;

"These things I do promise, and in proportion as I am faithful to this my oath may happiness and good repute be ever mine—the opposite if I shall be forsworn."

The next morning I drove by Julie's apartment to say goodbye before I left Birmingham for Mobile to serve my internship in general surgery at the Mobile General Hospital. We had decided to wait one more year before marrying so she could complete her master's degree in education at the University of Alabama in Birmingham and I could complete the grueling year of internship. When I drove up, Julie was busy cleaning her apartment. Her hair was pulled back and held with a rubber band, and she was wearing shorts and the Mickey Mouse T-shirt I had bought her at Disney World during the Christmas holidays. We talked for a few minutes about when she could visit me in Mobile, then she put a sack lunch and letter on the front seat of my car. She hugged me tightly, kissed me quickly on the cheek, then ran back into her apartment. I could still see her waving from the doorway as I pulled my U-Haul trailer out of the parking lot.

I had completed four years of college and four years of medical school and had absorbed volumes of medical information. I anticipated the demands of the years ahead, but, after watching the earnest expressions of older physicians reciting the Hippocratic Oath, I had a hint of the unspoken rewards of medicine.

CHAPTER 2

ALL I CAN ASK

PRECISELY AT TWELVE midnight on June 30, 1975, as I sat in the lobby of the Mobile General Hospital, I heard screams on the second floor. The echoes drifted down the hall and staircase to the main hospital entrance, where I was sitting with five other surgery interns who had been told to report to duty on July 1 at 12:01 A.M. I pictured victims of a car wreck being carried into the emergency room, their mutilated arms and legs spurting blood as they cried for help. Bloody sheets; broken bones protruding through torn muscles and ripped skin; dry, heaving breaths from blue faces gasping for air. More yells, shrill cries, and high-pitched shrieks. An emergency amputation in the E.R. followed by a dull thud as the leg fell on the floor, or perhaps a wife called to the bedside to identify a cold, dead body lying stiff on a stainless steel table. A screech. A patient awake enough to count the fingers of his bleeding hand and finding two missing. And then, a giggle. Chuckling. Laughter? I looked up to the top of the staircase and saw five men in rumpled gray uniforms slapping each other on the back, smiling, and racing down the hall and stairs toward the front door of the hospital. They passed us in the lobby but said nothing as they flung open the front doors of the hospital, crawled into a station wagon, and disappeared beyond the last light in the parking lot. Again there was silence in the lobby, and only a faint, stale odor of dirty clothes remained of the group that had rushed by.

"I think we're their replacements," mumbled Coke Richards, who was sitting next to me, sipping the first of seven or eight Cokes he drank daily. He was short, stocky, and a muscular 220 pounds. He looked more like a wrestler than a doctor.

"You're right," answered Dr. Whiting, the chief of surgery, who was standing at the end of the lobby behind us. He was at least 6'2" tall, looked about fifty, had a brown crew cut, and was wearing a white coat which was unbuttoned, exposing his green surgical scrub suit.

"Those men just completed their internships," Dr. Whiting explained. "I hope you do as good a job as they did."

Dr. Whiting called out our names and handed each of us an envelope containing a key to our sleeping room and a list of our assignments for the next twelve months. My schedule read: July and August, General Surgery Silver Team; September and October, plastic surgery and burn service; November and December, emergency room; January and February, neurosurgery service; March and April, cardiac surgery service; May and June, General Surgery Gold Team. The Gold Team was Dr. Whiting's private service; the Silver Team was the charity service run by a chief resident.

"Two of the chief residents are in the operating room now, finishing an operation on a gunshot wound to the heart," Dr. Whiting said. "They'll meet you in the cafeteria in about an hour to show you around the hospital and explain the assignments."

26

Dr. Whiting was paged to return to the operating room, so Coke and I wandered through the hospital looking for our sleeping room while we waited to meet our chief resident, E. B. Crow. Coke's assignment card read the same as mine, and both of us had been given a key to Room 402. Apparently the six interns had been split up into three pairs, and Coke and I had been matched for the year.

The sleeping rooms, we learned from a nurse, were located in the old nursing dorm, a four-story brick building located a hundred yards behind the hospital. Interns were housed on the fourth floor, junior residents on the third floor, senior residents on the second floor, and chief residents on the ground floor. This perk for the older residents provided fewer stairs to run down when emergencies occurred in the hospital. The elevators in the building rarely worked or moved too slowly when they were functioning.

Room 402 was at the end of the hall, an envied corner room with two windows instead of one. Though eight by ten feet, it seemed smaller because of the dark walls, faint yellow ceiling light, and brown venetian blinds. A wooden nightstand under each window served as a desk, and two cots folded down from the closet. The walls were peeling and the floor was missing some squares of linoleum. An old black telephone with a circular, clicking dial sat on the floor between the cots. We had no complaints about the room: the sheets were clean and we decoyed the roaches by stationing empty Coke cans in the bathroom.

E. B. Crow didn't finish operating in an hour, as we had expected. It was 7 A.M. before Coke and I found him making rounds on the fifth floor with his General Surgery Silver Team. He was easy to spot: tall, lanky, and concentrating intensely as he checked each patient carefully. He was all business, no small talk, just as the nurses had described him. The two junior residents were reporting the progress of his patients, informing him of their temperature, urine output, hematocrit, and amount of drainage from various tubes in their chests and stomachs. E.B. then made the final decisions concerning each patient's care: how many units of blood to transfuse, which tubes could be pulled, which tubes were to stay in another day, what new X rays the patient needed. When his rounds were completed, E.B. looked at Coke and me and asked, "Are you the new interns?"

"Yes," I answered, shaking his hand.

"This morning I have a hernia and two gallbladders to do," E.B. said, skipping additional introductions. "Meet me in Surgery when you finish your work."

Chuck Blackfoot, a junior resident, handed me a sheet of paper and left the ward with the nurses and other doctors. His notes, made on morning rounds, contained a series of instructions. Pull the chest tube on 14A—gunshot wound to the abdomen. Put a subclavian IV line in 16—ulcerative colitis. Put a Foley catheter in 17—cancer of the prostate (nurses can't get it in). Put a nasogastric tube in 18—post-op appendix still vomiting. Transfuse two units of blood into 20C—stab wound to the chest. Do a proctoscopic examination and check a stool specimen for blood on 21B—suspected cancer of the colon. Change the dressings on 14, 18, 20, 23, and 26. Do a history and physical examination on 15, 19, and 22. Pull the old medical records on 22 and get his X rays for the afternoon conference.

"Coke, do you know how to pull chest tubes or put in subclavian IVs?"

"Haven't a clue. You know how to do a proctoscopic examination?"

28

"No," I said.

"Hell, at this rate, they'll have us doing open-heart surgery next week."

"We have to learn sometime, Coke."

"Yeah," Coke said, staring at our work list, "but if we do everything on this list, this hospital is going to look like a ghost town."

"Don't jinx us, Coke."

"Okay. But we need some help. Look for an old nurse."

Debbie Moore, the trim and tan, twenty-year-old day-shift head nurse, was the only one available to help us. She gathered up the tubes and other supplies necessary to complete our work list, then joined us on the ward as we prepared to work on our first patient.

"Now, Willie, this won't hurt a bit," I assured the young black man who had been stabbed in the chest as I yanked out the two-foot-long plastic tube in the right side of his chest. The tube popped out, followed by a trickle of blood down his bare chest.

"Jesus!" Willie screamed as he took a deep breath. His eyes rolled back in his head, he fainted, and then crumpled onto the floor.

"What in the hell happened?" I asked as I tried to revive the unconscious man lying on the floor.

"He sucked air back into his chest and collapsed his lung again, Doctor," Debbie said. "He probably has a bigger pneumothorax now than he did when he came into the E.R. I'd suggest you put a chest tube back in quickly."

Coke and I pulled Willie back into bed and forced another tube through his chest wall into the thoracic cavity surrounding his lungs. His breathing became more regular, and in a few minutes he regained consciousness.

"We'll pull this chest tube tomorrow," I said. Since I had nearly assassinated my first patient, I thought it best to let him rest awhile.

Coke, Debbie, and I moved on to the patient in 16. I had been told to put an IV line into the large subclavian vein running under the clavicle toward the heart. Coke volunteered to try to hit the vein with a large 14-gauge needle through which we would thread the plastic IV tubing into the vein and downward toward the right side of the heart.

"Here's the nail," Debbie said as she handed Coke the needle.

"Nail?" Coke asked, unfamiliar with the term. But when he looked at the needle he understood. Almost the size of a ballpoint pen, the needle resembled a large construction nail. Coke shoved the nail under the clavicle, pierced the vein, and, continuing too deeply, punctured the lung. The patient grabbed his chest, became short of breath, gasped from the collapsed lung, and became unresponsive.

"Ah, Debbie, I think we'll need a chest tube for this patient too," I said.

Coke withdrew the needle slightly, found the subclavian vein, and threaded the IV line through the vein into the heart. I put a chest tube between the second and third ribs below the clavicle, connected it to suction and withdrew the air trapped between the chest wall and lung that was keeping the lung collapsed. With the air removed, the lung reexpanded, and the patient, Coke, and I began breathing easier again. We secured the IV by suturing it to his chest wall with two silk stitches, put a dressing over the chest tube, and moved on to the next patient on our list.

Working through lunch until the 4 P.M. conference, Coke and I spent the next eight hours finishing our work list. We put our fingers into noses and mouths to insert nasogastric tubes to drain stomachs, probed rectums to dig out fecal impactions, cleaned colostomies, transfused blood, changed dressings, and examined new patients admitted to the ward. We started IVs, and by the end of the day every patient that needed an IV had one. We prided ourselves on the fact that we hadn't asked for any help from the senior residents. However, another patient had required a chest tube because we had collapsed his lung putting in a subclavian IV line. We rationalized the complications by reminding each other that we now knew how to insert chest tubes.

The last patient on our list was Emma Sue Jones, a 375-pound patient admitted for evaluation of rectal bleeding which had been present for several weeks. We were told to perform a proctoscopic examination of her colon to see if a cancer was causing the bleeding. Debbie positioned her across the table like a center bent over to snap a football. As Debbie pulled one buttock over and I held the other back, Coke inserted the proctoscope, an eighteen-inch, rigid metal tube, into her rectum.

"I see it!" Coke exclaimed a minute later. "It's a huge, reddish tumor. I'll biopsy it and make the diagnosis."

"Great, Coke," I said, "but quit admiring it and get the biopsy. Debbie and I can't hold her apart much longer."

"Okay," Coke said. "Hand me the biopsy forceps." I handed Coke the alligator forceps, well named for the two sharp jaws for biting tissue.

Coke inserted the forceps down the tube and biopsied the mass. Emma Sue screamed, which startled Debbie so much she let go of the buttock she was holding and it bounced against the side of Coke's head. Coke didn't notice since he was so excited about making his first diagnosis. He pulled the bleed-

31

ing red tissue out of the proctoscope and held it up for everyone to see, like a fisherman proud of his catch.

"Mind if I take a look?" Coke and I turned around to see E. B. Crow, our chief resident, standing behind us.

"Sure," Coke answered. "Can you believe the size of that cancer?"

E.B. glanced into the proctoscope, stepped back, and leaned against the wall. "Congratulations," E.B. sighed. "You just biopsied her cervix. You're not in her rectum, Doctor, you're in her vagina."

By 7 P.M. the conference and evening rounds were over. E.B., Blackfoot, and Coke left to go home. I was on duty, so I went to the intensive care unit to see what problems awaited me my first night on call.

The I.C.U. was a sixteen-bed open ward filled with the sickest patients in the hospital. The "unit" contained the immediate post-op patients who had undergone complicated surgery that day. Patients recovering from open-heart surgery, neurosurgery, and lengthy abdominal operations were transferred from the wards to the unit for closer monitoring following their operations. The ratio of nurses to patients in the unit was one to two. On the wards it was one to six and sometimes as little as one to eight.

The I.C.U. nurses had tremendous responsibilities. They constantly monitored blood pressure, cardiac rhythm, urine output, temperature, IVs, and drainage from different tubes but still found time to provide emotional support for the patients and their families. At night, when the staff doctors were at home, the nurses observed the patients for any change such as a falling blood pressure, a cardiac arrythmia, or an alteration in the level of consciousness and then relayed this information to the intern or resident on duty, who made a decision concerning treatment. The nurses' experience was invaluable as they explained surgical complications to interns and suggested treatment. I learned early that an intern is taught during the daytime by residents and staff doctors but at night by the nurses.

June and July on the Silver Surgery Team provided an excellent beginning for my internship. With the help of E. B. Crow, Chuck Blackfoot, the nurses, and Coke, I made rapid progress in the skills of medicine. After a month of inserting chest tubes, IVs, arterial lines to monitor blood pressure, and endotracheal tubes for cardiopulmonary resuscitation and performing tracheostomies, I was ready to begin operating. At first I was instructed how to lance boils and remove hemorrhoids, then how to do appendectomies and hernia repairs. Finally I removed a gallbladder complete with a gallstone trophy the size of a marble, which normally was given to the pathologist. Instead, I kept it as a souvenir.

My day on the Silver Team started at 4 A.M., when Coke and I made intern rounds. From 4 to 5:30 A.M. we changed dressings, removed stitches, made sure that laboratory studies ordered the previous day were on the chart, and generally checked the patients to make sure no one had died during the night. At 5:30 A.M., rounds began with Chuck Blackfoot, E. B. Crow, and a night nurse. Resident rounds were completed by 6:30 A.M., at which time the residents went to the cafeteria for a quick breakfast before the operating room schedule began at 7:15 A.M. Interns were not expected to eat breakfast until they had transported all patients scheduled for surgery to the operating room.

Interns on the General Surgery Silver Team were taught to operate mainly at night and on weekends. That was when most trauma occurred and the victims of car wrecks, gunshot wounds, and stabbings were brought to the hospital. Often two operations were going simultaneously. Coke would scrub with either E.B. or Chuck, and I would operate with the other. Many of these patients were saved, but those who were obviously dying provided the laboratory in which interns were taught how to close intestines ripped apart by shotgun blasts, sew up lacerated arteries and torn veins cut by broken windshields, and remove kidneys ruined by knife blades. The origin of surgery for Coke and me was not operating under the guidance of a skilled attending surgeon at eight o'clock in the morning; it was performing operations in the middle of the night on patients whose massive injuries foretold their deaths.

In September, the interns were split up and assigned individually to different teams. Coke rotated onto the Cardiac Surgery Service, and I was transferred to the plastic surgery and burn service. The more superficial first- and second-degree burns were handled on the wards by the Silver and Gold Surgery Teams, but the extensive third-degree burns were managed by the intern assigned to the burn unit. The charred skin inside the six-bed intensive care burn unit smelled like an empty fireplace, and the painful screams of patients being dipped into the whirlpool baths to remove dead skin echoed off the steel tanks. Dressing changes were so painful that patients were premedicated with morphine. Once a week a plastic surgeon in private practice in Mobile came to the hospital and guided the interns through the multitude of skin grafts required for burned patients.

The first weekend in September, six businessmen were burned extensively, sustaining third-degree burns over 70 percent of their bodies, when their private plane crashed north of Mobile. All were brought to the burn unit, and for sixteen to twenty hours a day, seven days a week, I removed their dead skin, peeling them like onions. I kept their IVs running, changed their dressings, skin-grafted them in surgery, and talked to their families. Six weeks after the plane crash and twenty skin grafts later, five of the men were dead. The sixth wished he were. I turned the burn unit over to Coke at 12 P.M. on Halloween night and never went back into it again. I had great respect for plastic surgeons but never again considered the specialty for my career. I was too frustrated by the inability of medical science to save patients with extensive burns.

My two-month assignment in the emergency room began on November 1. Everyone hated the dark hole, the "pit" as we called it, that served as the E.R. Located on the ground floor of the hospital, it had no windows and was poorly lit. The green tile floors were dirty and caked with reddish-brown dried blood. With the bloody bandages and moans, the E.R. resembled a war zone. The Mobile General Hospital was the charity hospital for the area and received all trauma victims along the Gulf Coast from Biloxi, Mississippi, to Pensacola, Florida. Critically injured patients benefited from being brought to Mobile because interns and residents were constantly on duty in the E.R. The prompt medical attention saved many patients who might have died at a nonteaching hospital because of the delay resulting from surgeons in private practice driving to the hospital from their offices or homes.

Shifts for interns were twenty-four hours on and twenty-four hours off. Sometimes shifts were assigned from noon to noon, and sometimes from midnight to midnight. Days became nights and nights, days. It was difficult to decide when to eat, sleep, and exercise. Since I didn't know anyone outside the hospital, I usually spent off hours walking around Mobile for several hours, studying the architecture of the well-

35

preserved antebellum homes. Then I napped in my apartment for a few hours before walking the two blocks back to the hospital to eat dinner with my friends who were on duty. After months of odd hours, I had lost twenty pounds and felt chronically fatigued. At 6'1" and 160 pounds, I weighed thirty pounds less than when I had graduated from high school seven years earlier.

Many of the patients brought to the hospital had knives and guns in their pockets and occasionally razor blades hidden in their hair, an additional weapon if grabbed by the head in a fight. Policemen stationed at the front doors of the E.R. disarmed patients before they were brought to us for treatment, but sometimes a patient slipped through who still had a knife or gun. Patients tried to keep their weapons, hoping for a chance to retaliate against the person who had shot or stabbed them, should that person also be in the emergency room. At times a knife or gun was pointed at an intern, ensuring prompt medical service. No one was ever seriously hurt, though. The only injury I recall was a slight cut on the arm of an inexperienced intern who inadvisedly squeezed the testicles of a man to see if he was in a coma. He wasn't; he was merely sleeping off the effects of a generous supply of wine.

There were two main halls in the pit, each with ten rooms. The rooms were twelve-by-twelve-foot squares with a stretcher in the center of the room, a pole lamp plugged into the wall, humming neon lights overhead, and floor-to-ceiling aluminum shelves containing suture, drugs, bandages, and rubber gloves. The hall closer to the ambulance ramp was for those dying quickly; the other hall, about thirty feet away from the main E.R. doors, was for those patients stable enough to last an hour or so until they could be treated. In the back of the E.R., three rooms connected the two parallel halls. These

36

rooms were reserved for patients who died: victims of sui-
cides, car wrecks, drownings, and drug overdoses. Here, interns were taught how to insert tubes and needles into different parts of the body, techniques that would later allow us to
save the lives of more fortunate trauma victims. In these rooms
our respect for life was born, as we learned the fraility of the
human body and the thin thread that separates life from death.

During each twenty-four-hour shift I evaluated, X-rayed,
diagnosed, and treated about a hundred patients. I sutured
lacerations, set broken bones, delivered babies, and treated
shock, gonorrhea, and pneumonia. I removed foreign bodies
such as dimes, buttons, and chicken bones that children had
swallowed, inhaled, or put into their rectums or vaginas. I
pumped stomachs clear of barbiturates from patients attempt-
ing suicide. I counseled rape victims. I treated chest pain, heart
attacks, emphysema and asthmatic attacks. Always there was a
steady stream of patients with a multitude of problems. One
minute I would give a patient a shot of Demerol to ease the
pain as he squirmed trying to pass a kidney stone; the next, I
would see a child complaining of earache and remove a roach
from against his eardrum.

Some patients, like the Silver twins, were well known to the
E.R. staff. The brothers, "Sterling" and "Quick," were fifty-
year-old alcoholics who lived at the Y.M.C.A. and worked at
the docks. Sterling was addicted to Darvon, a pain pill, and
Quick was addicted to Dalmane, a sleeping pill. Years ago
Sterling and Quick had learned that interns rotated out of the
E.R. every two months, so they would show up each time new
interns were assigned. They would fake some new complaint,
such as stomach pain or dizziness, and receive new prescriptions from the inexperienced interns. The nurses told me the
Silver brothers kept a written list in their pocket of complaints

that would prevent the policemen at the front door from turning them away. They put a check by complaints they had used recently so they wouldn't repeat themselves. Their favorite complaints included chest pain, vomiting blood, coughing up blood, passing blood, peeing blood. They had also complained in the past of having tuberculosis, cancer, and worms. No doctor or policeman had the courage to turn the Silvers away when they complained of bleeding, but I was ready for them when they came in on my shift.

Sterling was complaining of vomiting blood, and Quick said he felt weak. I told them to come into the examining room and I would check them both at the same time. They were identical twins, thin men with drawn, wrinkled faces, wearing T-shirts, blue jeans, and sneakers. Sterling and Quick sat on the stretcher, folded their arms across their chests, and studied me.

"First I need to take your temperature," I said. I sat down on the stool by the door and watched them as they patiently held the thermometers under their tongues. Three minutes later, as planned, a nurse stepped into the room to check their pulses. She pointed to the thermometers in their mouths and explained to me that red tips on thermometers meant they were for rectal temperatures only.

"You should have used the blue-tipped thermometers for oral temperatures," she said.

Sterling and Quick gagged, spit the thermometers out onto the floor, and stormed out of the examining room, cursing me.

"Sorry," I said, "I thought the thermometers were just rusty."

Another frequent visitor to the E.R. was Sister Angelica. She wore a nun's habit and came about every three weeks to be checked after she had been "raped." The first time I saw

38

her, she was wailing and rubbing her rosary beads. I spent two hours examining her and counseling her about contraception and the feelings of anger and guilt common to many rape victims. I felt more upset than she did as I talked in low, soothing tones. When she quit crying, she listened to me while she drank a Coke filled with peanuts.

"Where's the intern?" I heard E. B. Crow ask outside the room.

"In Room twelve with Sister Angelica," the nurse answered.

E.B. stuck his head in the room, smiled, and said, "Hi, Sister. Here for your penicillin?"

"Yeah," she answered. "As soon as the doc finishes talking."

"Give her a shot of Bicillin and get back out front," E.B. ordered. "We've got a car wreck coming in."

"Bicillin?" I repeated. "What's that for? She's been raped."

E.B. grabbed my arm, pulled me out into the hallway, and said, grinning, "Sister Angelica is a schizophrenic prostitute who works Dauphin Street. She hears voices and talks to God. Whenever she gets gonorrhea she comes to the E.R. and says she's been raped."

"Jesus!" I said.

"Is He here?" shouted Sister Angelica from inside the room.

E.B. and I walked out to the ambulance ramp just as the first car wreck victims were unloaded from the ambulance. Two were blue, their mouths open, already dead. A third was awake, screaming, and bleeding from a deep laceration through his shoulder. The fourth person in the car, a young woman of about twenty-five, was in the best shape. She was awake and complaining of soreness from head to toe but wasn't in shock or severe pain. E.B. applied pressure to the man's bleeding shoulder and told me to take care of the girl.

Eva Roberts wasn't very different from a hundred other patients I had treated in the emergency room following car wrecks. She had briefly been knocked unconscious following the impact of the two cars. She was bruised and scratched all over her body, but I saw no broken bones on her X rays, and there was no internal bleeding. After observing her for four hours in the E.R. and repeating her blood count to be sure she wasn't bleeding, I released her to go home.

Several days later, the typed radiologist's report on Eva Roberts reached my X-ray box, and I read, with horror, his report of a badly fractured ankle which I had missed on the X rays the night I had seen her. I pulled her chart from the emergency room files, wrote down her telephone number, and prepared to call her. I began to dial the number, then hesitated, fearing I would only make matters worse for myself by calling to tell her that I had just discovered how badly her ankle was broken. I felt she probably had already obtained a second opinion, and, most likely, had received proper treatment from an orthopedic surgeon. If I called now, I feared it might provoke her and prompt a malpractice suit. But what if she had not gone to another doctor? What if she were still lying in bed with her foot elevated, as I had instructed her, waiting for her sprained ankle to get well? As I considered the choice, I thought of a lesson I had learned from my father while I was in college.

In the summer of 1969, six years earlier, my brother, Kelly, and I had stayed home while our parents vacationed in Florida. Kelly, who was two years older than I, was a junior at Auburn University, and I was a freshman. The weekend

40

before Mother and Dad were to return, we opened our house to our fraternity brothers for a Saturday night party.

About midnight we heard a crunch in the driveway, and we smelled smoke. Kelly and I walked outside to find two cars had locked bumpers, the result of a drunk who had backed into a car parked behind him. Unfortunately, the smoke was coming not from the cars, but from the air-conditioning unit, which was on fire.

"You idiot!" Kelly screamed at me. "I told you that was a goddamn stupid idea!" I had turned the thermostat in the house down to fifty degrees, making it so cold that all the girls had been forced to snuggle under blankets with their boyfriends to keep warm.

As Kelly continued yelling at me, a third car pulled into the driveway. "Turn those bright lights off," Kelly shouted at the driver, who courteously obeyed.

A moment later, the couple got out of the car and walked to where Kelly and I were smothering the fire with blankets.

"What's going on here?" Kelly and I didn't have to look up to see who had asked the question. It was our father, home a day early from vacation. He loomed above us, clenching his fists and hissing through gritted teeth as he struggled to control his rage.

Dad didn't wait for an answer. He guided Mother away from the window where she was cautiously peeking into the house. I glimpsed her shocked expression and pale face as she walked by. Kelly and I, standing by the back door, could hear Mother ranting in the den and Dad growling in the living room as they ordered the partially clad couples sprawled on the floor and sofas out of the house. Then we heard a scream. Mother had found one last couple astride in her own bed. As

41

Dad calmed Mother, Kelly and I used the time to pick up the remaining beer cans and clothes scattered throughout the house.

"You've really screwed up this time," Kelly whispered to me as he pulled a sweater out from under one of the sofa cushions. "I told you not to let the fraternity know Mother and Dad were gone."

"You're not blaming this on me," I retorted. "Dad's been mad at you for two months, ever since you made a D in physics."

After the tow truck had pulled the two locked cars out of the driveway, Dad came outside to talk to us.

"It makes me mad that you boys had a party here when you knew you weren't supposed to," Dad said, his flat top bristling. "It makes me mad that you trashed the house and burned up the air conditioner. And it makes me mad as hell that a bunch of college kids were using my house as a motel, but it goddamn infuriates me that they were screwing in your own mother's bed!"

Kelly and I remained standing at attention, our faces pale in the early morning moonlight.

Dad glared at each of us for several seconds and then said, "I want both of you packed and out of this house before your mother wakes up in the morning."

"But," Kelly protested, "we don't have any money to pay for our college tuition. We don't have jobs. We don't even have a place to live."

"Besides," I added, "we couldn't possibly pack everything into our Volkswagen."

"You'll have plenty of room," Dad assured me.

Dad stormed into the house, threw a suitcase at each of us,

and then said, "You can take whatever you get in that suitcase. Everything else stays."

Packing went much quicker than we had anticipated as we left our stereos, books, bikes, and even our dog at home. Thirty minutes later we were on our way.

We napped in the car until dawn and then spent the morning looking for an apartment we could afford. Finally we found a trailer for forty-five dollars a month, on the outskirts of Auburn behind the Shoney's Big Boy restaurant. The main problems with living here, we both knew, were the frequent stabbings and shootings that occurred in this trailer park. But our financial situation outweighed the risks, so we decided to rent the trailer.

The trailer was perched unevenly on concrete blocks and hadn't been lived in for years. It was only twenty feet long, so the one window in its center provided enough light until we got the electricity turned on two days later. The rusty aluminum siding blended well with the red clay surrounding the trailer. Inside, the gold shag carpet was soggy and mildewed; the bare mattresses in each bedroom were stained. The ceiling was only six feet high, and we both had to stoop whenever we moved about.

I took a job at Lee County Hospital working as an orderly. Kelly chose to rely on the goodwill of his female acquaintances to keep him afloat. Consequently, there were always college girls around the trailer, although they were now considerably less impressed by our station in life. Loretta came over most often, bringing dinners from the dorm cafeteria where she served meals. Friends from our neighborhood came by on weekends with brownies Mother smuggled to us without Dad's knowledge.

Shortly before Christmas, six months after we had been evicted from home, Dad sent word to us through an intermediary that if Kelly and I thought we could show proper respect for our parents, our home, and the money they had spent for our college education, we could move back home. I was delighted; I could quit my job and wouldn't have to give any more enemas. Kelly was ecstatic; he wouldn't have to worry about missing any more meals. We gave the required fifteen minutes' notice at the trailer park and moved out that night.

Dad met us in the driveway. We walked stiffly toward him and then shook his hand as he welcomed us home. "All I can ask of you two boys," he said, "is that you be honest. If you're honest, you can keep our name good, no matter what may happen in your lives."

I looked back down at Eva Roberts' chart in front of me and decided to call her to tell her about her fractured ankle and make sure she had received correct treatment.

"Yes," Eva answered, "I went to an orthopedic surgeon the day after I saw you in the emergency room. It was such a bad fracture, he operated that afternoon and put pins in my ankle. I'm in a full leg cast now." The conversation seemed to last forever, although I'm sure it was brief.

"I'm glad you got it taken care of," I said. "I'm sorry I didn't see the fracture on the X ray."

"I'm sorry, too!" she replied angrily, then hung up the phone.

That night I reported the conversation to Dr. Whiting, the chief of surgery, who advised me that he would wait to contact the hospital attorney until he found out whether the patient had retained an attorney. Three days later, Dr. Whiting informed me that Eva Roberts' attorney had scheduled a meeting with us for the following morning. All night my stomach burned as I sat at the desk in my hospital room reviewing Eva's chart and worrying about the prospect of a malpractice suit and its adverse effect on my appointment to a surgical residency.

Dr. Whiting and I met Eva Roberts' attorney in the paneled hospital board room. Dr. Whiting sat at the head of the oblong mahogany conference table which seated twenty. I sat several seats away from Dr. Whiting, directly across the table from the attorney. A secretary sat behind us, making notes of the conversation as Dr. Whiting and the attorney discussed the supervision of interns working in the emergency room.

Finally the attorney put down his coffee, looked across the table at me and said, "Doctor, I was prepared to file a two-million-dollar medical malpractice suit against you, but my client changed her mind this morning. She said you were honest enough to call her to make sure she received proper medical care." The attorney paused, and then continued. "Doctor," he drawled, "you have a lot of luck."

To avoid an argument with the attorney, I said nothing. Odd, I thought. I've made a thousand correct diagnoses and never received any money or even a compliment. I miss one diagnosis, and a lawyer wants two million dollars. I wondered, too: how many lawyers would still be in practice if every mistake cost them two million dollars? How many lawyers could stay awake thirty-six out of every forty-eight hours, seven days a week, and never make a mistake? When it was clear that neither I nor the attorney had anything else to say, Dr. Whiting dismissed me.

As I went back to work on the ward, I continued to think about what the attorney had said. "Luck," he had called it. Maybe, I thought to myself; but I believe my father would have called it integrity.

CHAPTER 3

TO KNOW IS SCIENCE

IN THE SHADOWY back hallway of the emergency room, Coke Richards tilted the man's head back, turned on the suction machine to clear his mouth of saliva, passed a tube into his windpipe, and connected it to a respirator. The machine moved the man's chest, expanded his lungs, and breathed for him, but his ashen complexion didn't change. I plunged a needle between his ribs, lodged it in his heart and injected stimulants as I watched the cardiac monitor on the wall above me. A straight line; no heartbeat at all. Coke threaded an IV through the subclavian vein into the heart and flooded glucose and fluids into the vein. Still no blood pressure. I inserted a catheter into the bladder, and Coke slid a tube through the man's nose into his stomach to empty it. Together we cracked the ribs apart and opened his chest beside the bullet wound over his heart. I squeezed the heart with my gloved hand for a few minutes, then stepped back while Coke took over. I reached for a knife to open the man's abdomen where several other bullet holes were located but paused when E. B. Crow stepped into the room.

46

"That's enough," E.B. said. "The morticians from the funeral home are complaining that you've kept them waiting forty-five minutes while you practiced on their stiff. Give them the body; they've got work to do too."

Coke and I pulled the tubes out and followed E.B. outside the emergency room to the ambulance ramp. The soggy January evening was warm, with no hint of winter. We stood in our shirtsleeves, sipping coffee, as E.B. told us about the car wreck victims en route to the hospital.

"The paramedics called on the C.B. radio a few minutes ago to tell us to be ready," E.B. said. "There was a two-car, head-on collision on Government Street. Two people are dead. They're bringing in the other three. One man is in shock from an amputated leg. I'll take care of him. A woman with a broken arm is awake and talking. Coke, you take care of her. The other man is unconscious with an obvious head injury. The neurosurgery service will take care of him. Aren't you the intern on the brain team now?" E.B. asked me.

"Yes," I answered. "This is my first week."

"Well, do what you can," E.B. said. "Get the blood work, chest X ray, EKG, skull X rays, and CT scan of the man's head; then call the neurosurgeon on call for the emergency room to find out what to do next."

The first patient carried out of the ambulance was E.B.'s. A bleeding knee was all that remained of his left leg. The second patient was crying and writhing on the stretcher, a white splinter of bone protruding through the skin of her right arm.

"The other man is still pinned behind the steering wheel," the paramedic informed E.B. "He's unconscious but his breathing and blood pressure are stable."

"Okay," E.B. answered. "We'll have a doctor waiting for him when you cut him free."

E.B. and Coke disappeared with their patients into the emergency room. I sat down on the edge of the ramp, waited for the ambulance to return, and thought about my patient: an unconscious, critically injured man who probably had a blood clot in his head that would require brain surgery. Ironic, I thought: an intern with no experience practicing a five-thousand-year-old specialty perfected by famous physicians: Hippocrates, Celsus, Galen, Vesalius, Paré, Horsley, Cushing, Dandy.

Neurosurgery was a new field to me but a specialty whose Stone Age origin predated all written records of history's most celebrated surgeons. Three thousand years before the birth of Christ, the ancient Incas had treated war injuries by cutting holes into the skulls of fallen warriors, either as a surgical attempt to save lives or as a religious rite, before burying them near the great mountain fortresses. The Edwin Smith Papyrus, dating from 1700 B.C., described skull fractures and convolutions of the brain, and recognized the hopeless prognosis of paralyzing spinal cord injuries following dislocated, crushed vertebrae. Hippocrates, writing in 400 B.C., first recorded a systematic approach to the treatment of head injuries: opening the skull (trephining) over skull fractures, closure of the scalp, and dressing the wound.

In 30 B.C., Celsus, physician to the Roman emperors Tiberius and Caligula, detailed the ominous signs of head injury —wandering of the mind, vomiting, visual loss, bleeding from the nose or ears, and paralysis. Galen (A.D. 131–201), physician to the gladiators at Pergamon in Asia Minor, examined gladiators' wounds—since dissection of cadavers was tabooed—and advanced the treatment of head injuries by developing a trephine which wouldn't plunge into the brain and by paying more attention to closure of wounds with silk, linen, and catgut. His writings remained unquestioned for nearly thirteen centuries, until the Renaissance.

During this revival of learning, Vesalius (1514–1564) advanced medical knowledge through his keen interest in anatomy and emphasis on human dissection. The only bodies legally available to him for study were those of executed criminals, which were difficult to study because many had been tortured, dismembered, or decapitated. By careful anatomical observation on stolen bodies, Vesalius corrected many of Galen's anatomical errors. Paré (1510–1590) contributed to the surgery of the brain by applying skilled art rather than new information and summed up his contributions to medicine by saying, "I have labored more than forty years to throw light on the art of surgery and bring it to perfection."

No major advancements in surgery emerged until the advent of anesthesia and antisepsis three hundred years later. The demonstration of ether in 1846 and chloroform in 1848 as anesthetic agents, and the description of the antiseptic method by Lister in 1867, revolutionized surgical therapy.

In 1884, the first recorded removal of a brain tumor was done in London by Sir Rickman Godlee. The patient died a month later from meningitis. By 1890, neurosurgery emerged as a surgical specialty when Sir Victor Horsley, operating at the National Hospital for the Paralyzed and Epileptic, Queen Square, began devoting the bulk of his time to surgery of the brain and spinal cord.

Neurosurgery was propelled into the twentieth century by Harvey Cushing (1869–1939), Yale graduate, Harvard M.D., and Johns Hopkins surgical resident, who operated on more than two thousand brain tumors in twenty-five years. His pupil, pioneer neurosurgeon Walter Dandy, was an assistant resident surgeon on Cushing's service at Hopkins. A personality clash and quarrel between them climaxed when Cushing, who had accepted the chair of surgery at Harvard in 1912, told Dandy he would not take him to Boston to continue his training. Dandy remained at Hopkins and made his own significant contribution to neurosurgery, particularly in the diagnosis and removal of brain tumors, which he described in 160 articles and eight books.

Watching the ambulance race into the parking lot and back up to the emergency room door, I prepared to attend the head-injured patient lying unconscious inside. He was pale and barely breathing. I wished I could be sure of giving him proper treatment, but I was an intern with only three days of neurosurgical experience. Where were the three thousand neurosurgeons in the United States now? Why couldn't one be here to attend this man? I wheeled him into the closest trauma room and cut his shirt and pants away to look for other injuries. He was in shock, but his blood pressure improved with IV fluids. His breathing was shallow but sufficient when oxygen was added. I shaved his head, letting the matted hair drop to the floor as I held pressure on the arteries pouring blood from the cut behind his left ear. I drew his blood work and rolled him quickly into the X-ray department. He was comatose, bloody, paralyzed. But at least he stood a chance. In 1910 he would have died. Then there were only four neurosurgeons in the country, none of them in Mobile.

"His name's Robert Simpson," the paramedic said.

"How did the accident happen?" I asked.

"He swerved across the median and hit the other car head-on."

"Was he speeding?"

"No."

"Drunk?"

"No."

"Think it was a suicide attempt?" I asked.

"No," the paramedic answered. "His wife and daughters are outside. They said nothing's bothering him. He teaches biology at Sacred Heart High School and was on his way to a basketball game."

The X-ray technician completed the skull X rays and hung them on a view box for me to see. There was a jagged skull fracture behind his left ear. The chest X ray showed several rib fractures but no heart or lung injury, so we carefully moved Mr. Simpson into the CT scanner to check for blood clots in the brain. Twenty minutes later the CT scan was completed and produced pictures of the inside of the brain as clear as Polaroid snapshots. There was a blood clot the size of an orange pressing on the frontal and temporal lobes of the brain directly beneath the scalp laceration and skull fracture next to his left ear. The blood clot had pushed the brain toward the opposite side of the skull, leaving the brain indented as if an orange had been pressed into clay. The blood clot would have to be removed to reduce the pressure on the brain if Mr. Simpson were to have any chance of living.

I moved Mr. Simpson back to his stretcher and pushed him to the emergency room to make final preparations before surgery. He needed a blood transfusion, antibiotics, a tetanus shot, and an EKG. While the nurses administered the medications, I walked out to the waiting room to talk with Mr. Simpson's wife and daughters.

The waiting area was an old trauma examining room which had been enclosed with concrete block walls. There were no windows and only one white neon ceiling light. Twelve wooden theater chairs, bolted to the floor, filled the middle of

51

the room, and a Coke machine and pay phone crowded one corner. At least twenty people were milling about the room, drinking Cokes and coffee and talking softly in small groups.

"Mrs. Simpson?" I called out from the doorway. Immediately she stood up and walked over to the door with her two daughters. I guided them outside to the ambulance ramp, where there was some privacy and fresh air.

"He's very seriously injured," I told them after introducing myself. "He has a blood clot in the left side of the brain which must be removed."

"Will you do it?" Mrs. Simpson asked. She reached for both daughters' hands and began crying quietly.

"No. I'll call the neurosurgeon on call for the emergency room, Dr. Clark, to do the operation," I answered.

"How long will surgery take?" she asked as she wiped the corner of each eye with her fingers.

"About four hours."

"How dangerous is the operation?"

"The blood clot's not too deep in the brain, which should make it easier to remove," I explained. "The operation isn't as dangerous as a blood clot from a ruptured artery, like an aneurysm, where the bleeding is deeper inside the brain and more difficult to stop."

"Do you think he'll make it?" Mrs. Simpson whispered.

"The operating room is ready, Doctor," a nurse informed me from the door of the emergency room.

"I'll have to get things started, Mrs. Simpson. I'll talk to you as soon as we've finished."

I walked back inside the emergency room with the nurse. "I haven't even called Dr. Clark yet," I said.

"You better hurry," the nurse said. "Mr. Simpson isn't breathing well."

52

I called Dr. Clark's home and his wife told me he was in surgery at the Mobile Infirmary.

"Damn!" I mumbled. "I've got a patient at the Mobile General Hospital who has a blood clot in his brain and I need help."

"Call the operating room at Mobile Infirmary. That's all I know to tell you," Mrs. Clark suggested.

When I reached an operating room nurse at the Mobile Infirmary I explained the situation to her and she arranged for Dr. Clark to come to the phone, even though he was in the middle of an operation.

"Dr. Clark," I said. "I've got a patient who was in a car wreck an hour ago. He has three fractured ribs, a skull fracture, and a large blood clot in the left side of his brain. He's unconscious and paralyzed in his right arm and leg and now he's about to quit breathing. I've got to get this clot out. Can you come help me?"

Dr. Clark's voice was muffled by his surgical mask. "Of course," he said. "I can be there in about thirty minutes. I'm just about through with this operation. Take your patient to the operating room, shave and prep his head, then make an incision over the skull fracture and start removing the blood clot. I'll be there to help you shortly."

"Thanks."

"Are you sure the blood clot is from the accident?" Dr. Clark asked.

"What do you mean?"

"Sometimes a brain tumor will bleed, or an aneurysm will rupture and cause a blood clot inside the brain."

"The clot is under the skull fracture," I answered. "I'm sure the blood clot resulted when he had the car wreck and hit his head."

53

"Okay," Dr. Clark replied. "Just remember that occasionally an aneurysm ruptures suddenly and bleeds into the brain,
resulting in a car wreck, rather than the impact of a car wreck
causing the blood clot in the brain. Did you do an arteriogram
to rule out the possibility of an aneurysm?"

"No, sir," I answered. "But I don't think he has an aneurysm. I think he just struck his head on the windshield, cracked
his skull, and bled from the fracture into his brain."

"All right, I'll see you in about thirty minutes," Dr. Clark
said.

Inside the operating room, I felt alone. There were two
nurses opening the brain instruments, a nurse-anesthetist at
the head of the table, and an orderly in the room, but I was
the only doctor. I scrubbed Mr. Simpson's head with alcohol,
then spread sterile surgical sheets over him from his neck
down. I delayed for fifteen minutes, then five minutes more,
but still Dr. Clark had not arrived. There was nothing else to
do but start the operation.

The nurse handed me the cold, sparkling knife and I extended the cut behind Mr. Simpson's ear forward, toward his
forehead for about three inches. I cauterized the bleeding
arteries with electrical forceps and gradually stopped all the
blood oozing from the scalp. Underneath the scalp I felt the
rough edge of the skull fracture, and slowly, carefully, I began
prying up the in-driven skull fragments from the surface of the
brain. Sweat soaked through my surgical cap as I glimpsed the
thick, black blood clot lying beneath pieces of the shattered
skull.

"Quick, stop!" Dr. Clark shouted.

I looked up and saw him looking at the CT scan hanging on
the view box in the operating room.

"Most of this blood clot is inside the brain; only a little of it is on the surface," he said. "If this were a blood clot from a car wreck most of the clot would be on the surface of the brain. This man's ruptured an aneurysm."

My face flushed. I had not done an arteriogram. There would be no way of knowing where the aneurysm was located, or how big it was.

"Don't suck off any more blood clot," Dr. Clark ordered. "That clot is like a scab over the aneurysm. If you knock the clot off before we find the aneurysm, he'll bleed to death on the table."

For eight minutes I stared at Mr. Simpson's open head in front of me while Dr. Clark scrubbed his hands and put on a sterile surgical gown. The operating room remained deathly quiet as Dr. Clark approached the head of the table. He glanced at me, then focused on the open head in front of him.

"From the location of the blood clot, I think this is a middle cerebral artery aneurysm," he said. "Extend the incision up higher on his head and take the bone of his forehead out."

"Me?"

"Yes."

I lengthened the skin incision, and within seconds Dr. Clark had stopped the bleeding from the scalp edges with the electrical forceps. He handed me the air drill, pointed to the corners of the forehead, and instructed me to drill four burr holes. The instrument screamed, jumped and wavered, then gnawed into the skull.

"Hold it with two hands," Dr. Clark suggested. He positioned both my hands on the power shaft. I turned on the drill and it cut the skull precisely where he had marked it, remained steady, and pierced the skull like a hot knife through butter.

"Normally I connect the four holes with a Gigli saw wire to cut the bone free," Dr. Clark said. "But tonight we better use the power saw to save time. This patient can't last much longer with this clot in his brain."

Dr. Clark changed the power drill bit to a straight hacksaw blade. He slipped the blade into a burr hole, turned on the drill, and pushed the blade forward. The saw whined and smoked as it cut the skull, but in thirty seconds Dr. Clark had connected all four holes and lifted the bone of Mr. Simpson's forehead free from the rest of his skull. He cut the final covering of the brain, the dura, with scissors, and exposed the brain. Instead of its normal pulsating, pale yellow appearance, it was swollen, discolored and mottled red from the hemorrhage.

"It's an angry brain," Dr. Clark said as he stared at the tight red brain. He cauterized the small vessels on the brain's surface and then inserted a metal retractor and pulled the frontal lobe back from the inside surface of the skull.

"Why are you working on the frontal lobe under the forehead when the blood clot is by the left ear?" I asked.

"I want to find the origin of the artery that bled," he explained. "Then I can clamp the main trunk to stop the bleeding if the aneurysm ruptures while we're looking for it."

"But if you clamp the main artery to the brain, won't that leave Mr. Simpson with a permanent stroke? Wouldn't he be paralyzed and unable to talk forever?" I asked.

"Not if we can find the aneurysm, clip it off from the artery, and then open up the main arterial trunk within four minutes."

"Four minutes? Is that all the time we'll have?"

"Maybe four and a half."

"Isn't there some other way to clip the aneurysm without having to rush?"

"Yes, you can try to clip it without clamping off the main feeding artery. That's risky because the aneurysm is more likely to bleed, but you'll have more time since the blood supply to the brain won't be cut off."

"I'd rather try it that way," I said.

"Fine," Dr. Clark answered. "The first step is to remove the rest of the blood clot in the brain so you can see the artery underneath."

Dr. Clark handed me the sucker and a syringe full of water. I squirted the clot with water to loosen it up, then gently sucked it away from the brain. The sucker gulped the clot, burped itself clear as the clot passed through the tubing, then grabbed more. Ten minutes later I had removed most of the clot except for a faint rim over an artery four inches inside the brain, at the bottom of the cavity the clot had left in the brain.

"That's the aneurysm," Dr. Clark said.

The artery looked normal except for a swelling projecting from one side. The marble-sized aneurysm, a weakness in the arterial wall, had ballooned outward like a weak spot on a car tire. It would be necessary to place a steel clip across the neck of the aneurysm so blood could no longer enter the weakened, swollen sac, but at the same time the clip must not occlude the artery that supplied blood to the brain.

As I sucked away the remaining blood clot covering the artery, the aneurysm burst and hemorrhaged again into the brain. Blood welled up and flooded over the edge of the skull and poured onto the floor.

"Aneurysm clip," Dr. Clark said calmly.

A nurse put a second sucker into my other hand but blood continued to pour out faster than two suckers could remove it. The anesthetist reported the falling blood pressure: "100, 80, 70, 60."

"Quick, give him more IV fluid to keep his blood pressure up," I yelled to the anesthetist.

57

"No, leave it alone," Dr. Clark said. "The lower blood pressure will slow the bleeding down."

Dr. Clark opened the jaws of the aneurysm clip, lowered it deep into the brain, and closed the clip over the main trunk of the artery feeding the aneurysm. All bleeding stopped.

"We're committed now," he said. "Keep up with the time; we've just got a few minutes to clip the aneurysm, then open up the artery feeding his brain."

Dr. Clark took one of the suckers from me and quickly cleaned all the blood out of the brain.

"Thirty seconds," a nurse said.

Next, with various instruments, Dr. Clark followed the course of the artery into the aneurysm and away from it to find the exact location of the neck of the aneurysm.

"Ninety seconds."

"I'm losing his blood pressure," the anesthetist reported.

Dr. Clark continued working. The entire swollen, throbbing aneurysm could now be seen projecting from the artery.

"Two minutes."

He tried a straight clip, but each time he squeezed the neck of the aneurysm the clip pinched the artery as well, depriving the brain of its blood supply.

"This clip won't work. Let's try a clip curved upward," Dr. Clark said.

"Two and a half minutes."

The clip obliterated the aneurysm but curved upward and pressed on a vital area of brain, forcing Dr. Clark to remove the clip.

"Well, let's try a clip curving downward," he said.

"Three minutes."

The clip fit perfectly. The aneurysm was pinched off from

the artery which remained open. No brain was caught between the jaws of the clip.

"Three and a half minutes."

"Hand me the clip remover," Dr. Clark told the nurse. "I still have to remove the temporary clip on the main arterial trunk."

The nurse handed him the instrument.

"No, that's the wrong clip remover," Dr. Clark said quietly.

The nurse gasped and dropped the instrument on the floor.

"That's okay," Dr. Clark reassured her. "We've got plenty of time."

"Four minutes."

The nurse surveyed her instruments. Four clip removers lay in front of her. She reached for one, then hesitated. Dr. Clark remained silent. Her hand rested on another one and she glanced up. Dr. Clark nodded and winked, and she passed him the instrument. His hand glided into the brain and removed the temporary clip on the main artery feeding the brain.

"Four minutes, fifteen seconds," the nurse reported.

"This patient will do fine," Dr. Clark said.

Dr. Clark complimented the nurse assisting us, then helped me close Mr. Simpson's head. We closed the dura, replaced the skull of his forehead, then sewed up the scalp. Next, I dressed the wound.

"Sorry I didn't recognize this was a blood clot from an aneurysm," I told Dr. Clark as I wrapped Mr. Simpson's head with bandages.

"Apologies don't help dead patients," he replied bluntly.

Mr. Simpson lay in the noisy intensive care unit flat on his back, his head wrapped in a white turban, his arms and legs tied with leather straps to keep him from thrashing about in

59

bed and pulling out critical tubes. A cardiac monitor beeped with each heartbeat; a respirator sighed each time it pushed air into his chest. Two IVs dripped in unison, delivering glucose and antibiotics. A plastic tube in an artery in Mr. Simpson's wrist pulsated as it monitored his blood pressure. A catheter drained his urine. A small refrigerator in one corner contained his medications, and a rocking chair in the other corner provided me a place to rest as I watched Mr. Simpson in the critical hours following his operation.

"Good morning. How's he doing?" Dr. Clark asked.

I glanced at the clock. It was 6 A.M., five hours after we had finished the operation. Dr. Clark didn't look tired, although I knew he couldn't have slept more than four hours. He was dressed in a light blue parka, his graying hair neatly parted and brushed back from his forehead. I grabbed my white coat, which I had been using as a blanket, and slipped it over my dirty scrub suit.

"I didn't know you would be here this early," I said, "or I would have cleaned up before you made rounds."

"That's okay," Dr. Clark replied. "I'd worry about my patients if the intern taking care of them looked fresh."

Dr. Clark leaned over the bed and rubbed Mr. Simpson's shoulder. "Robert," he shouted, "squeeze my hand."

Mr. Simpson squeezed Dr. Clark's hand tightly, first with his left hand and then with his right hand, which had been paralyzed just six hours earlier. He followed all of Dr. Clark's commands but couldn't talk because he was still attached to the respirator.

"We'll get you off the respirator this morning," Dr. Clark told him. "Everything is going well, and you're doing fine."

Mr. Simpson nodded that he understood. Despite the blood

clot in his brain and the surgery to remove it, there had been no permanent damage.

"That's an excellent result from a bad disease," Dr. Clark said to me after we left the room.

"Next time I'll be more careful to be sure what caused the blood clot," I said.

"Keep in mind what Hippocrates wrote," Dr. Clark replied. " 'To know is science, but merely to believe one knows is ignorance.' "

By 7 A.M. we had finished rounds. Dr. Clark suggested we stop by the operating room to get some coffee.

"How much longer do you have in your internship?" Dr. Clark asked.

"Five months."

"What will you do next year?"

"I'll do a residency in general surgery, cardiac surgery, or neurosurgery," I answered.

"Neurosurgery is the hardest residency," Dr. Clark said.

"Why?"

"Long hours, long years, difficult operations to learn, and lots of dead patients."

"I can accept deaths from strokes, malignant brain tumors, and head injuries," I said.

"I'm not talking about deaths from disease," Dr. Clark replied. "I mean deaths from operations you're trying to learn."

"Oh," I mumbled.

"Well, if you choose neurosurgery, and if you finish the residency, give me a call. I may need a partner by then."

"If I choose neurosurgery, I'll finish the residency," I assured Dr. Clark, then returned to the ward to begin my morning work, buoyed by his interest in my future plans.

61

LEARNING THE CRAFT

PART II

CHAPTER 4

JUNIOR RESIDENT—1976

T HE METHODIST HOSPITAL in midtown Memphis stood thirteen stories higher than any surrounding building. Its red brick facade, sprawling over two city blocks, provided continuity for the seven separate hospital wings and towers which combined to form the one-thousand-bed hospital. The Mississippi River lay six blocks to the west, inner city slums to the north, blue-collar row houses to the east, and smokestacks and railroad tracks to the south.

I pulled the letter I had received two months earlier out of my coat pocket and read it again as I stood in front of the main hospital entrance.

"You have been appointed junior assistant neurosurgical resident at Methodist Hospital effective July 1, 1976. Report to the senior resident, Dr. Peter Bone, for further instructions. Congratulations, Richard T. Harkness, M.D., Professor and Chairman, Department of Neurosurgery, The University of Tennessee Center for the Health Sciences."

Methodist Hospital was one of five hospitals participating in the neurosurgery residency. Others included Baptist Hospital (the largest private hospital in the world), the Veterans Administration Hospital, City of Memphis Charity Hospital, and LeBonheur Children's Hospital. The medical center served a large rural area including the bootheel of Missouri, eastern Arkansas, northern Alabama, and western Tennessee. Thirty neurosurgeons practiced in Memphis, making it one of the largest neurosurgical centers in the world and a highly respected four-year residency training program.

"Lost?"

I glanced up from the letter at a nurse who had spoken to me. "Yes. I need to find the neurosurgical ward."

"Which one?" she asked. "There are four neurosurgical floors in the Thomas Wing, one in the East Wing, one in the Sherard Wing, and a seventh ward for charity patients in the Brinkley Wing."

"I guess the charity ward," I answered. "I'm a new resident."

"I'll show you the way."

The open, two-story ground floor was a mall, complete with restaurant, gift shop, drugstore, anytime bank tellers, and doctors' dining room. I followed the nurse up an escalator to the second floor, where there was a large teaching auditorium to our left and a two-block-long hallway running the length of the hospital. Fifty yards down the hall we entered the Brinkley Wing and walked through the charity wards until she saw Peter Bone, who was looking at X rays on a view box beside the nurses' station.

I introduced myself, and Pete shook my hand firmly. He was about my height, six feet tall, but he was thinner. His thick black hair was graying. He was thirty-three, nine years older than I, and had two years left in his residency. His father and brother were neurosurgeons, and he planned to practice with them in Chattanooga. His nickname, "Bones," suited him.

"Glad to have you on board," he said cheerfully. "Let me introduce you to a patient we need to operate on."

Pete led the way to a four-bed ward where a black woman was propped up in bed knitting a blanket. Two young children were quietly drawing pictures on a table beside her.

"Hi, Leola," Pete said, waving to her as he walked in the room.

"My favorite doctor!" Leola chuckled as she put down her knitting. "I bet you're here to tell me about my test results."

"Yes," Pete answered, sitting on the bed beside her. "The vomiting you've had this last month isn't due to gallbladder trouble or a stomach ulcer, like your other doctors thought. The X rays show you have a brain tumor. It needs to come out."

"Are you sure it's not my gallbladder?" Leola asked. "French fries and potato chips make me vomit. My sister had the same problem, and she had gallstones."

"No, it's the tumor building up pressure inside your head that's making you feel so bad."

"Is that why I have headaches and dizzy spells?"

"Yes."

"Maybe it's the change of life."

"No, Leola. You're just thirty-eight."

"Where is the tumor?"

"In the back of your head, just behind your right ear."

"Is it big?"

"It's about the size of a lemon."

"Is it cancer?"

"No, I think's it's benign. But we have to take it out and look at it under a microscope to be sure," Pete explained.

"What happens if I don't have the surgery?" Leola asked.

"The tumor will keep growing and cause more headaches, dizziness, and vomiting. Eventually it will cause too much pressure in your head and you'll go into a coma and die."

"Do you think I'd make it through an operation?"

"Yes, I do. You're young, and except for high blood pressure you're in good health. Every surgery has risks like infection or bleeding, but I think you'll come through the operation fine."

"What are the odds?"

"About ninety percent in your favor."

"Okay, I'll have the operation, but do a good job. Will you have to shave all my hair off?"

"No, just the back of your head."

"How long will the operation take?"

"About six to eight hours."

"When are you going to do it?"

"I can do it this afternoon, about one P.M., or later in the week."

"If I have to have an operation, I'd rather get it over with," Leola sighed.

"Okay," Pete said as he glanced at the pictures her children had drawn. "I'll see you in the operating room."

Outside the room Pete asked if I had found my way around yet.

"Not yet," I answered. "Memphis is a big city."

"No, I meant the hospital," Pete laughed. "You don't need to know your way around Memphis. You'll never see the city."

After we finished seeing the other charity patients, Pete

68

took me to the five floors reserved for neurosurgical patients and the intensive care unit reserved for head injuries and postoperative brain patients. We made rounds for three hours, checking sixty private patients whom he saw each day for the three neurosurgeons in private practice he was assigned to. He seemed tireless as he asked each patient how he or she was doing, checked the charts, and ordered medications and X rays.

"Ready for lunch?" Pete asked finally.

"Sure. Point me toward the cafeteria."

"We can't take that much time. Ask the nurse if there were any deaths on the floor last night."

"Why?"

"So we'll know which trays to pull off the patients' lunch cart."

Sixty-four operating rooms stretched along the third floor of the Thomas Wing like an ancient Roman catacomb. Eight rooms bordered each side of the four main hallways, which connected to form a square. The halls and rooms were cold and smelled of disinfectant. There were no outside windows, so only harsh white light flooded the rooms. Nurses and surgeons passed quickly through the halls, pausing occasionally for warmth beside the autoclaves, the large steel ovens where surgical instruments were steamed and sterilized.

Rooms 20 through 24 were neurosurgical operating rooms, especially equipped with X-ray machines, microscopes, and operating tables that could be cranked into a sitting position for operations on the neck and back part of the brain.

Pete and I entered Room 20 as the anesthesiologist was preparing to put Leola to sleep.

"See you in the recovery room," Pete said to her as the anesthesiologist pushed pentothal into her IV. Leola tried to

69

answer before the tranquilizer worked, but she was asleep in six seconds.

Pete shaved the back of Leola's head, first with clippers, then more carefully with a razor blade. Next he screwed the steel pins of the metal C-clamp headrest into her skull to hold it steady. As I held her head, he turned two cranks underneath the operating table, forcing the back of the table up. He screwed the headrest into a steel frame anchored to the operating table with eight separate bolts, completely immobilizing Leola's head. When finally in position, Leola looked as if she were sitting comfortably in a lounge chair, asleep with her hands folded on her lap.

One nurse began scrubbing Leola's head with soap while the other nurse continued preparing the instruments. Pete and I left the room to scrub our hands for ten minutes.

"You've been assigned to three surgeons," Pete said as he soaped his hands. "I'll work with three other surgeons and run the charity service and get you to help me when I get bogged down. Sometimes we get a general surgery resident to rotate with us, but so far this year no one has volunteered. That means you and I will be on call every other night."

Pete walked over to the door, cracked it open with his foot as he continued to scrub his hands with a brush the size of a bar of soap, and looked into the operating room to make sure everything was about ready. Then he stepped back over to the scrub sink.

"There are several rules on the brain team," he said. "Every patient admitted to the neurosurgery service must have a history and physical examination done by you or me before the next morning's rounds. We see every patient who comes to the emergency room before the staff surgeon is called. The resident on duty at night makes evening rounds on every patient who had surgery that day. We write all the preoperative orders for patients scheduled for surgery, arteriograms, and myelograms. We do all the arteriograms and myelograms for the staff neurosurgeons and assist on all their operations. One of us must prepare the Monday evening X-ray conference, Wednesday morning journal conference, and Friday morning morbidity and mortality conference. Be sure to make rounds on your patients every day, and twice a day on patients in the intensive care unit. On Wednesday afternoons we work the charity outpatient clinic."

"What time do you usually finish your work each day?" I asked.

"When I'm on call or off call?" Pete replied.

"Both."

"Two or three o'clock in the morning on the nights on duty, and about ten P.M. on off nights."

Pete spread a blue sheet over Leola's head with a six-inch-wide hole cut in the center. Only Leola's right ear and the back of her head were visible now, since the rest of her body was covered with other sheets. Pete made a straight, eight-inch incision behind her ear and through the scalp, until the knife blade ground against the skull. He handed me the bone pliers and told me to remove the thick skull bone in the back of her head.

"I want to keep my hands fresh for removing the tumor once we're inside the brain," Pete said.

Carefully, I nibbled away small flecks of bone over Leola's brain. The skull cracked as I bit it with the pliers, but even the larger chips of bone I chipped free were no bigger than dimes. Gradually the hole in the skull enlarged, but it needed to be as big as a saucer. I stopped every few minutes to rest and shake my hand and stretch my fingers before squeezing the pliers again to break off more bone.

"How did you choose neurosurgery?" Pete asked as he watched me crack away more skull.

"It was a process of elimination," I answered. "I didn't enjoy sewing up bullet holes in intestines all night long on the general surgery service, and I got bored with bypass surgery on the cardiac service. That left neurosurgery."

When the skull opening was wide enough, Pete cut the dural covering of the brain and pulled it up like a veil, exposing the yellow, pulsating face of the brain. He took a soft metal retractor shaped like a spoon and gently pushed the cerebellum up, then pulled it down and moved it from side to side as he searched for the tumor.

"I just answered a page for you, Dr. Bone," a nurse said, opening the door slightly and leaning her head into the operating room.

"Who was it?" Pete asked.

"It was Dr. Wright. He wanted you to make rounds with him but I told him you were operating."

"Thanks."

"Surgery and emergency room calls take precedence over all other responsibilities," Pete explained to me as he continued looking for the tumor. "If you're not in surgery, then you're expected to do arteriograms and myelograms for the staff surgeons and make rounds with them. After rounds, you can do histories and physicals on the new patients admitted to the hospital or help me with the charity patients. But your first priority is to be in the operating room, learning to be a surgeon."

"How do you find time for all the work?" I asked.

72

"I've followed a schedule for two years that works well. I make charity rounds at four-thirty A.M., before the staff neurosurgeons get to the hospital and begin calling me. I make private practice rounds for the staff surgeons from five-thirty to seven A.M. before I go to the operating room at seven-thirty. Usually I get out of the O.R. around three P.M. and do a few histories and physicals before the five o'clock afternoon conference. I eat supper from five-thirty to six and then go to the E.R. to see the patients that have been waiting during the day. At eight P.M. I finish the ten or fifteen histories and physicals I have left, and about ten P.M. I make evening rounds and check all the post-op patients. From midnight to one A.M. I write orders on patients going to surgery or having myelograms and arteriograms the next day. I go back to the E.R., check for patients, then try to sleep from two to four A.M. before starting the next day's work."

"That's a full day."

"Some days are busier than others. Basically, I just come to the hospital and stay until I finish my work."

"Do you get home much?"

"Once or twice a week."

"Are you married?" I asked Pete.

"Yeah. I've been married eight years. We have four children. How about you?"

"Ten days," I answered. "Julie and I married the day after I finished my internship. We skipped the honeymoon and drove straight to Memphis so we'd have time to settle into our new home."

"Did you have a good week?" Pete asked.

"We sure did," I answered, smiling. "We went out to eat and saw two movies and drank daiquiris every night when we got home."

73

"I'm glad you had a good week," Pete said. "It's the last free time you'll have for a while."

I inched closer to Pete to get a better look through the skull opening. Red arteries throbbed on the brain's surface, and the crystal-clear spinal fluid surrounding the brain continuously bubbled up like a spring, filling the back of the head before it was suctioned out. The cerebellum, which controls coordination, was nestled in the back of the brain under the two cerebral hemispheres above, revealing only a half of its full fistlike size. In front of the cerebellum lay the brain stem, a long gray stalk conveying all information from the brain to the spinal cord. Thin white filaments, the cranial nerves, draped along the inside of the skull on each side of the brain stem like a spider web, providing hearing, swallowing, and feeling and movement in the face. Scattered about the brain, blue veins converged to form larger channels draining blood from the head.

"There's the tumor," Pete announced.

It looked like a gray tennis ball with rough, irregular ridges resembling fish scales on its surface. It was stuck to the skull under the right ear on one side and indented the brain stem on the other side. The nerves stretched around it were so thin they were glistening and pale rather than milky white.

"What do you think it is?" I asked.

"It looks like a benign meningioma because it's shaped like a round ball. Malignant tumors usually spread into the brain and you can't tell where they start or stop."

"Will it be hard to take out?"

"All brain tumors are; some are just harder than others."

"How long can she live with this type of tumor?"

"About five years if I get part of it out, but if I'm able to remove it all she should live out a normal life."

74

Pete unlocked the wheels of the microscope, pulled it toward the operating table, and centered it over the brain. The instrument was seven feet tall and covered completely in clear plastic to keep it sterile and protect it from dust. It had two long, spidery arms, one for the surgeon to look through and one for the assistant. Pete sat down on a stool, rested both arms on the operating table, and began twisting the binocular eyepieces to bring the brain into sharp focus. After turning up the intensity of the microscope's light and increasing the magnification to ten times normal, he began removing the tumor. With nine-inch-long electrical forceps, he cauterized the arteries feeding the tumor until they had shriveled, collapsed, and hardened. Once they were no longer able to bleed, he cut the vessels and peeled them away from the tumor. After nine or ten arteries feeding the tumor had been cut, the tumor had lost much of its deep gray color. He cut a hole in the side of the tumor ball and stuck a sucker into its center. With sweeping movements of the sucker back and forth, he cored out the center of the tumor. As the mushy center was removed, the outside capsule of the tumor began to collapse back onto itself, away from critical nerves. With the tumor deflated and lying on the brain stem like an empty balloon, Pete slowly slid the nerves off its surface. But the remaining rim of tumor along the brain stem had burrowed into critical areas of the brain and was stuck. Each tug on the tumor pulled on the brain stem and caused it to malfunction, with abnormal heartbeats, falling blood pressure, and loss of respirations.

Pete persisted, but when he looked up at the clock and saw it was 10 P.M., nine hours after we had started, he murmured, "This is taking forever."

Two more hours drifted by, and still Pete had an area of

tumor the size of a silver dollar pinned between the cerebellum and brain stem.

Around midnight Dr. David Wright, a forty-five-year-old senior staff neurosurgeon, came by the operating room to see how the case was going. He was a ghostlike figure, known to show up at odd hours to help residents or other staff surgeons on difficult operations. He would disappear when the surgery was over, avoiding thanks for his help. Pete stepped back from the operating table to rest and drink a Coke, while Dr. Wright inspected the remaining tumor and poked and stroked it with a long, slender instrument with a hook on the end.

"You've done a nice job removing this tumor, Pete," he said ten minutes later when Pete returned to the operating table.

"Thanks," mumbled Pete, but Dr. Wright didn't hear him. He had already left the room.

Pete resumed the operation. Several minutes later he suddenly lifted the remaining tumor out of the brain and handed it to the nurse.

"All out," he said.

The nurses congratulated Pete on the total tumor removal. By 1 A.M. Leola's head was closed. We plopped down in the surgeons' lounge to rest.

"How did you get the rest of the tumor out so easily?" I asked Pete.

"I didn't. Dr. Wright apparently stripped it off the brain stem while I was drinking a Coke. When I looked back in the brain, the tumor was sitting in a little ball next to the brain stem. I just picked it up and gave it to the nurses."

"Why didn't he stay and talk to us?"

"He probably has a date. He works hard and plays hard. He

76

races Porsches and spends a lot of nights partying. But he can sure operate."

"Are you sure his life is as fast as he puts on?"

"I don't know, but last Christmas the residents and nurses got together and gave him a gag gift—one hundred prophylactics wrapped up in a shoe box. He just laughed and thanked us for the week's supply."

"Is there any work left to do?" I asked.

"I've got three patients to see in the E.R., and I need to make post-op rounds and write orders on the patients going to surgery tomorrow. I'll finish it up. Why don't you get some sleep?"

"I'll stay and give you a hand. I'll make the post-op rounds and then meet you in the I.C.U. to check on Leola."

The intensive care unit was a room the size of a tennis court, filled with patients with shaved heads. Two ten-bed rows faced each other across a narrow aisle. Many patients were unconscious, and some were vomiting. Most were lying still in bed, listless, with glazed eyes and heavy eyelids, looking as though they were falling asleep. They lay on their backs, tethered by tubes, staring at the ceiling or the machines beeping around them.

Without windows the air was heavy and warm, and the sweaty smell of patients with fever mixed with the odor of urine, feces, pus, and disinfectant was unpleasant.

There were no clean, crisp, white uniforms. The nurses were dressed in loose-fitting, wrinkled surgery scrub suits like those worn in the operating room. Vomit, blood, and infected sputum from the tracheostomies spotted their clothes. They wore no makeup, and their hair was pulled back. Each nurse cared for two patients, constantly standing between the beds and emptying tubes and bags, giving shots, and monitoring blood pressure and temperature. This was a working room, the engine room of the hospital: steamy, noisy, throbbing with energy, isolated from the rest of the hospital.

"Squeeze my hand!" Pete shouted at Leola to make sure she was conscious.

"What year is it, Leola?"

"1976."

"Who is the President of the United States?"

"Ford."

Pete sat down on the edge of her bed, felt her pulse, listened carefully with his stethoscope to her heart and lungs, and took her blood pressure.

"Follow my finger," Pete said to Leola as he moved his index finger up, down, and side to side.

Leola tracked his finger perfectly with her eyes, indicating three of the cranial nerves in her brain were functioning normally.

"Stick out your tongue; swallow; shrug your shoulders; close your eyes; bite down like you're chewing food," Pete instructed Leola as he checked five more nerves.

"This will sting, Leola," Pete said before he pricked her finger with the sharp point of a razor blade. He squeezed the end of her finger and forced the drop of blood to swell, and then filled a thin glass tube with it. After he spun the tube around inside a centrifuge, he read Leola's hematocrit—thirty-eight, a normal blood count indicating she hadn't bled much during the operation and wouldn't need a blood transfusion.

"Your blood pressure is fine, you don't have any fever, and all the nerves in the area where we took the tumor out are working fine. We got all the tumor out and it wasn't malignant. You're fine, and you'll be home in a week."

"What time is it?" Leola asked.

"Four o'clock in the morning," Pete answered.

"Tuesday?"

"No, Wednesday."

"I've lost a day."

"Well, you were asleep for twelve hours while we removed that tumor."

"Is it all out?"

"Yes."

"Was it cancer?"

"No, Leola. Just rest now; we can talk more later."

Pete wrapped Leola's head with a fresh bandage, then sat down in the nurses' lounge adjoining the I.C.U. for a cup of coffee.

"Her thinking is still fuzzy," Pete said to me. "It's like a boxer who has been knocked out. It takes a few hours for the mind to clear."

I studied Pete as he chatted with two of the night nurses who were on a break. His clothes were wrinkled, his eyes puffy, but he was smiling and in good spirits. He wasn't slumping in his chair or complaining about the fact that he'd been awake for twenty-four hours and had another eighteen to go before he could sleep. He seemed oblivious to the hours and looked like any man at 5 P.M. at the end of an eight-hour work day.

"Pete, why are you in such a good mood?" I asked.

"Because we've got a good day ahead of us. There are two interesting brain tumor operations today, and it's just four A.M. now."

"What do you mean, it's just four A.M.?"

"Normally I start rounds at four-thirty, but today I'll get a thirty-minute head start."

Pete and I walked down three flights of stairs to the spacious, forty-bed, ground-level emergency room, and he introduced me to Mrs. Bohanon, the fifty-year-old head nurse on the 11-P.M.-to-7-A.M. shift. Pete had warned me that she could be a powerful ally or a formidable enemy because the frequency of her phone calls determined how much sleep a neurosurgery resident got at night. If Bohanon liked you, she examined the patients herself, ordered the blood tests and X rays, and then saved up four or five patients until 4 or 5 A.M. before calling the neurosurgery resident to come down to the E.R. Since all the workup had been done, the resident could nap from 2 to 4 A.M., then come to the E.R. and admit the patients before the staff surgeons came to the hospital around 6:30 A.M. If Bohanon didn't like you, she called immediately each time a patient arrived, leaving you no time to sleep between hourly calls as the patients filtered in. Two hours of sleep a night were a blessing for neurosurgical residents; many nights there was none. The only time a resident could expect more sleep, Pete had explained, was during ice storms, which closed roads and bridges and prevented patients from getting to the hospital. The resident couldn't get home either, but after a few months on the brain team most residents preferred a night with six hours of sleep rather than a chance to go home.

Bohanon walked down the hall with us, pointing out the patients waiting to be seen by a neurosurgeon.

"This first patient has a deep four-inch cut on the top of his head," Bohanon said. "He said God bit him."

Pete glanced in the room at the chubby, middle-aged man sitting on a metal stool. His shoulder-length, brown frizzy hair was pulled back and tied with a red ribbon. Black high heels and stockings matched his black, V-necked dinner dress. His fresh shave was highlighted by penciled eyebrows, rouge, and glossy lipstick.

"How would you like to wake up next to that each morning?" Pete asked me.

"You don't think I'm pretty?" the man retorted, standing up and folding his arms under his padded bra.

"You can't help being ugly," Pete replied, "but you could stay home."

The next patient had been struck on the right side of his skull, and the fractured bone was caved in and pressing on the brain. However, he was awake, alert, and not paralyzed. Emergency surgery to lift the chips of broken bone off the brain would be necessary.

"What happened to you?" Pete asked the man.

"Doc, I had just gotten home from a tent revival. I was sitting in my living room reading my Bible when a television broke through the window and hit me on the head."

"Can you believe the story that guy came up with?" Pete said to me out in the hall. "He was probably drunk, in a bar fight, and got clubbed with a pool stick."

"The other patient you need to see has been shot in the head," Bohanon told Pete.

"How did he get shot?" Pete asked one of the policemen beside the unconscious man's bed.

"He broke into a pawn shop and shot the owner," the policeman explained. "We yelled at him to stop, but he kept running down the street. Just before I shot him he threw a TV through the window of some man's house. He's here in the emergency room, too."

Pete told Bohanon to prepare the man with the fractured skull for surgery while he continued to examine the man who was shot in the head. The bullet had entered the back of the head, just above the neck, and had exited the brain in the middle of the forehead, leaving a half-dollar-sized hole oozing brain and blood. The man was unconscious and breathing shallowly.

"The man with the skull fracture is ready for surgery," Bohanon informed Pete fifteen minutes later.

"Good," answered Pete. "Wrap this man's head, Bohanon, and don't put him on a respirator if he quits breathing."

"Yes, sir."

"Why are you operating on the skull fracture before the gunshot wound?" I asked Pete. "The man shot in the head is in much worse shape. The patient with the skull fracture is awake and talking."

"The man shot in the head will probably die with or without surgery. The bullet passed through the center of his head and destroyed too much brain. The man with the skull fracture may die if we delay his operation, but he'll make a full recovery if we remove the bone fragments in his brain quickly. I'm going to operate on the patient who has the best chance to live."

"That's a tough decision."

"Surgeons decide every day who lives and who doesn't."

"Do you ever worry you've made the wrong decision?"

"I can't waste time worrying."

"But what if you're wrong?"

"It takes sixteen years to become a neurosurgeon," Pete answered. "If I'm wrong after that much training, anyone else would have been wrong too."

"Is that confidence or conceit?"

"A surgeon without confidence is dangerous."

"A conceited surgeon is too."

"It takes both to be a neurosurgeon."

82

"Why?"

"Confidence keeps your hands steady; conceit keeps you confident."

Two hours in the operating room assured the recovery of the man with the skull fracture and the death of the man shot in the head, who was cold, blue, stiff, and expressionless when we returned to the E.R. Only one man stood beside the bed, gazing intensely at the corpse.

"At least he had some family," I mumbled.

"Nope," Pete replied. "That's the coroner."

Within days, time had blurred. A steady stream of head-injured patients requiring lengthy brain operations, together with the scheduled, nonemergency operations, produced twenty-four-hour days without a starting or stopping point. Three and four days at a time passed without a breath of outside air. After a month on the neurosurgical service, the intense volume of surgery numbed our minds and we thought only of medicine.

On Thanksgiving morning, I met Pete in the emergency room to help him with a seven-year-old girl who lay thrashing and screaming on a blood-soaked stretcher. The right side of her head was cut open and caved in, and gray, swollen brain throbbed out of the gaping wound and slid down her cheek. Nurses wiped the brain off her face each time it mushroomed out of her head. Pete told me to wrap her head while he finished putting in the IVs.

"Her blood pressure is responding to the IV fluids," a nurse reported to Pete. "She's out of shock now."

"And I've got the scalp bleeding stopped with the Ace wrap," I said.

"Good," Pete answered. "She's jabbering and moving, so some of her brain is still working. Give her a tetanus shot, antibiotics, and a blood transfusion, and get the operative permit signed. I'll go to the operating room and make sure the nurses have all the brain instruments ready."

Under the spotlights in surgery we inspected the extensive wound in the right side of the brain. The major arteries, which were spurting blood, were cauterized with electrical forceps until all bleeding stopped. Skull fragments driven into the brain were freed from the brain, then carefully pulled out. The brain remained swollen, however, leaving no choice but amputation of the right frontal lobe to provide enough room for the rest of the brain to fit inside the head. The frontal lobe, considered "silent" because even after its removal the remaining brain appears to function normally, clogged and choked the suction tubing as we sucked it out of her head. Thirty minutes later, the baseball-sized frontal lobe had been removed and the rest of the brain fit easily inside the skull. We made the child a new skull out of acrylic since much of hers had been destroyed by the injury, sewed up the scalp, and moved her to the recovery room.

"That must have been a terrible car wreck this girl was in," I said to one of the nurses in the recovery room.

"It wasn't a wreck," the nurse answered.

"What happened?"

"Her father was cutting wood, and the girl ran up behind him into his chain saw."

Pete winced. My stomach burned. We left the recovery room to talk to the child's parents but said nothing as we walked down the three flights of stairs to the E.R.

The parents were divorced, and the father, who was a farmer, was raising his daughter by himself. Pete talked at length with the father and reassured him his daughter was out of immediate danger, but explained the severity of the injury might leave her permanently paralyzed in her left arm and leg. The father remained expressionless.

"We'll make it," he said simply as he brushed the back of his sleeve across his eyes.

The holiday weekend ensured more injuries. At midnight Pete and I returned to the E.R. to see a sixteen-year-old boy who had careened his car into a bridge embankment. His head had slammed into the windshield and split his brain with dozens of shattered skull fragments. Broken ribs punctured both lungs, his legs and pelvis were fractured, and he had bled into shock from a ruptured spleen. When I saw the boy in the emergency room, I knew immediately he would die. I called and awakened his parents at home and told them their son had been in a car wreck and would require emergency surgery on his head, chest, abdomen, and legs. I didn't tell them he was drunk, with a blood test showing an alcohol level twice the limit of legal intoxication. The police would tell them later. The tragic injuries were enough for them to hear tonight.

Six surgeons surrounded the boy on the operating table. Pete and I opened the head and removed the bone fragments from his brain. Two general surgeons opened his abdomen and removed the bleeding spleen. Orthopedic surgeons straightened the broken bones in his legs. Our blue surgery gowns were red from the massive bleeding from his brain, spleen, and legs, and blood puddled on the tile operating room floor. Four IVs poured blood into the boy, but he never responded and remained in shock. The chest was already open when he had a cardiac arrest, so the thoracic surgeon simply squeezed the heart with his right hand to keep blood circulating throughout the body. For hours we tied off arteries, sewed up lacerations, and transfused blood in an attempt to save his life. Finally, the boy's blood pouring out of his body became thin and watery and no longer had the thick red look of normal blood. We had run out of blood to transfuse, and he was bleeding the clear IV fluids we were running into his veins.

After nine hours of surgery, everyone knew it was time to quit. When multiple injuries are associated with a head injury, the decision to stop treatment is made by the neurosurgeon. The other surgeons looked at Pete. At 10 A.M., he returned their looks with a nod. Without comment the surgeons backed away from the dead teenager on the operating table, stripped off their rubber gloves, and left the room quietly. I sat down on a stool in the corner of the room and watched Pete wrap the boy's head with clean bandages and cover his mangled body with a hospital gown.

I followed Pete out of the operating room to the prayer room, which was located two floors above the O.R., next to the intensive care unit. The room was small and seated only six people. There were three chairs grouped around a sofa, and a kneeling bench in front of a crucifix. Thick blue carpet darkened the windowless room and hushed the sounds.

Ten people had crowded into the room. The parents sat holding hands on the sofa next to their pastor. A brother and sister sat in chairs facing their parents. Pete and I squeezed into the hot, cramped room and closed the door behind us.

"Your son had severe injuries," Pete began, standing stiffly and looking only at the father. "He had a fractured skull, broken legs, collapsed lungs, and a ruptured spleen. We were never able to get his blood pressure up. His heartbeat got weaker and weaker until finally his heart stopped and we couldn't get it started. He passed away a few minutes ago."

The mother screamed, then sobbed, gasping for air. The children cried, shivered, and buried their faces on each other's shoulder. The father mumbled a thank-you to Pete, then cried silently. I opened the door and stepped outside. Pete followed a few seconds later.

"Telling people someone's dead is tough," I said to Pete.

"You better get used to it," Pete mumbled, staring at the floor, and shaking his head, as he walked down the hall.

The months quickly lapsed into a routine: long days in the operating room; nights working on the wards. Off nights allowed library time for studying and preparing conferences, and weekends provided either a Saturday or Sunday afternoon, but never both, to spend a few hours away from the hospital.

Whenever possible, Julie and I went for walks together in Memphis' spacious Overton Park. If the weather was cold or raining, we worked inside our three-bedroom home, painting rooms, refinishing floors, preparing a nursery and planning for our first child. Most of our free time was spent together. Our friends in Memphis were also in residency and seldom off duty at the same time.

In December the normally smooth running of the brain team was interrupted by an argument between Pete and me. For months he had performed all the difficult brain operations, leaving the easier spinal operations for me with the explanation that tradition allowed the senior resident first choice on operations and the privilege of bumping junior residents from doing surgery.

At ten o'clock one night, after we had finished the day's work, I invited Pete into my sleeping room and closed the door behind us.

"Pete, goddammit, I've had enough!" I shouted. "You're doing all the surgery and taking my cases, too. How do you expect me to learn to operate on the head if you're doing all the brain cases?"

"That's the way it's always been around here. I got bumped on my surgery two years ago when I was a junior resident, and now I'm making up for lost cases."

"Listen, Pete. I cover for you when you need to go home. I do the charity work when you're tied up in surgery or snowed under with ward work. I prepare the conferences for you when you're tired. I do everything I can to make things run smoothly, and I'll be damned if you're going to steal any more of my surgery."

"Well I'm sorry, but you're not ready to do delicate brain operations."

"Give me a chance!" I yelled. "It's time I used my hands for something besides holding a sucker."

I walked over to Pete, stood inches from his face, and said in a low, monotone voice, almost a whisper: "Let me tell you something. I'm going to operate on Shirley Roberts, the charity aneurysm case scheduled tomorrow. I saw her in the E.R. when she came in with a headache. I admitted her, did the arteriogram, made the diagnosis, and got her through the first three days when she was sick as hell from a brain hemorrhage. She didn't meet you until today when you got back from the medical meeting, and she wants me to do the surgery, not you. You never saw her before today, and I don't think it's fair to me, or the patient, if you do her surgery."

"The reason it's fair," Pete answered, "is because I know how to do aneurysm surgery, and you don't!"

"I told Shirley this morning that you were planning on doing the operation and she said she wouldn't sign the operative permit unless I was the surgeon. She has confidence in me, Pete; she doesn't know you."

"Okay, you do it. But if you kill her, we'll both get fired."

Pete glanced at the list of patients he kept in his pocket to see how much work he had left to do. He underlined ten or twelve names on the list, at least two more hours of work. When he opened the door, I assumed he was returning to the ward to finish his work.

"Let's go down to the library and go over the operation," he said. "I don't want you needing books during surgery tomorrow!"

The library was a small cubbyhole which had once been a four-bed ward. Floor-to-ceiling bookshelves lined the walls and partitioned the room, and a small, round table and four chairs were crammed into the corner to the left of the door. Despite the hundreds of thick medical books and musty smell, it still looked like a hospital room. Metal runners for the curtains dividing the beds were still fixed to the ceiling; four green oxygen outlets remained where the beds had been; the linoleum floor was still scratched and dented from the heavy steel bed frames.

"Let's start with these," Pete said, pulling two large text-books, Kempe's *Operative Neurosurgery* and Poppen's *Atlas of Neurosurgical Techniques,* off the shelf.

We sat down at the table, and Pete flipped to the chapters on aneurysm surgery without studying the table of contents.

"You've got to do aneurysm surgery right," he said. "You can screw up other operations but not this one. Mistakes result in paralysis, coma, or death. It's right or wrong; there's no in-between."

"Why do the books always picture the surgeon pulling the frontal lobe instead of the temporal lobe back to find the aneurysm?" I asked.

"Because the aneurysm is usually stuck to the temporal

lobe," Pete explained. "If you pull on the temporal lobe, you break off the top of the aneurysm and your patient bleeds to death."

"I've got a lot to learn."

"In seven hours," Pete mumbled.

While I studied the pictures showing the major arteries and aneurysms in the brain, Pete went upstairs to the operating room and returned a few minutes later with a large metal tray the size of a cookie sheet. A hundred clips used to pinch the aneurysm off the artery feeding it were laid out in five rows of twenty each. The clips were about an inch and a half long, varying in configuration, curving to the left, right, up, or down; each one for use depending on which direction the aneurysm ballooned from the artery.

Pete broke a thick rubber band and tied a knot in its middle to simulate an aneurysm.

"Now practice placing the clips across the knot without touching the rest of the rubber band," Pete instructed.

Each time I squeezed the clip holder, the jaws of the clip opened and allowed me to get around the knot without touching it. Then, as I gently released my grip on the holder, the jaws of the clip closed on the knot in the rubber band and pinched it flat.

"That's not so hard," I said to Pete after successfully clipping the knot for the first time.

Pete looked at the rubber band and several seconds later the clip popped off.

"You put the clip too far out on the knot. It has to be closer to the rubber band."

I tried again. This time the clip pinched the knot *and* the rubber band.

"No good," Pete said. "Remember, in the operation the

90

rubber band will be a major artery feeding the brain. The knot will be the aneurysm. If the clip pinches the artery, the patient will have a stroke. If your clip pops off the aneurysm, she'll bleed to death. Keep practicing."

For two hours I experimented opening and closing each of the hundred clips over the rubber band. I tried clipping the knot at arm's length and up close, a few inches from my chin. I cocked my hand at odd angles to experience the different ways the holder could release the clip. I turned off the bright overhead neon lights and worked only by the faint yellow desk lamp to practice with poorer lighting in case the brain blocked part of the light during the operation. And, at Pete's suggestion, I tried clipping the rubber band inside a Mason jar to simulate the small opening I would have in the brain to reach the aneurysm. About 2:30 A.M. Pete returned to the library.

"Got it down?" he asked.

"I think so."

"Work another hour then. When you're clipping an aneurysm you have to be sure you know how to do it, not *think* you know how."

"Okay."

"When you finish," Pete added, "why don't you get some sleep. I'll see you in the operating room in the morning."

"I'll help you finish your work," I volunteered. "I won't sleep well anyway, thinking about this operation."

"All right. You want the ward work or the E.R.?"

"I'll take the emergency room," I answered. "Maybe I can find another aneurysm."

Pete forced a smile but said nothing.

Three hours later, at 7 A.M., I walked into the main neuro-surgery operating room. It was cold, quiet, and businesslike as four nurses opened the brain instruments for the operation and the anesthesiologist prepared Shirley for the anesthetic. She was shivering since she was wearing only a hospital gown. I walked over to the narrow operating table and spread a blanket over her.

"Did you get plenty of sleep last night?" she asked.

"I sure did," I lied.

"Good. I don't want a sleepy surgeon opening my head."

"See you when you wake up, Shirley," I said as I felt her pulse.

She tried to continue talking, but within five seconds the pentothal had put her to sleep. I watched the anesthesiologist put a tube into her windpipe and connect her to a respirator for the five-hour operation. I shaved her hair, positioned her head in the headrest, outlined the incision on her head with a purple pen, and then took a needle and syringe and injected her scalp with epinephrine to decrease the bleeding from the wound edges when I made the incision.

Outside the operating room, in the adjoining hall, I began washing my hands in the scrub sinks. Pete still hadn't arrived, and I wondered if he planned to come in late to make me realize I needed help. After the ten-minute scrub, I backed through the door into the O.R. and saw Pete inspecting the patient on the operating table. He checked the IV tubes, Foley catheter, arterial line monitoring blood pressure, and the direction in which Shirley's head was turned. He made sure her eyes were covered to avoid injury to her corneas and bent her legs slightly to avoid stretching the nerves to her legs, which might result in paralysis during a long operation.

"Attention to detail," Pete said to me, "avoids complications."

I covered Shirley with surgical drapes and was ready to

begin when Pete finished scrubbing his hands. Pete took the knife and made the incision, returning the same favor I had given him for three months: opening the head for the primary surgeon, who rested his hands for the main part of the operation. He pulled the scalp down over Shirley's forehead, removed the skull, opened the dura, and exposed the surface of the brain.

"It's all yours," Pete said stepping to one side.

I stared at the hemorrhagic, swollen brain; fiery red instead of its normal pale yellow color. I pulled in the microscope but still couldn't see the aneurysm since it was hidden under the optic nerve. Injury to this nerve while dissecting the aneurysm would blind Shirley. At age forty-eight, with two teenaged children, blindness could ruin her life.

To see the aneurysm better, I slowly removed bone from the base of the skull. I steadied my hands as I ground down the bone with an air drill. The drill was only millimeters away from the optic nerve and carotid artery, and one slip, even a slight tremor of my hands, would tear the brain, nerve, or artery, either blinding or killing her. I worried constantly that the aneurysm would rupture again and hemorrhage into the brain before I clipped it.

After two hours of tedious work, I saw a portion of the aneurysm peeking out from under the optic nerve. Pete carefully pulled the optic nerve to one side to show me the entire aneurysm. It looked like a cherry-red plum, although slightly bigger, and I could see blood swirling within it, pulsating and bulging the dome of the aneurysm and threatening to explode it at any second.

"Take your time; you're doing fine," Pete encouraged me.

I hesitated and continued to look at the angry, throbbing artery in front of me.

"Don't let that aneurysm intimidate you," Pete said. "You're bigger than it is."

Forty-five minutes later I had finished dissecting the aneurysm, and its connection to the parent carotid artery was evident. I was ready to clip it but waited while the O.R. nurses put sheets under my feet on the floor to provide a steady footing as my hands approached the aneurysm. The room was so quiet I could hear air blowing through the vents. I opened the jaws of the clip and gently closed them across the neck of the aneurysm. Suddenly the aneurysm ruptured, and blood gushed out of the head and spilled onto the floor.

"Jesus!" Pete shouted. "Give me another sucker!"

Now Pete had a sucker in each hand and could do nothing else to help me. Blood continued pouring out of the head faster than he could remove it, and within seconds Shirley had lost four units of blood.

"She's in shock!" the anesthesiologist reported.

"Transfuse more blood," I ordered.

"No use," he answered. "By the time the blood gets here from the lab, she'll be dead."

"Hang on," I said. "I can get another clip on this aneurysm."

"You've got the wrong angle on the aneurysm," Pete said. "I could get it from where I'm standing but I can't stop sucking. Dammit! You just can't get to it with your right hand!"

"Her heartbeat's irregular," the anesthesiologist warned. "She's fibrillating! You've got about thirty seconds to stop the bleeding, Doctor; then you've got a dead patient."

"Give me the clip in my left hand," I instructed the scrub nurse. Pete looked at me and nodded, knowing it was my only chance. With the clip in my left hand, I had a perfect angle to clip the aneurysm without injuring the carotid artery or optic nerve. The problem was that I couldn't see well since she was bleeding so badly.

"Good luck," Pete mumbled, his steady hands continuing to suck blood and providing me some vision.

I took the clip in my left hand, passed it six inches inside the skull into the brain, and then, once again, closed the jaws over the neck of the aneurysm. This time the aneurysm wall didn't tear, the clip held, and immediately the bleeding stopped. The anesthesiologist got Shirley out of shock, and with her blood pressure restored, her heartbeat became regular again.

"Outstanding!" Pete said. "I didn't know you were ambidextrous."

The nurses congratulated me too, but I didn't reply until my heart slowed down and my breathing started again.

"Thanks," was all I could muster when finally I could talk.

"Scared the hell out of you, didn't it?" Pete said.

"Sure did. You didn't cover this last night."

"I didn't want to take all the fun away today."

"I can do without this kind of excitement," I mumbled, then began closing Shirley's head.

A week later, on Christmas Eve, I discharged Shirley from the hospital. Except for the black silk stitches and incision on her head, she didn't even look like she had been sick. She stood staring into the mirror, puckering her lips to smooth her lipstick, as I walked into her room.

"Ready to go home, Shirley?"

"I sure am. When are you going to take my stitches out?"

"Right now."

"Are there any instructions to follow?" Shirley asked as I sat down on the bed next to her and began removing the stitches.

"I don't want you to exert yourself until your brain has

healed up from the operation. That means no housework, no driving, no sex until I see you in one month," I answered.

"Two of those won't be hard. But the other may be impossible," Shirley said.

"You've got to try. I don't want you to have another brain hemorrhage."

"I know," Shirley answered. "But I hate a messy house."

Outside the room in the hall I heard Pete giving instructions, too: "Don't go out of town until I check her again."

I glanced up to see who he was talking to. A thin young girl limped slowly by the open door, dragging her left leg, steadying herself by holding hands with Pete and her father. The right half of her head was still bald over her incision. The hair on the left side of her head was pulled into a pony tail and tied with a rubber band over her left ear. She was wearing faded blue jeans and a sweat shirt, but I recognized her immediately as the child who had run into her father's chain saw.

I asked Shirley to excuse me for a minute and walked out to the hall to say good-bye to the girl and her father. Pete stopped and I bent down in front of the girl to say good-bye.

"Take care of yourself," I said.

The right side of the child's face was paralyzed and twisted grotesquely to the side. Her right eye was now a glass marble. Saliva drooled out of the corner of her mouth. She made a garbled, gurgling sound, trying to answer me, but had no useful speech. A pink pit on the right side of her head was all that remained of her amputated right ear. She faced her father, held both arms up in the air, and he leaned over, picked her up, and cradled her whole head with his left hand.

The father, wearing a red flannel shirt and overalls, shook hands with Pete and then, before leaving, said, "Thank you for making my daughter well."

96

. . .

In February, Dr. Richard T. Harkness, professor and chairman of the department of neurosurgery at the University of Tennessee Medical Center and head of the residency program, assigned me to talk to the journal club of the Memphis Neuroscience Society. Each month forty or fifty neurosurgeons, neurologists, and scientists at the medical school who were interested in the brain gathered at a restaurant for a private dinner and an academic talk by a visiting professor. If the guest canceled, a resident was drafted to fill in. I happened to be the first resident Dr. Harkness saw the day his secretary told him the neurosurgeon scheduled to speak from the Mayo Clinic had postponed his February visit.

"Come here," Dr. Harkness barked when I passed him in the hall outside the operating room. He was a tall, muscular man with a commanding voice and a threatening scowl. I stopped immediately and turned to face him, almost as if I were standing at attention. "Dr. Walters canceled his talk for the journal club next Tuesday night. You fill in for him, and talk on trigeminal neuralgia."

"Yes, sir," I answered, but Dr. Harkness wasn't listening. He expected no other reply from a resident.

In the next six nights I prepared a forty-page, hour-long discussion on trigeminal neuralgia: a severe, sharp, stabbing facial pain. I discussed the different causes of the pain, including brain tumors and abscessed teeth, and outlined drug treatment with Dilantin and Tegretol, which sometimes relieved the pain, making brain surgery unnecessary. I concluded the talk with the current operation used to treat the disorder, in which the trigeminal nerve is not cut but rather separated from the surrounding, pounding arteries that produce lightning pains in the face each time they pulsate and strike the nerve.

97

The new operation, I stressed, now allowed the neurosurgeon to relieve the pain without producing permanent numbness in the face.

When the meeting was over, Dr. Harkness asked me to talk to him alone. I waited outside the restaurant for the last doctor to leave, wondering what I had done wrong. I hadn't killed anyone in the operations I had done, and there had been no major complications from my surgery in the first eight months of my residency. But I knew a private talk with Dr. Harkness was a bad sign. Good news didn't require privacy.

Dr. Harkness stepped outside, lit a cigarette, and waved to me to come over to where he was standing.

"I've decided to keep you an extra year," he said bluntly. "Your residency will now be five years instead of four."

"No, sir," I replied sharply. "You promised four years when I applied. It's not fair to change it now."

Other residents had advised me to stand up to Dr. Harkness during confrontations. He abhorred weak personalities and instinctively attacked whenever he sensed a resident was willing to compromise his position.

"I don't give a goddamn what you think is fair!" Dr. Harkness shouted.

"Do you think I need an extra year to learn the operations?"

"No."

"Then you're just keeping me because we're short on residents."

"We have enough residents," Dr. Harkness replied.

"*Eight* residents to cover five hospitals and thirty neurosurgeons?"

"You can't learn surgery from a book. You've got to do it. And that means staying in the hospital and working."

98

"Does sleeping four hours every two days make you a better surgeon?"

"You have to be able to operate when you're tired."

"And leaving the hospital one afternoon a week—what does that do?"

"It makes medicine your first priority. You can't learn neurosurgery if you're interested in other things."

"Medicine *is* my entire life; I can learn neurosurgery in four years."

"It's going to be five years now," snapped Dr. Harkness. "I've made the decision and there won't be any more discussion of it. You can leave in 1981, or you can leave tonight."

"Well, then I'll leave now, Dr. Harkness. I don't mind staying an extra year if I'm not progressing in my ability, but I won't stay just for you to have another resident to get the work done."

Dr. Harkness ignored my last comment, then said, "In addition, I've made a new policy for all residents. No one completes this residency until they've passed the written examination given by the American Board of Neurological Surgery. That means the two chief residents will be around for another year if they don't pass the exam this spring. So don't feel sorry for yourself. You're not the only one I've talked to."

I returned to Methodist Hospital, paged Pete, and asked him to come down to our sleeping quarters to talk with me. About 1 A.M., when he finished making post-op rounds, he joined me in our room and sat down on the edge of the bed.

"Pete, Dr. Harkness told me tonight he's keeping me an extra year. He promised me a four-year residency when I came to Memphis, and I don't think it's fair to change now."

"Why's he adding a year to your residency?" Pete asked.

"He says for more experience, but I think it's because there aren't enough residents to do all the work."

"What are you going to do?"

"I told Dr. Harkness I would leave Memphis if he made me do five years," I answered. "It's not the extra year that bothers me as much as the principle. If I needed the year to become a competent surgeon, that would be fine. But he's keeping me because he only has eight residents."

"Well, we are short on residents," Pete said. "But the truth is, Dr. Harkness is interested in only one thing: graduating residents that are superbly trained neurosurgeons. And I'm sure he believes you'll be a better surgeon if you have an extra year of training."

"What do you think, Pete? Do you think I need another year?"

"No, I don't. You have natural ability, a delicate touch inside the brain that can't be taught. And you're operating better now than most of the other residents."

"What should I do?"

"Hold him to his word: that he told you four years," Pete answered. "And if he doesn't change his mind, transfer to another residency."

"Okay, Pete, I'll think about it for a few days. Thanks for the advice."

"Whatever you do, keep Dr. Harkness informed," Pete said walking out the door on his way back to the ward. "Don't do anything behind his back. He's honest and he expects the same of you. Whether you like what he says or not, at least he'll tell you what he's thinking. And if you ever have a problem—an operative death or complication, a malpractice suit, a personal problem, or a personality clash with another neurosurgeon—you can count on Dr. Harkness to support you. He stands by his residents."

Three days later, on Friday afternoon, I reached a decision to leave Memphis and transfer to a residency program that would allow me to finish in four years. I wrote to Dr. Charles Matthews, the chief of neurosurgery at the University of Alabama. I asked him if I could come back to Birmingham to complete my training. If not, I requested that he help me find another residency. I photocopied the letter, took it to Dr. Harkness' office, and left it with his secretary. A week later I received Dr. Matthews' reply. He told me there were no openings in Birmingham for a second-year resident, but he had talked to a friend in St. Louis who had agreed to accept me as a second-year resident beginning on July 1, 1977. He wished me well and asked me to stay in touch.

"When are you leaving?" Pete asked when I showed him the letter.

"I'm going to ask Dr. Harkness to let me complete my first year here. If he does, I'll leave at the end of June," I answered.

"Why don't you talk to him right now?" Pete said. "I think it would be a good idea for you to show him Dr. Matthews' letter before he hears about it from someone else."

"Okay," I muttered, feeling nauseated at the prospect of confronting Dr. Harkness about leaving the residency.

At 6 P.M., when Dr. Harkness' last patient had left, his secretary ushered me into his spartan office containing only a small desk and two chairs. There were no pictures or certificates on the bare walls and no family pictures in the small, ten-foot-square room. Patient charts and unfinished correspondence cluttered the top of his desk. A skull sat on the windowsill, its bleached white bone speckled with blue ink spots where he had explained different operations to his patients. He leaned forward in his chair and stared at me, tapping the charts with a rubber reflex hammer. I sat down in the red leather chair in front of his desk.

"Did you hear from Dr. Matthews today?" Dr. Harkness asked.

"Yes, sir. How did you know?"

"He called me last week when he got your letter and asked me what kind of resident you were. He didn't want to recommend you for another residency if you had screwed up here," Dr. Harkness explained.

"What did you tell him?"

"I told him you were an excellent resident, and you'll be a competent neurosurgeon, but that you and I had a disagreement about the length of your residency."

"Dr. Matthews has arranged for me to finish my residency at Barnes Hospital in St. Louis, but I'd like to finish my first year in Memphis, if that's all right with you."

"Did you know my professor kept me an extra year when I was a resident?" Dr. Harkness asked.

"No, sir."

"He sent me to Boston Children's Hospital. The extra year was very important for me. It matured me and fine-tuned my surgical judgment. The decision to operate can be very difficult. Sometimes experience is all that you have to go on; knowing how the patient will do if you let the disease run its natural course, and knowing how the patient will do if you intervene with surgery. You can't teach that. It's only learned by living with disease."

"Yes, sir."

"I've decided to let you finish in four years if you wish. But if you decide to finish in four years, then I'm going to condense five years of training into four. So you better move into the hospital if you hope to survive."

"Yes, sir."

I repeated the conversation to Pete that night after we finished evening rounds.

"I guess I should congratulate you for standing up for yourself," Pete said. "But somehow I think you may have stepped into a firefight."

"There's no doubt about it," I said. "He's going to try to break me. But no matter what happens, I won't let him."

"Well, put it behind you. You've spent the last week worrying about it. It's time to get back to learning neurosurgery."

"Okay," I answered. "Why don't you let me operate the brain tumor you have scheduled tomorrow?"

"Maybe you should worry one more day before you get your mind back on operating," Pete answered, grinning.

"At least you're consistent, Pete. It's harder to get a brain case from you than it is to get change from a whore."

In May I took the written examination of the American Board of Neurological Surgery, along with the other seven residents. We sat together around an oval conference table in the Semmes-Murphey Clinic library across from Baptist Hospital. I sat next to Pete and across the table from the two chief residents. They sat motionless, their lined faces frozen with worried frowns. Both were married and had children in school. Their $12,000-a-year resident's salary had left them thousands of dollars in debt. They had arranged private practices and needed to leave the residency to begin work and clear their debts. They were anxious to spend time with their families again, but each chief had been told by Dr. Harkness he must pass the examination before leaving the residency.

"You guys will do fine," Pete said to the chiefs as the exam was passed out.

"I don't know," one chief replied. "Running the neurosurgery service at the charity hospital this year didn't leave much time for studying. We spent most nights operating gunshot wounds to the head."

"You've been in the brain more than anyone in this room," Pete said. "This test will be easy for you."

"Thanks for the encouragement," the chief said, "but look at the first question."

Pete and I looked at the test booklets in front of us. We broke the seal and read the first question: What artery forms the border of the hypothalamus in the center of the brain?

"See what I mean?" the chief replied. "The only way a neurosurgeon would ever see that area of the brain would be if he's lost or performing an autopsy."

Five hours later we turned in the exams, and all eight of us walked across the street to the Holiday Inn to drink beer and discuss the test. After a single sip of beer the chiefs were beeped to return to the charity hospital emergency room.

"Two fine surgeons, and two fine men," Pete said after they had left. "I've never heard either one complain about the residency."

"Think they'll pass the exam?" I asked.

"I don't know," Pete said. "That test measures trivial knowledge, not surgical ability. We'll just have to wait and see."

Pete and I returned to Methodist. That evening I vomited, ran a low-grade temperature, and ached in all my muscles. Pete diagnosed me as having a "virus," a very unsophisticated diagnosis coming from a brain surgeon. He remained in the hospital with me and took my calls that night. The next morning I was worse, with a 104-degree fever and swollen, golf-ball-sized lymph nodes in my neck. I stayed in bed, and Pete brought me some soup from the cafeteria. He turned on the light, then yelled, "My God!"

"What's wrong with me?" I asked.

"You have huge red splotches all over your face and neck," he answered. "Take off your shirt and let me look at your chest and back." The red circles were there, too, and on my legs, palms, and soles of my feet. I had a terrible headache. We both thought I had meningitis. Pete called Dr. Mock, a specialist in internal medicine, to see me. He came up to the resident sleeping quarters, listened to my heart and lungs, felt the swollen lymph nodes in my neck, drew some blood, then wheeled me down to radiology for a chest X ray. He came back to my room about 2 A.M. with the diagnosis: infectious mononucleosis complicated by encephalitis.

"It's a virus," Dr. Mock said. "Antibiotics won't help. Fortunately, the brain infection is mild, with only headache and unsteadiness, so the encephalitis should resolve completely in a couple of weeks. There's no treatment except bed rest. Pete, tell Dr. Harkness he's lost a resident for a month."

For two weeks I lay in the darkened call room with the curtains closed since light hurt my eyes too much to read or watch TV. The third week I began taking short walks in the hall, and by the fourth week I felt strong enough to go outside for walks.

By the time I returned to work it was the last week in June, and all residents were scheduled to rotate to new hospitals on July 1. I had received a letter from Dr. Harkness informing me my next rotation was six months of neurology at the Veterans Administration hospital. I returned to the operating room on June 25, feeling well, although wobbly, and determined to make it through my last week without asking for help. Although Pete was exhausted from doing his work and mine for a solid month, he greeted me enthusiastically outside the operating room and suggested I go back to the call room and lie down after the scheduled surgery was finished.

"I'll keep working the nights until you're full steam," he said.

"Thanks, Pete, but I'll take the calls tonight. I'm fine."

"Okay, but I'll sleep in the hospital, so call me if you need me."

"I sure will. Thanks."

I looked at the surgery schedule and saw I was assigned to assist Dr. Thomas in removing a brain tumor. The tumor was located in the back of the brain next to the cerebellum and required a lengthy, microscopic dissection. Several times during the ten-hour case, Dr. Thomas encouraged me to sit down and rest. I had no fever or headache but had lost my energy and endurance. I struggled through the operation and was thankful he didn't ask me to do it. At 5 P.M. he finished closing the head and I left to begin my night duties. I made rounds on the post-op patients, admitted the patients waiting in the emergency room, skipped dinner, and fell into bed. The phone didn't ring all night, and I felt better the next morning. As I was making morning rounds, I saw an order on a chart, signed at 3 A.M. by Pete. I realized then that he had taken my calls.

Our final week at Methodist Hospital ended on June 30. Pete and I packed the books and clothes in our call room and prepared to move to the V.A. hospital for our next year of residency. Pete was the new chief resident there, and I was assigned to the neurology service.

"You did a great job at Methodist," Pete told me as we walked out the front door.

"Thanks. By the way, how did the exams turn out?"

"Everyone did fine," Pete answered. "Both chiefs passed."

"Fantastic! How did you do?"

"I passed too."

"Congratulations, Pete! How did I do?"

"You did fine," Pete answered. "But you'll do better next year."

I squeezed into Pete's Datsun for the ride over to the V.A. and stared out the window, thinking of the advice one of the chief residents had given me on the afternoon of the board examination: never lose your confidence, or you won't survive the residency. It must be good advice, I thought; it saw him through.

CHAPTER 5

NEUROLOGY AND
LABORATORY RESIDENT—1977

THE MEMPHIS VETERANS Administration hospital was a stately thirteen-floor, 882-bed, gray stone building covering a square block in the center of the University of Tennessee Medical Center, midway between Methodist and Baptist hospitals. The grounds were immaculately groomed, with edged lawns and clipped shrubs. A giant United States flag fluttered from a tall flagpole beside the circular driveway in front of the hospital. Ambulances packed the ramp leading to the emergency room. Visitors in cars with license tags from a dozen different states slowly circled the front driveway and parking lots, looking for empty spaces. Paraplegics and quadriplegics lounged in wheelchairs on the patio connecting the parking lot and outpatient clinic entrance on the east side of the hospital. V.A. staff physicians in long, flowing white coats ambled about the main lobby speaking to waiting patients and welcoming them to Memphis.

Inside the bowels of the hospital where the interns and residents worked, the V.A. was not a prestigious referral medical center, but rather an inefficient government hospital. Laboratory tests and X rays required days, rather than hours, to be done. Often the operating room closed for government holidays, delaying surgery. The hospital census influenced funding, so there was no incentive for efficient diagnostic workups, treatment, and patient discharge. The V.A. remained a popular rotation, however. Staff physicians allowed residents to perform all surgery.

"You'll love the V.A.," Pete said as we pulled into the parking lot.

"Why?" I asked.

"Because here you're a doctor, not a resident. You can do what you want to the patients without having to wait for a staff physician to give you permission."

"But I'm stuck on neurology for six months," I answered. "There's not a lot I can do except talk to patients. I'll be bored to death without operating for that long."

"Make the most of it," Pete said. "Take the neuroscience courses at the medical school in the morning, and it will help you pass the written board exam. In the afternoon you can operate with me. It won't be bad, and it's a good six months to catch your breath."

"But neurosurgery gets all the interesting brain diseases. On neurology I'll just have the problems that can't be helped."

"It's still good to understand multiple sclerosis, Parkinson's disease, Alzheimer's dementia, meningitis, encephalitis, stroke, and all the other diseases seen on the neurology service. You'll be a better neurosurgeon if you're a competent neurologist too," Pete replied.

"A CT scan can do everything a neurologist can, and quicker."

109

"We know that, but don't let the neurologists hear you say it," Pete warned. "Or you'll flunk the neurology rotation."

"What is the neurology schedule like?" I asked.

"Neurologists get to the hospital about eight A.M.," Pete answered. "They eat breakfast and read the newspaper until nine-thirty. Then they make morning rounds, break for lunch at noon, attend conferences from one to three P.M., and leave for home about four."

"It's going to be a boring six months," I repeated to myself as Pete left for the operating room.

I waited patiently beside two veterans for an elevator to 8 South, the neurology ward. Both men were wearing surgery masks, a protection against infecting others with tuberculosis. They looked about sixty, were unshaven, and had thinning hair that wasn't combed and stood straight up. Inside the elevator they stood in one corner staring at the elevator floor and avoiding the worried looks of three women visitors standing opposite them. The masks muffled their coughs, but their chests rattled when they breathed. When the elevator stopped, the women rushed out. The doors closed but the elevator started slowly, and we could hear the women talking.

"Imagine! Those men on a public elevator. They should be on a special ward."

As the elevator glided up I watched the two men. Their expressions remained frozen. They said nothing about the women being on the wrong elevator. This one was reserved for patients with infectious diseases. Visitors never read the instruction signs on the main floor.

The T.B. ward was on the seventh floor, but when the elevator stopped on the sixth floor both men got off. One of the men held the other by the elbow and helped him across the threshold between the elevator and the floor. They

110

shuffled toward a door beside the elevators. As other visitors crowded into the elevator, I watched the two men hold on to the stair rail, wheeze, cough, and then take a deep breath each time they climbed another step. The door closed behind them and hid their illness, but not their desire to protect others from the tuberculosis infection.

On 8 South I walked down the main hall and glanced into the open eight-bed wards. Each veteran was dressed identically in brown and white seersucker bathrobes and tan slippers. They hobbled about the ward with amputated legs, blind eyes, paralyzed limbs. Some sat beside their beds listening to radios; some read Bibles; most stared blankly out the window.

At the end of the hall a thirty-year-old veteran lay flat on his back, tied to the four corners of his bed with leather restraints. From the window of his locked room I watched him scream and struggle to free himself.

"It's stress syndrome," a neurology nurse said behind me.

"What's that?" I asked.

"Nightmares and marital problems."

"Is keeping him tied down in a room by himself supposed to help that?"

"He's receiving tranquilizers four times a day. What else can we do?"

"Sit on the edge of his bed and talk to him."

Inside the residents' office I introduced myself to Dr. Anderson, to whom I had been assigned. He was a tall, broad-shouldered, fifty-year-old midwesterner with thick sandy hair and half-rim glasses sitting low on his nose. He was dressed neatly in a white shirt, plaid bow tie, khaki pants, and a starched white lab coat. He sat behind an army-green metal desk, assigning patients to the other two neurology residents.

When I sat down beside him, he swiveled his chair toward

me and said, "I'm assigning you a multiple sclerosis, a schizophrenia workup, three strokes, and a patient with amyotrophic lateral sclerosis."

"What are their names?" I asked.

"I don't know. It's the disease that's important," he answered.

"Is the night call schedule made out, Dr. Anderson?" one of the other residents asked.

"It's once a week for you two," Dr. Anderson answered. Then he turned back to me and said, "You're not on the call schedule."

"Why?" I asked.

"Dr. Harkness called and told me he wanted you to continue taking neurosurgery night call. That's never happened before. Why's he doing that?"

"We're short on residents," I answered.

"I see. Okay, you're free until three P.M. I suggest you do a history and physical examination on your patients."

I wandered through the main ward, studying the patients, trying to find one who looked sick enough to have amyotrophic lateral sclerosis. This degenerative, incurable disease of the spinal cord produces muscle weakness in the arms and legs, eventually weakening the respiratory muscles. It is an agonizing death over months or years, ending in suffocation. The cause is unknown; perhaps a slow viral infection of the nervous system.

It wasn't hard to find the patient with A.L.S. His flesh crawled like a thousand worms under his skin. This sign, called fasiculations, was due to the gradual loss of nerve function in his muscles.

He sat next to his bed, beside a window, talking to another patient. The sun penetrated his gray hair, accentuating his gaunt face and shriveled arms and hands. He looked about sixty and held his left hand straight up to keep his copper wedding band from sliding off his thin finger. His arms were frail and spindly. He stretched his stiff legs straight in front of him, unable to bend his knees easily.

I introduced myself and sat on the foot of his bed to talk to him. He told me his name was Norman Bell, but he preferred to be called Bud.

"What did the other doctors say is wrong with you?" I asked.

"I can't remember what they called it. But I know some people call it Lou Gehrig's disease. Do you know anything new?" Bud asked.

"A little," I said. "It used to be called A.L.S., but now it's believed to be three different diseases."

"No, I mean, do you know anything new about Lou Gehrig?"

"I know he played 2,130 consecutive games in fourteen years with the New York Yankees."

"What was his batting average?" Bud asked.

"Three forty-one."

"What did he do after he retired from baseball?" Bud grinned when I hesitated.

"I don't know, Bud."

"He was parole commissioner of New York City from 1940 to 1941."

"I see you've read a lot about Lou Gehrig."

"Yes. I wanted to know how the disease affected him, so I'll know how I'm going to die."

"How long have you had symptoms?"

"About a year."

"How did they start?" I asked.

113

"I was leaning over the fireplace putting a heavy log on the fire, when I felt a sharp pain in my neck. It hurt every time I moved my neck for about a month, and then the pain went away. After that I started getting weak in my arms and legs, and my muscles wasted away. I think the doctors called it atrophy. About six months ago I started twitching in my arms, and the doctor who saw me in the outpatient clinic called them fasiculations, and told me I had Lou Gehrig's disease."

"What tests have been done, Bud?"

"I had an EMG, some sort of electric muscle test where doctors stuck needles in my muscles and shocked the nerves to see if they worked. Then they did some blood tests and biopsied the deltoid muscle in my left arm."

"Have you had a myelogram?" I asked.

"What's that?"

"It's a spinal tap test where dye is injected into the spinal canal and run up into the neck to see if you have a ruptured disc or pinched nerve."

"No, I haven't had that test."

"Take your pajamas off and let me examine you."

"Okay, Doc. But you're not going to like what you see."

Bud stood up in front of me wearing only his underwear. His legs were thin and stiff and didn't bend when he walked. The muscles in his arms and legs could barely be seen, and his thinned-out chest wall quivered with each heartbeat. The twitching fasiculations were present in both arms but, oddly, were absent in his legs. His neck hurt when I tilted it back, and it sent an electrical shock down his spine into his legs.

"Bud, how long have you been in the V.A.?"

"Three weeks."

"What are the doctors doing for you?"

"I go to physical therapy twice a day to strengthen my legs

114

and help me walk. And they take me to lots of conferences and show me to interns and residents."

"I want you to get another opinion about what's wrong with you. I don't think you have A.L.S."

"How can you say that? I've been here three weeks and examined by several doctors. You come in and in fifteen minutes tell me they've got the wrong diagnosis. That's not fair to get my hopes up, Doc." Bud paused, and then blurted, "The other doctors have even sent the psychologist to see me, to counsel me about dying."

"It won't hurt to get another opinion. Your symptoms started suddenly and didn't build up slowly like most people with A.L.S. You have neck pain, which is unusual, and you have fasiculations in your arms but not your legs. Patients with A.L.S. have them everywhere."

"What do you think is wrong with me, Doc?"

"I think you've ruptured a disc in your neck, and it's pressing on the nerves going to your arms and putting pressure on the spinal cord, which explains why your legs are weak."

"What kind of doctor should I see?" Bud asked.

"A neurosurgeon."

"Is there one here at the V.A.?"

"Yes. There's an excellent neurosurgeon here named Dr. Bone, but you can't see him."

"Why?"

"Because he has to present his patients to a combined neurology and neurosurgery conference, and the doctors on this floor will find out I told you I thought they had the wrong diagnosis," I explained.

"What should I do then?"

"I want you to see a neurosurgeon at Methodist Hospital named Dr. Paxton. He has a special interest in neck disease and is one of the few neurosurgeons in Memphis who operates through the front of the neck, rather than from behind. If you have a ruptured disc in your neck it will be large, and it would be safer to remove it from the front. Dr. Paxton's the best surgeon to do that operation.''

"I don't have any insurance, Doc. I can't go to another hospital.''

"If you want to give up and be paralyzed and then die without trying, then that's fine, Bud. But if I were you, I'd do something about this. Maybe you have a treatable problem.''

"How much would it cost me to see Dr. Paxton?''

"The operation would cost about twenty-five hundred dollars, and the hospital bill would be about five thousand dollars.''

"Okay, Doc. I'll borrow the money and give it a try.''

"Remember, Bud. Don't say anything to anyone. Residents aren't allowed to do this.''

"I understand,'' Bud said.

That afternoon Bud requested home physical therapy, so Dr. Anderson discharged him from the hospital. Three days later he saw Dr. Paxton, who agreed Bud should have a myelogram. It was done the next morning and showed a complete blockage in the neck, consistent with a large ruptured disc. Two days after the myelogram, Dr. Paxton operated on Bud's neck and removed a massive fragment of ruptured disc pressing on the spinal cord. Dr. Paxton called me that night to tell me Bud had come through the surgery fine, there had been no complications, and he thought Bud might regain much of the strength in his arms and legs over the next six months.

"Thanks for sending the case over,'' Dr. Paxton said before hanging up.

Two weeks later, Bud called from home to tell me how well

116

he was doing. "Thanks, Doc! Dr. Paxton told me it might take me months to get better, but that I definitely wouldn't get worse. Even if I never get better, you can't imagine how great it is to know I'm not dying."

"I'm glad everything turned out well," I said.

"Doc, what would have happened to me without the operation?"

"You would have become quadriplegic—paralyzed in your arms and legs," I answered.

Bud was silent for a few seconds, and then said, "Is Dr. Anderson your boss?"

"No, why?"

"I wanted to write and tell him what you did for me. Who is your boss?"

"Dr. Harkness. But don't bother him with this, Bud. He's a very busy surgeon. You're going to get well now, so let's just forget about it."

"Okay, Doc. But you'll never know how much I appreciate what you did for me."

July and August were hot in Memphis, and I didn't venture outside much. Gradually my energy returned following the mononucleosis, and by fall I was able to work nights on the neurosurgery service without feeling exhausted the next morning. The medical school neuroscience courses were scheduled to begin in September, and the written board examination was announced for March 30, 1978. I decided to start my study routine on September 1. That would give me seven months to prepare and two more months to rest, feel better, and concentrate completely on neurology.

Each morning Dr. Anderson joined the residents on rounds. For two hours we walked through the wards examining the paralyzed, speechless, helpless patients. He checked their reflexes, looked into their eyes, stuck them with a safety pin, vibrated a tuning fork beside each ear, and searched for muscle wasting. He felt their thyroid glands, listened to their hearts and lungs with a stethoscope, and pressed on their abdomens. He checked the strength in their arms, hands, fingers, legs, feet, and toes. But never did he say "Good morning" to a patient or ask him how he felt. He knew no patient's name or occupation. To him they were simply diseases.

Each morning we ended rounds by stopping at Randy White's locked-up room at the end of the ward. Dr. Anderson would peer through the window in the door for a few seconds, then pronounce to the other doctors that there was no improvement in Randy's "stress syndrome."

"Why don't we go inside and talk to him?" I asked Dr. Anderson one morning.

"Because there's nothing to see," Dr. Anderson replied. "He doesn't have any abnormal reflexes, muscle weakness, or numbness. It would be a waste of time to examine him."

"The attention might do him some good," I persisted.

"Okay," Dr. Anderson sighed, shrugging his shoulders.

A nurse unlocked the door, released Randy from the leather restraints around his ankles and wrists, and then propped him up on the edge of the bed. Immediately Randy began thrashing about with his arms as if he were trying to keep his balance. Seconds later he fainted and fell back across the bed.

Dr. Anderson felt his pulse, then pulled his stethoscope out of his pocket and began listening to his heart.

"He has a heart murmur," Dr. Anderson said while still listening to Randy's heart. "His pulse is irregular, and his lungs sound wet. What does his EKG show?"

"An enlarged right ventricle," a resident reported.

"This man doesn't have stress syndrome," Dr. Anderson said standing up and facing the residents around the bed. "He's in heart failure. He's acting crazy because he's not getting enough blood up to his brain."

"I'll call a cardiologist," a resident said, leaving the room.

Each morning after rounds, beginning on September 15, I walked four blocks to the medical school and took the neuroscience courses with the sophomore medical students. The lectures covered neuroanatomy, physiology, and brain pathology and were an excellent review for the neurosurgery written board exam scheduled for March. I typed my notes, expanded them with information from more advanced texts, and passed them out weekly to the other residents who were preparing for the exam. In the afternoons I worked in the anatomy lab helping medical students dissect the brain. At 5 P.M. I went back to the V.A., made evening rounds, finished my work, and then, two or three nights a week, went to the Baptist or Methodist hospital at seven o'clock to be on neurosurgery night call. After working nights, I studied in the library from 3 to 5 A.M., before beginning the next day's work.

On off-duty nights I arrived home about 8 P.M. Julie and I ate a light dinner—soup, salad, or a sandwich—then walked around the block before going to bed. We talked mostly about her job teaching early childhood education at Memphis State University. She was thoroughly enjoying her work and looking forward to raising children of our own. We planned for the day we would have children and decided on names: Laura Page or John Kenyon, Jr. Julie always asked about my day, but I remained vague. There was no remedy in reliving the death of a patient; no compliment necessary for saving a life.

One cool fall evening Julie seemed especially happy as we walked down the sidewalk. She had her shoulder-length black hair tucked under a knitted cap and her maroon sweater pulled tightly around her. At the end of the block she turned and faced me. Her tears glistened in the car headlights passing by. She hugged me tightly and whispered in my ear that she was pregnant.

"Great!" I exclaimed. I held her at arm's length and then added, "I wonder when that happened."

"I have a good idea," Julie laughed, opening her sweater and wrapping it around me as she pulled me to her. "You've only been home once in the last six weeks."

One morning in October I arrived at 5:30 at the V.A. and found a new patient had been admitted to the ward about midnight. The neurology resident on duty had been called at home, and he had admitted the patient but hadn't come to the hospital to see her. It was my day to do a history and physical examination on new patients, so I read the brief note written on the chart by the emergency room doctor: "Lieutenant Commander Ruth Hester, fifty-five years old, career Navy, headache and weakness in left arm and leg. Neurology resident Mertins contacted. Diagnosis: migraine. Demerol hypodermic, 100 milligrams every four hours as necessary for pain."

There was no record of how long the headache had been present, the severity of it, whether or not she had fallen and hit her head, what medications she was taking, what her overall health was like, her blood pressure, temperature, level of alertness, or how long she had been paralyzed on the left side of her body. No CT scan had been done to rule out a life-threatening cause of the paralysis, such as a blood clot in the brain, that would require immediate surgery. Worse, she hadn't been examined by the neurology resident on call but rather admitted to the hospital by telephone.

120

I walked down the hall to her room, knocked on the door, and went in to examine her. She had been assigned a private room since all the other patients on the floor were male. I found her lying in bed reading a paperback. I introduced myself, then took her history and discovered she had a long history of migraine headaches, which had probably accounted for her admitting diagnosis.

"But," she said, "this headache wasn't as bad as my migraines. My whole head hurts now, not just the right side like a migraine. And I never got weak in my arm or leg before, although doctors have told me that migraines sometimes cause temporary paralysis."

"That's right," I said. "Has your weakness cleared up?"

"Yes. It always does."

"Has this happened before?"

"About five or six times this week. My right eye goes blind, then I get weak in my left arm and leg and my head hurts, and in about thirty minutes it always clears up."

I leaned over the bed rail, listened to the right carotid artery in her neck with my stethoscope, and heard a loud noise, like the rush of rapids, indicating severe hardening and narrowing of the artery. Her diagnosis was therefore not a migraine headache, but rather a transient ischemic attack, or T.I.A., which is the warning sign of an impending stroke. She needed an immediate arteriogram, an X ray made after dye is injected into the artery, to determine how clogged the artery was. If the carotid artery wasn't completely closed, an operation could be done to clean the artery out and remove all the cholesterol narrowing it. Keeping the artery open was her best chance to avoid a permanent stroke.

I left Ruth's room and called the radiologist, explaining the situation to him and emphasizing the need for an arteriogram.

"Fine," he said. "I can do it day after tomorrow. I'm booked up until then."

"It's not safe to wait two days," I said. "She may have a stroke if she doesn't have surgery."

"Two arteriograms a day," the radiologist replied. "That's all I do. She'll have to wait."

I started Ruth on heparin, a blood thinner, to help blood circulate through the clogged artery while we waited forty-eight hours for the arteriogram. At 7 A.M. I finished writing the history and physical examination and explained to the nurses the doctor's orders I had written on the chart.

"Please don't delay on starting the heparin," I instructed the nurses. "Heparin is all I have to protect her from a stroke until I can get her X rays made and a neurosurgeon to operate on her."

I spent the morning at the medical school and returned that afternoon to check Ruth before leaving for night duty at Methodist Hospital. As I walked onto the ward, I saw a flurry of activity outside her room. Nurses were running back and forth from the room to the nurses' station. Several residents trying to start IVs were bent over Ruth, who was lying motionless on the bed. A nurse was on her knees next to the bed, taking Ruth's blood pressure, and Dr. Anderson was watching from the doorway.

"What happened?" I asked Dr. Anderson.

"The nurses found your patient unconscious. They didn't know how to contact you at the medical school, so they asked the other residents for help. Dr. Mertins read your diagnosis of T.I.A. on the chart and thinks she's had a stroke."

I walked over to the bed and saw Ruth lying flat on her back, shallowly breathing, and chalky white. I felt the pulse in

122

her wrist. It was racing at one hundred forty beats per minute instead of her normal eighty. I pulled her gown down and saw a softball-sized blood clot over the right femoral artery in her leg. A pulsating geyser of blood was spurting from a puncture site in her groin.

"Jesus!" I yelled. "She's hemorrhaging from her femoral artery. She hasn't had a stroke; she's in shock. My patient's dying and none of you even checked her closely!

"Quick," I ordered the nurses, "put her head down and put shock blocks under the foot of the bed."

I pushed the neurology residents out of the way and said, "She's in shock, so her veins are collapsed. You'll never get an IV in her arm. Get me a subclavian IV."

I stuck the needle under Ruth's clavicle, thinking of all the lungs Coke and I had collapsed during our internship. The IV tubing slipped easily into the large subclavian vein, and I threaded it into the heart and turned the IV fluids wide open. In minutes she was out of shock. I pressed the femoral artery until the bleeding stopped, and five minutes later Ruth began thrashing about in bed asking what had happened.

"Lie still," I told her. "You're okay."

"Why does she have a puncture wound in her femoral artery?" I asked Dr. Mertins who was standing next to me.

"I drew arterial blood gases to check the oxygen concentration in her blood. I couldn't hit the radial artery in her wrist," he explained.

"Why did you draw blood gases?" I asked. "She doesn't have any history of asthma, emphysema, or any shortness of breath. She doesn't even smoke!"

"I'm doing a research paper studying whether or not giving oxygen to patients with strokes helps them," Mertins answered. "I gave her some oxygen this morning and then drew blood gases four hours later to see how much her oxygen had increased in the bloodstream."

"Did you hold pressure on the artery after you took the needle out?"

"Yes," Mertins answered. "For four minutes."

"That's not long enough to prevent bleeding, since she's on heparin."

"She's on blood thinner?" Mertins gasped.

"Yes," I mumbled as I wheeled Ruth's bed out of the room and toward the intensive care unit.

After I stabilized Ruth's blood pressure in the I.C.U., I called Raoul Pérez, a second-year neurosurgical resident.

"Raoul," I said, "I've got a woman at the V.A. that Mertins nearly assassinated this afternoon. I've got her out of shock now and I think she's stable, but I'm on call tonight at Methodist and I'm afraid to leave her alone. Can you cover for me tonight?"

"Sure," he said. "I'm over at the charity hospital. I'll walk over to the V.A. and pick up the beeper from you."

"Thanks. I'll probably make it over to Methodist about midnight."

Fifteen minutes later Raoul sauntered into the V.A. intensive care unit. He was a handsome, impeccably dressed Mexican of pure Mayan descent, about 5'8", a portly 230 pounds. His father was a neurosurgeon in the Yucatán Peninsula. He had studied under him for three years before coming to Memphis for formal training, making him one of the most experienced neurosurgical residents.

"Hi, Raoul," I said when I saw him come in. "Have any good operations today?"

"I operated all day on a drug addict who had a brain abscess."

"How's he doing?"

"Fine," Raoul answered. "He told the nurses in the I.C.U. after the operation he'd just take his own drugs when he hurt."

I handed Raoul my beeper. When he pulled his white coat back, I saw he already had the John Gaston Charity Hospital beeper clipped onto one side of his belt and the Baptist Hospital beeper hooked onto the other side. My beeper made three.

"I'm sorry, Raoul. I didn't know you were covering two other hospitals tonight."

"It's no problem. I'll wait for you at Methodist until you're free, and that will still give me plenty of time to get back to the charity hospital before the people start coming in who are shot in the head."

Several hours later, after I transfused four units of blood, Ruth's blood count was thirty-five, still below the normal forty but safe. Her blood pressure stabilized at 110/70, and there was no more bleeding in her groin. She was alert and able to drink some orange juice. At 11 P.M. I left for Methodist.

Six hours later I returned to the V.A. and found Ruth feeling much better and stable enough to have an arteriogram. It wasn't safe to wait two more days for the radiologist to do the test, so I called the X-ray department and told them I had a patient who needed an emergency arteriogram.

"We don't do emergency arteriograms at the V.A.," the X-ray technician replied.

"Well, goddammit! You're going to do your first one today," I shouted into the phone. "Now either help me or I'll do it myself. I'm bringing my patient from the I.C.U. now, and I want the room set up before I get there."

In fifteen minutes I had Ruth in the X-ray department for the arteriogram. The technician had all the equipment ready and I started the test about 5:30 A.M. I stuck a needle into each carotid artery in her neck and then injected dye into the arteries while the technician took the X rays. In twenty minutes I had finished the test.

"I can't believe it," the X-ray technician said. "It takes our radiologist two hours to do an arteriogram."

"Yeah, they make a big deal out of it. That's why it made me so mad to risk Ruth's health while we waited two days for a twenty-minute test."

The technician developed the X rays while I held pressure on the carotid arteries I had stuck with the needles. When all the X rays were on the view boxes, I pushed Ruth's stretcher out into the hall so she could see them too. There was a 99 percent blockage of Ruth's right carotid artery. She was less than one millimeter away from completely occluding the artery and having a massive stroke. The artery never would have stayed open for two days until the radiologist did her arteriogram. I paged Pete Bone, who was making rounds, and asked him to come down to radiology and look at the arteriogram.

It took Pete thirty seconds to reach the same conclusion: emergency carotid surgery was necessary. He called the operating room and told them to be ready within the hour. Next he talked to Ruth, listened to her history carefully, then explained the operation to her.

"I need to clean out the artery in your neck to prevent it from clogging up completely and causing a stroke," Pete explained to Ruth. "There is a risk of having a stroke during the operation while the artery is clamped off and I'm cleaning the cholesterol out of it, but the risk of stroke from surgery is much less than your risk of stroke if we do nothing."

126

"I don't want to have a stroke. When will you do the surgery?" Ruth asked.

"In about an hour."

Pete and I started the operation at seven. He made a six-inch incision down the right side of her neck, spread the muscles, and identified the carotid artery, which was pulsating below the obstruction but not above it. Yellow cholesterol glistened through the thickened wall of the artery. The diameter of the carotid, about the same as that of the thumb, was sufficiently large that we could bypass the obstruction with a shunt tube, ensuring that blood flow to the brain continued while Pete peeled the rock-hard, yellow chunks of cholesterol from the sides of the artery. Once the artery was cleaned out, he sewed it up with nylon stitches. The carotid could now be seen to bound, throb, and pulsate along its entire course.

Two and a half hours after the operation had begun, Ruth was in the recovery room talking, moving her arms and legs, and smiling when she realized she had not suffered a stroke.

"Is this all behind me now?" she asked Pete.

"Yes, it is. You'll be able to go home in a week and not have to worry about strokes anymore."

I was leaving the recovery room with Pete when the hospital operator paged me and told me Dr. Harkness wanted to talk to me. I picked up the phone and said, "Yes, sir."

"Come over to my office," he said gruffly.

There were no patients waiting to see Dr. Harkness, so I was sent in immediately. I sat down in the red chair in front of his desk and looked at his icy stare.

"Dr. Anderson called me last night and told me you nearly killed one of his patients!" Dr. Harkness said. "He's mad as hell, and goddammit, I am too!"

"What did Dr. Anderson say exactly?" I asked.

"He said you put a woman with migraine headaches on heparin, and she bled into shock after you ordered arterial blood gases on her. He also said no one knew where you were when she got into trouble, and she would have died if his neurology residents hadn't been there."

"That's not what happened."

"I'm not through," Dr. Harkness barked. "Anderson called back this morning and told me you did an emergency arteriogram on this woman, contrary to all V.A. regulations. Give me the woman's name. I'm going to review her chart, and if Anderson is right, I'm going to kick your ass out of this residency! Now get out of here."

"Let me tell you what happened."

"I don't want any excuses."

"I don't have anything to excuse," I persisted.

"I don't want to discuss it further until I review the chart." Dr. Harkness swung his arm through the air, motioning me out of the room.

That evening I finished checking my patients at the V.A. about six o'clock and joined Raoul for dinner in the Baptist Hospital cafeteria. Raoul wasn't going home either, since he was covering the charity hospital while the chief resident, Jim Molton, was on vacation for a week. We sat down in the small room beside the cafeteria reserved for interns and residents and began eating our hot dogs while we waited for the french fries to dry on napkins. We were eating ice cream sandwiches when Dr. Harkness marched into the dining room.

"Raoul, I need to talk to you," he growled.

"Yes, sir," Raoul answered, standing up.

"I just got a call from a surgeon in Dallas. It seems Jim Molton was out there moonlighting during his week's vacation. Did you know he was that short on money?"

"No, sir," answered Raoul.

"The surgeon told me Molton nearly bled to death from an ulcer and had to have surgery. He's stable now, and I'm sending a plane for him tonight so we can get him back to Memphis and his family. Molton's going to be out of work at least six weeks, so I want you to continue filling in for him as chief resident at the John Gaston Charity Hospital."

"Yes, sir," Raoul mumbled.

Dr. Harkness looked at me, then to Raoul, said, "Pick two nights a week for Rainer to cover for you at John Gaston. That will give you a break from night work."

Dr. Harkness left without saying anything else, and Raoul sat back down at the table. The other residents in the room resumed their conversations. Raoul and I said nothing as we finished our coffee and ice cream sandwiches.

Several minutes later Raoul looked up from his plate and said, "How do you want to work the night calls?"

"I don't care, Raoul," I answered. "I'll take the calls when you're tired, and you can take them when I need some sleep."

"That's a better idea than trying to work out a schedule," Raoul agreed.

"Why don't we move into the same call room?" I suggested. "That way I'll run into you more often, and it will make it easier to figure out who's working at night."

"Good idea," Raoul said. "Molton had a room by himself at John Gaston. There's enough room for an extra cot. He's got a desk in there and a closet, and it's right next door to the bathroom on the floor."

"That will work out well," I said. "We'll also be able to study together for the board exam. I'll go get my toothbrush and shaving kit from my room at the V.A. and meet you in Molton's room."

"I'll walk over to the V.A. with you. Some fresh air will feel good," Raoul said.

In the V.A. call room, Raoul and I ran into Pete, who was reading a *Playboy*.

"I had to read neuroanatomy for three years until I passed the board exam," Pete explained. "Now I can read something worthwhile."

"I'm moving to a room at the John Gaston," I told Pete as I picked up my books and shaving kit. "Raoul and I are filling in for Molton until he gets well."

"I'll be happy to take some nights for you," Pete said. "Just let me know."

"Thanks," I answered.

"By the way," Pete said. "Dr. Harkness was over here today raising hell about Ruth Hester's care."

"What happened?" I asked.

"I told him the full story and that you saved her from having a stroke. That settled him down."

"Good," I said going out the door.

I was glad Dr. Harkness had heard the facts. For months, Dr. Anderson had resented my constant requests for neuro-surgery consultations on neurology patients. He sensed my boredom and my desire to operate again. I respected his neurological knowledge but resented his reluctance to consult surgeons. I regretted the confrontation, but when I saw Ruth Hester leave the discharge office I knew it had been worth-while.

Most nights, Raoul and I both slept in the call room and shared the calls. On quiet nights we studied for the board exam scheduled for March. We tried to study two or three hours a night, before taking a break at midnight to eat a snack in the cafeteria with the other residents on duty. Each Saturday morning, from eight to nine, we attended the resident board review conference, after which Raoul always hurried home until noon to see his five-year-old son, Raoulito, who liked to watch Saturday morning cartoons on TV. After watching *Tarzan,* Raoulito's favorite program, at 11 A.M., Raoul rushed back to the hospital to help me with any work I was doing.

"Stay home longer," I pleaded with Raoul every Saturday when he returned to the hospital.

"No, I want to carry my load," Raoul always answered. "Anyway, three hours a week is probably more than any other resident is getting home."

One weekend in October, Raoul took the Friday night calls while I slept. At eight Saturday morning I found him in the John Gaston emergency room beside a bleeding policeman. There had been a shoot-out in the early morning hours, when police were called to a house in south Memphis where a drunk was beating his wife. When the police arrived, the drunk shot one of them in the stomach before they shot him in the head.

The policeman shot in the abdomen was dying from shock. The man shot in the head had received a glancing wound to the brain that would require surgery, but he wasn't in shock or in immediate danger of dying. He could probably last several hours without surgery; the policeman had only minutes.

"Operate on the policeman first," I heard Raoul tell the general surgery residents as I walked up.

"Aren't we going to operate the head injury now, too?" I asked Raoul.

"No. There are only enough personnel to run one operating room on Saturday morning, so we'll wait until they're through with the policeman."

That afternoon, Raoul and I operated on the man shot in the

head and removed the dead brain tissue, blood clots, and bullet fragments. The man regained consciousness in the intensive care unit and immediately began cursing the policeman in the bed across from him.

Five days later, the drunk ran a 104-degree fever, then became unconscious. A spinal tap showed he had bacterial meningitis, but, despite antibiotics, he died twenty-four hours later. The next morning Dr. Harkness summoned Raoul and me to his office.

"The mayor called me this morning and said the family of the man you operated on who was shot in the head is threatening to sue the police department," Dr. Harkness said. "He asked me why the man died. I reviewed the medical record and it seems he died from meningitis. Is that right?"

"Yes, sir," I answered.

"Why did he get infected?" Dr. Harkness asked.

"He had an open head wound with brain coming out his forehead where the bullet entered," Raoul explained.

"What time did he come into the E.R.?"

"About five-thirty A.M.," Raoul answered.

"Who did his surgery?"

"I did," I said. "Raoul was off call."

"What time did you start?" Dr. Harkness questioned me.

"Noon."

"How in the hell do you account for a six-hour delay?" Dr. Harkness shouted, standing up and leaning over his desk as he glared at me.

"We only have one operating room available on Saturday mornings at John Gaston," I explained. "The policeman was operated on first."

"You should have demanded the hospital open another operating room. Your patient deserved prompt surgery as much as anyone else. You're a surgeon, not a goddamn ethicist! No wonder he died with that length of delay on an open head wound. If Raoul had been there he wouldn't have waited, and that patient would be alive now."

"But, Dr. Harkness," Raoul said.

"Don't interrupt me," Dr. Harkness said, and then staring at me added: "One more mistake and you're out. Now both of you get back to work."

Raoul and I walked back to the John Gaston in silence. Finally Raoul said, "I'm sorry I got you into that mess. I'll talk to Dr. Harkness when he cools down."

"That's okay, Raoul. But you know, I don't think the delay caused the meningitis. I think it was just a contaminated wound that would have gotten infected no matter when we operated."

"Of course it would have. And Dr. Harkness knows that."

"We'll just have to try harder for better surgical results," I said.

"We have hundreds of excellent surgical results," Raoul replied, "but Dr. Harkness never comments on those."

Late in November, when Jim Molton returned to work at the John Gaston, Raoul and I dropped back to three nights a week on duty. On free nights we continued studying together, reading fifty pages a night in the three-volume *Youman's Textbook of Neurological Surgery,* hoping to complete the 2,024 pages in three months. We studied neuroanatomy, embryology, pathology, physiology, neurology, radiology, anesthesia and surgical techniques and reviewed previous board questions. If we were operating and missed a night studying, we got up the next morning at 2 A.M. to make up for the lost time.

We took a break from studying on Christmas Day and were watching TV in the cafeteria, when Raoul was beeped. The paging operator told Raoul that Dr. Harkness wanted to talk to him in the surgeons' lounge at Baptist Hospital. We turned off the TV and walked out the back door of John Gaston and across Madison Avenue to Baptist. Dr. Harkness was drinking coffee by himself when we walked in. Raoul caught his eye and said, "Yes, sir?"

Dr. Harkness handed Raoul a beeper and said, "Here's the chief resident beeper for Baptist Hospital. I fired Chen Lee this morning, and I want you to fill in for him the rest of the year. You've had the most experience, and you're the only one I can trust. Work out whatever you want to with Rainer concerning night work."

"Yes, sir," Raoul said, and both of us hurried out of the room.

We walked up to the chief resident's call room at Baptist and found Chen packing his medical books in a cardboard box.

"What happened, Chen?" Raoul asked.

When Chen turned around to answer, only his pale complexion gave a hint of his emotion. His stoic expression remained unchanged.

"A general practitioner called me last night from Jackson, Tennessee," Chen said. "He wanted to transfer a patient with back pain to the Baptist charity service. I was home with my family, so I told him to have the patient call the outpatient clinic on Monday and make an appointment. Apparently the G.P. is a good friend of Dr. Harkness, and he called him at home to complain that I wouldn't accept the transfer. Dr. Harkness had warned me that if I made one more mistake, I was out. I guess this was it."

"What will you do now, Chen?" Raoul asked.

"I'll spend the rest of the year studying for the board exam

134

and then try to find a residency somewhere else," Chen answered.

Chen handed his room key to Raoul, then picked up his box of books. Out in the hall he said good-bye to the other neurosurgery residents, who had come over from the other hospitals when they heard the news. Raoul and I walked down the stairs with Chen and helped him put his books in the back seat of his Volkswagen.

Chen took a list of charity patients out of his shirt pocket and handed it to Raoul, saying, "Come on. Let's make rounds on these patients so I can introduce you and explain what needs to be done for them."

An hour later Raoul and I watched from a window of the hospital as Chen's navy blue VW slid down snow-covered Madison Avenue as he headed home.

On January 1, 1978, I completed my neurology rotation at the V.A. Hospital, glad to finish such a concentrated exposure to untreatable diseases. For six months on neurology I'd seen patients with multiple sclerosis, Alzheimer's dementia, A.L.S., muscular dystrophy, and Huntington's chorea. I was anxious to get back to the neurosurgical service, where I could tell patients how they could be helped instead of how they would die. But Dr. Harkness assigned me to the Cerebrovascular Research Laboratory for three months and instructed me to devise experiments to study stroke.

The Cerebrovascular Lab occupied an entire floor of an old, unused wing of the John Gaston Hospital. One hundred thousand dollars' worth of microscopes and other equipment glistened in rooms with unpainted concrete-block walls, dusty shelves, and linoleum floors. Dulled sunlight filtered through rows of screenless windows, now translucent rather than transparent because of the buildup of grime on the panes. The air was thick with dust particles, making the room hazy. The lab smelled like a gas station bathroom, and even the pages in the research texts on the shelves were soiled. Research animals were kept in cages at the end of the hall, in a converted autopsy suite which had a red tile floor sloping to a drain in the center of the room to collect the animals' urine.

Though CT scanning was still primitive in 1978, it was important to obtain an accurate CT scan on stroke patients because some strokes had treatable causes such as brain tumors, aneurysms, and blood clots in the brain. Some strokes didn't show up for several hours on the scan, so I decided to investigate when most strokes were visible on the CT scan.

I chose mongrel cats as subjects since they were smaller than dogs and simpler to anesthetize. In addition, their skulls were thinner and easier to open than dogs', making the experiments faster. I submitted a proposal to Dr. Harkness, who sent it to the chairman of the Animal Experimentation Committee of the medical school. With the cats asleep, I proposed to tie off an artery in their brain and produce a stroke. Then, I planned to CT scan the cats at one hour, two hours, four hours, and eight hours after the stroke had been produced in order to determine the average length of time it took for a stroke to be seen on a CT scan. This would enable physicians to understand the CT scan better and avoid misdiagnoses.

My proposal was approved, and I was funded two hundred dollars for the project. Cats were donated by the city pound, and I spent most of the money on Nembutal, a tranquilizer used to anesthetize the animals. I operated on most cats at 4 A.M. to allow time for the eight-hour follow-up CT scan, which had to be done before the X-ray department at John Gaston Hospital closed at 5 P.M. The logistics of the experiment worked well, except for an occasional patient who complained when he or she spotted me positioning the sleeping cats in the hospital's CT scanner.

I operated on four cats each morning, and three weeks into the experiment I had accumulated data on sixty brains. I noticed, however, that each week I was becoming more allergic to the cats. At first I was troubled only by red, itching eyes. Later on I began to sneeze, and in the third week I began to wheeze when I breathed. On Friday morning of the third week the allergic reaction worsened. Large red splotches covered my face and arms. My chest tightened and the wheezing increased until I became short of breath. I felt dizzy, my heart raced, then I slumped out of the chair onto the floor.

Fortunately, Raoul came by to see if I wanted to eat breakfast with him. He found me blue, unable to talk, and gasping for air. Immediately he dragged and carried me down the stairs, through a back door into the John Gaston emergency room, and shouted for help. Interns ripped off my clothes and put IVs in both arms. They pulled a tracheostomy tray to the bedside, and I saw Raoul opening the knives and putting on gloves as he instructed the nurses to give me epinephrine. Even though they covered my nose and mouth with an oxygen mask, I continued to have difficulty breathing. The room began spinning and turned yellow, and the voices of the doctors and nurses around me echoed before I lost consciousness.

When I awoke, Raoul was sitting next to me taking my blood pressure. I was still on the stretcher in the E.R., but there was no commotion around me. I reached up to touch my throat and smiled when I realized I had not required a tracheostomy.

Raoul winked at me and said, "You scared the hell out of me. You quit breathing and went into shock before the epinephrine worked. Did you know you were that allergic to cats?"

"I've had trouble with them before, but not this bad."

"You're not wheezing anymore. Do you feel short of breath?"

"No."

"Good. I'm going to write you two prescriptions that you should take for three days to prevent the allergic reaction from coming back. And stay away from those cats!"

"I've got to finish the experiment," I said. "Dr. Harkness expects me to publish a paper on my findings."

"Not anymore, he doesn't," Raoul said. "I've already told him what happened."

"What did he say?"

"He said you'd do anything to get out of work!"

"He doesn't think much of me, does he?"

"He was kidding. He said to tell you to get out of the lab and work on the neurosurgical service at Methodist Hospital."

"Why Methodist? They've got two residents; he's never assigned three there before."

"One of the first-year residents quit and moved home," Raoul explained. "He told everyone he was homesick, but Dr. Harkness thinks he's depressed and needs psychiatric help."

"I think quitting shows he's sane."

"Me, too," Raoul agreed. "I would have quit a long time ago, but I knew my father would have been disappointed in me."

"Well that knocks us down to eight residents," I groaned. "If we can just hold on until three new residents come in July, we'll be back up to eleven."

"Not really." Raoul added more bad news. "Nancy Barton is quitting at the end of this year. She's going into emergency room work; says she doesn't want this lifestyle. So in July there will just be ten of us, five residents short."

"At least we'll get to operate more," I suggested, trying to sound optimistic.

On March 27, at 4 A.M., after ten hours of labor, Julie delivered our first child—a healthy, eight-pound, dark-haired, dark-eyed daughter, Laura Page. I kissed them both, held Laura for about five minutes, and tried to rub the red forceps marks off her face. When Julie fell asleep, I started studying again. The written examination of the American Board of Neurological Surgery was three days away.

Six weeks later Raoul and I were notified of our passing scores. We headed to the Holiday Inn after work to celebrate with a few beers.

"Well, at least the exam is behind us now," Raoul said.

"Yeah," I answered. "I'll be glad when the residency is, too."

There were two years of residency left, many more sleepless nights, and dozens of operations to perfect. But on this spring afternoon, I decided to put it all out of my mind for a few hours. I asked Raoul to cover for me until 8 P.M., handed him my beeper, and then drove home to take Julie—and Laura—out for dinner.

CHAPTER 6

SENIOR RESIDENT—1978

O N JULY 1, 1978, Pete Bone completed his residency and entered private practice in Chattanooga, Tennessee. I became senior resident in neurosurgery at Baptist Memorial Hospital, and Raoul received the senior appointment at Methodist Hospital. Two chief residents ran the John Gaston, V.A., and Children's hospitals, and six junior residents were assigned to various clinical services in the five hospitals. Neurosurgery residencies nationwide had now increased to five years, and Memphis was approved for fifteen residents. We had ten.

Advancement to senior resident carried added responsibilities. Night call increased from four nights a week to every night. Junior residents filtered the phone calls, but senior residents were responsible for patients who were admitted at night after attending surgeons had gone home and had to make sure they were properly evaluated, X-rayed, and treated. Patients were seen in the emergency room by junior residents, who did a history, physical examination, laboratory studies, and skull and cervical spine X rays. For patients with diagnoses of stroke, head injury, or headache, an emergency brain CT scan was done. With this information, the junior resident then called the senior resident for advice on further treatment.

The senior resident year was a transition from junior resident years of constant supervision and assisting in surgery to the chief resident year of no supervision and performing all surgery. Twelve months as senior resident included supervised operations by attending surgeons on their private patients and unsupervised operations on charity patients. This allowed senior residents to learn the surgical craft from fully trained surgeons and then build confidence by operating on charity patients alone.

Each senior resident at Baptist and Methodist hospitals ran a charity service of about twenty-five patients. In addition, each senior covered three surgeons, totaling about eighty patients to be seen daily. He was also responsible for teaching junior residents basic surgical procedures such as spinal taps, myelograms, arteriograms, opening and closing head, neck, and back incisions, insertion of skull tongs, and tracheostomy. The senior was expected to set the example for junior residents: thorough patient workups, skilled surgery, close postoperative care, and constant textbook study.

The senior resident at Baptist Hospital was always assigned to Dr. Harkness, who had twenty-five to forty patients hospitalized at all times and had the busiest neurosurgical practice in Memphis. His interests included pituitary tumors and stroke, so patients with difficult problems requiring tedious operations were constantly being referred to him. In addition, Dr. Harkness was a member of the American Board of Neurological Surgery, which required him to travel extensively and left the senior resident to run his service at Baptist Hospital

141

while he was out of town. He operated on Thursdays from 7 A.M. until 7 P.M., leaving eight or nine critical post-op patients for the resident to take care of when he left town on Friday morning.

The six-month rotation on Dr. Harkness' service was the flashpoint in a resident's training. Not only did Dr. Harkness scrutinize the senior's care of his private patients, he also supervised charity patient surgery. Residents weren't allowed to become chiefs until Dr. Harkness was satisfied with their performance on his service. Consequently, a resident's most intense work was done during these six months. Resident rounds to check incisions, change dressings, write orders and progress notes began at 4 A.M. to ensure they were finished before Dr. Harkness made rounds at 5 A.M. At night, after Dr. Harkness' work was completed, the senior resident did his own work: running the charity service. The emergency room, operating room, and hospital wards became the senior's entire world. Summer and winter clothes weren't necessary. Inside the hospital it was never hot and never snowed. I watched the seasons change from the hospital windows and Laura grow through pictures Julie saved for me.

The night before I rotated onto Dr. Harkness' service, he admitted eighteen patients to the hospital from the afternoon clinic in his office. The senior rotating off his service had received Pete Bone's appointment as chief resident at the V.A. and had forty patients to become familiar with before the next morning, so I volunteered to work up Dr. Harkness' new admissions. I began after supper at 7 P.M. and finished the last history and physical examination about 1 A.M. I slept until four, made rounds, and then met Dr. Harkness at the nurses' station on the 14 Madison Ward at 5 A.M.

He was dressed neatly in a dark, vested suit and inhaled deeply on his cigarette as he leafed through the charts. He frowned at me when I walked up, and glanced at the clock. Then, without speaking, he marched down the hall to see his first patient. I chuckled quietly as I walked a few yards behind him. Other residents had told me his bedside manner was worse than his treatment of residents. With Dr. Harkness, any amusement was welcome. He entered the patient's room without knocking and began talking before the door closed.

"You have a tumor in the pituitary gland," he blurted out to the young woman, Mary Hurst, who was lying in bed. She jumped straight up, startled by his commanding voice. "It can be treated with a medicine named Parlodel, which will shrink it down but won't get rid of it, or I can operate and take it out. I recommend surgery."

"I just want to be free of this tumor forever," Mary stammered as she hurried to put her bathrobe over her lacy white nightgown.

"Then surgery is the only option," Dr. Harkness replied.

"Okay, I'll have the operation. When will you do it?"

"Tomorrow."

Dr. Harkness turned abruptly and left the room. Outside, he said to me, "Go back after rounds, sit down with her, and make sure she understands the surgery. If she doesn't, cancel the surgery and I'll talk to her again."

"Yes, sir," I answered.

He stared at me, making sure I understood. Then he went to see the next patient. As morning rounds proceeded, I noticed Dr. Harkness checked each chart to see if the history and physical examination had been completed. My fatigue from staying up until 1 A.M. vanished when he looked at the last chart and realized I had done all eighteen workups. He turned to me and glared at my smiling face. I expected a compliment, the first day on his service.

"Goddammit!" he said. "You didn't record the weakness in this patient's right biceps muscle. That's a sure sign of a ruptured cervical disc, and you didn't even pick it up. You've got to be more thorough!"

I wanted to remind him of all the correct observations I had made on the other seventeen new patients, but instead I gave my standard reply: "Yes, sir."

After rounds I went back to Mary Hurst's room to explain the operation Dr. Harkness would perform to remove her pituitary tumor. She was twenty-six years old and the daughter of a prominent trial attorney in Memphis. She had been married for four years but had been unable to get pregnant. Her gynecologist recognized that she had the pituitary tumor syndrome: the absence of menstrual periods and presence of breast milk in a woman who is not pregnant. The gynecologist obtained blood tests, including a serum prolactin level which was abnormally high, suggesting the possibility that a pituitary tumor was secreting the hormone prolactin, which was causing her symptoms and infertility. She had been referred to Dr. Harkness, who had X-rayed the bone surrounding the pituitary gland. There was erosion of the skull, which confirmed the presence of a small pituitary tumor.

"Hi, Mary," I said. "Dr. Harkness asked me to come back and talk to you and see if you had any additional questions that he didn't cover this morning."

"Yes, I do," Mary said. "The nurse brought me an operative permit to sign, and I don't understand it. The operation is called transsphenoidal removal of pituitary tumor. I don't understand what that means."

144

"There are two ways to remove pituitary tumors," I explained. "One is through the top of the head, pulling the frontal lobe back and approaching the pituitary gland between the optic nerves from the eyes. That's called a craniotomy. The other approach is transsphenoidal. That means Dr. Harkness won't open your head. Instead, he'll go through your upper gum, along the nasal septum under your nose, through the sphenoid sinus, into the base of the brain from below, instead of from above. It's a much easier approach for the patient because the surgeon doesn't have to pull on the brain to reach the pituitary gland."

"Is there any chance this tumor might be malignant?" Mary asked, wrinkling her forehead and rubbing her temple.

"No," I reassured her. "It's a benign tumor. The main reason to remove it is to decrease the hormone prolactin circulating in your bloodstream and let you get pregnant."

"What's the chance the operation will work for me?"

"There's about a seventy-five-percent chance you'll get pregnant after the tumor is removed," I answered.

"Will I hurt after surgery?" Mary asked.

"No," I said. "Your nose will feel stopped up, like you have a cold. But after three days the nasal packs will be removed and you'll feel better."

"Well, thanks for talking to me. I have all the confidence in the world in Dr. Harkness, and I believe I have the best surgeon doing my operation."

Each Thursday at 7 A.M. Dr. Harkness began a marathon operating schedule. Usually he did two or three pituitary tumors, two extracranial-intracranial bypass operations, a brain tumor, and several laminectomies for ruptured cervical and lumbar discs. Often he operated twelve to fourteen hours, but he never complained of fatigue. Each patient, whether first or

145

seventh on the schedule, received the same intense attention. He scheduled the more complicated operations in the morning and the easier operations in the afternoon and evening, when he knew he would be tiring.

Mary Hurst was scheduled first. Dr. Harkness carefully positioned her on the operating table with her head tilted back. Her head was fixed in the headrest, and she resembled someone in bed, propped on her elbows and trying to wake up in the morning. An incision was made in the gum over the upper teeth and extended under her nose. At a depth of four inches, the skull under the pituitary gland was opened with a hammer and chisel by tapping on the bone until the skull fractured inward toward the pituitary gland. The operating microscope was pulled into position to provide additional light and magnification for the tedious work ahead. After X rays were made in the operating room to confirm that the hole in the skull was directly underneath the pituitary, Dr. Harkness widened the opening to the size of a quarter. The grape-sized pituitary gland was now visible and appeared uniformly gray on its surface, without any obvious tumor. Dr. Harkness explored all sides of the pituitary, gently raising it, pulling it down, and pushing it from side to side with thin, twelve-inch-long stainless steel forceps.

After ten minutes he still had not found the tumor, and he said, "I'll have to fillet the gland. Sometimes these tumors are burrowed into the substance of the gland, and can't be seen unless the gland is cut open."

He took a clean knife and cut the gland five times. The gland remained intact but could now be spread apart like a fan. A yellow, pea-sized ball was evident in the left lobe of the gland. Using a small hook and scooping movements, Dr. Harkness took the tumor out of the pituitary gland. Then he

146

sealed the opening in the skull with cartilage from the nose and closed the gum incision with six catgut stitches. The operation was over in ninety minutes. The older method, a craniotomy, would have taken four hours. Mary awoke immediately in the recovery room and, except for the nasal packing in her nostrils, complained of no discomfort.

"We got the whole tumor out, Mary," Dr. Harkness told her in the recovery room. "You'll be able to get pregnant now, so you better just fool around with your husband from now on."

She smiled and drifted off to sleep. Dr. Harkness returned to the operating room for six more operations and ten hours of surgery.

After he removed two more pituitary tumors, Dr. Harkness began the first of two extracranial-intracranial, or E.C.-I.C., bypass operations. This operation, popularized in 1967 by Dr. Gazi Yasargil in Switzerland, involved sewing the superficial temporal artery from the scalp to a branch of the middle cerebral artery inside the brain. This allowed restoration of blood flow to the brain following a stroke, when the carotid artery in the neck was occluded, or when major arteries in the brain were blocked. The delicate surgery could be done only under a microscope and involved sewing two arteries together that were only two millimeters in diameter. The nylon suture used to sew the arteries was finer than human hair, couldn't be seen with the naked eye but only through a microscope, and was so delicate that the suture floated, instead of falling, when dropped. The slightest tremor in a surgeon's hand made the operation impossible because the work was so precise. Dr. Harkness was one of three neurosurgeons in Memphis with the ability to perform the surgery.

Dr. Harkness began the E.C.-I.C. bypass at 1 P.M., after

147

finishing the three transsphenoidal pituitary tumor operations. The patient, B. B. Dawkins, was a retired seventy-five-year-old carpenter who had remodeled Dr. Harkness' antebellum home in midtown Memphis.

"Why is he called B.B.?" I asked Dr. Harkness.

"He was delivered by a midwife in Tunica, Mississippi, and all she wrote on the birth certificate was Baby Boy. His mother began calling him Baby Boy, and when he got older he shortened it to B.B. Ready to go to sleep, B.B.?" Dr. Harkness asked his patient lying on the operating table.

"Goddamn son of a bitch," B.B. answered evenly without emotion.

"Okay, put him to sleep," Dr. Harkness instructed the anesthesiologist.

"Not very friendly, is he?" I said to Dr. Harkness after the patient was anesthetized.

"Well, he really is," Dr. Harkness answered as he began scrubbing his hands with pHisoHex at the scrub sinks overlooking the O.R. "He had a stroke six months ago that left him unable to talk except to curse."

Dr. Harkness explained that the more primitive portions of B.B.'s brain, such as the area controlling cursing, had survived the stroke, while higher cortical centers, such as those responsible for fluent speech, had been destroyed. The effect on his brain was similar to being drunk. Alcohol affects the frontal lobes, which normally inhibit the primitive areas of the brain. Once free of frontal lobe inhibition, the primal brain surfaces, accounting for why some drunks change into lovers or fighters and their mood becomes euphoric or depressed.

Man's drives are the same as those of animals. He eats, sleeps, mates, and is motivated only by self-interest, which in animals is called survival. The only difference is that man's darker emotions are hidden behind a mask of intelligence and inhibition resulting from a more highly developed brain. Drugs, alcohol, and strokes unmask the hidden recesses of the brain, and the animal instincts surface. This is why stroke victims or brain tumor patients sometimes laugh and cry inappropriately, lose their temper and curse, or masturbate in public. The powerful, primeval forces in the brain have been unleashed.

"Will the bypass restore the higher cortical centers and help B.B.'s speech return to normal?" I asked.

"It might," Dr. Harkness answered. "But when a patient or family asks you if a brain bypass will return normal function, always answer 'No.' Stress that the bypass operation is designed to prevent another stroke and stop deterioration, not to make the patient better. With this operation, all you can reasonably expect is to keep a patient from getting worse."

Dr. Harkness finished scrubbing his hands and began the four-hour operation. He made a six-inch incision over the visibly pulsating superficial temporal artery located in the scalp just in front of the ear. Carefully he dissected the tortuous artery from its wandering course across the forehead. Next he split the temporalis muscle, the powerful muscle over the temple that can be seen contracting on chewing. A silver-dollar-sized hole was drilled in the skull, and the bone was cracked free, exposing the arteries on the surface of the brain. A large branch of the middle cerebral artery was selected and the operation began. Dr. Harkness steadied his arms and hands on a Mayo stand as he sewed. The surgery was so delicate, the movements of his hands so slight, and the needle and suture so difficult to see that, to the uninitiated eye, he looked as if he was sewing the Emperor's new clothes. There was no bleeding, no tissue removed from the brain, no power

149

saws or noise, and no talking in the operating room; just intense concentration as he stared through the microscope at the grayish-yellow, pulsating brain. He completed sewing the two arteries together an hour later. The additional blood flow into the brain could be seen expanding the cerebral arteries. Thirty minutes later the head was closed, and Dr. Harkness was ready to begin the fifth operation.

At 5 P.M. Dr. Harkness began a second E.C.-I.C. bypass, and at nine o'clock he started his last case, a ruptured lumbar disc which he removed in forty-five minutes. At 10:30 he left to go home, and I returned to the charity ward to make rounds and finish the work on my own patients. At midnight the hospital operator paged me and told me I had an outside call. It was Colt Jackson, an alcoholic who tended bar at Huey's, a beer and pizza parlor a few blocks from Baptist Hospital, where residents and nurses met in off-hours to unwind.

"Doc, my leg feels numb," Colt said.

I had known Colt for two years, and he always complained to any resident in Huey's that would listen. I had become his favorite after I took care of him at the V.A. when he nearly died following delirium tremens. I had nursed him through the D.T.s with massive doses of the tranquilizer Librium, stopped his convulsions with phenobarbital, and transfused him with eight bottles of blood, saving him from an operation when he hemorrhaged from an ulcer. He had found the Lord and been a model citizen for two months. He attended Alcoholics Anonymous, went to Bellevue Baptist Church every Sunday, and had given up alcohol and women he didn't know. When he returned to bartending, he found Jim Beam bourbon and lost the Lord. At midnight, after twelve hours of surgery and with two more hours of work ahead of me, I didn't pay much attention to his complaint of a numb leg.

150

"Colt, you've had back surgery before. Most patients have some numbness in their legs afterward," I said.

"Okay," he answered.

The next morning he called back and said, "Both my legs are numb now, Doc. I think I'm having a stroke."

"No, you're not," I reassured him. "You're just having a flare-up of your back trouble."

"I don't know, Doc," he said. "This has me scared."

I was tired of listening to him complain and needed to get to the operating room, so I said, "If you're having that much trouble, come on down to the emergency room, and I'll check you."

"Thanks, Doc," he said.

That evening I finished my work about eleven. I was too tired to drive home, and I had just stretched out on the cot in my hospital room when the phone rang. The E.R. nurse told me Colt had just arrived, and he was drunk.

"Admit him to the charity ward and I'll see him in the morning," I told the nurse. I needed the sleep and knew I couldn't do a thorough workup on him until he was sober.

The next morning I checked Colt first. He had just been given a bed bath by an orderly and was lying naked in bed.

"Why didn't you take a shower in the hall bath?" I asked.

"Can't move, Doc. I'm paralyzed," he answered.

"What do you mean, you're paralyzed?" I asked, thinking he was joking.

"I can't move my arms or legs," Colt replied.

I looked at him closely. He was frightened, breathing shallowly, and totally paralyzed from the neck down. His eyes were opened wide, and he was looking directly at the ceiling. His nostrils flared and his head bobbed as he struggled for air.

151

"Get me some oxygen and a spinal tap tray—now!" I shouted down the ward to the nurses' station.

A nurse rushed into the room with a spinal needle and helped me roll Colt over on his side. She pulled his knees up toward his chest and pulled his neck forward, to flex his spine for the tap. I shoved the five-inch needle through his skin and into his spinal canal. Cloudy fluid gushed out the needle. I ordered protein, glucose, and cell counts on the spinal fluid. In a few minutes a lab technician called me the results. Colt had Guillain-Barré syndrome, a disease of nerves thought to be due to a virus, that ascends the body, causing paralysis first in the legs and then in the arms, sometimes paralyzing the respiratory muscles and resulting in death if not quickly and correctly treated. His alcoholism had made me complacent, resulting in a critical delay in making the proper diagnosis. And now, because I had judged his character and not his disease, he was in danger of dying.

"Get him a bed in the intensive care unit, and ask the chief resident in internal medicine to meet me there," I instructed the nurse.

In the I.C.U. I asked the medicine resident to keep a close eye on Colt so if he stopped breathing he could be put on a respirator. One peculiarity of the disease is its total remission. Even after paralyzing a patient, the disease usually resolves spontaneously, leaving a patient who eventually recovers completely from the paralysis. I stressed to the medicine resident to treat Colt aggressively, emphasizing he could survive the illness with thorough care.

I operated all day and late that night and didn't see Colt until the next morning at 4:30. I was walking into the I.C.U. drinking some orange juice when a nurse grabbed me and shouted, "Come in here, quick! He can barely breathe!"

152

I ran to Colt's bedside and found him sweating and gasping. His lips were blue, his eyes glazed. I grabbed a laryngoscope, stuck the metal blade down his throat, pulled his tongue to one side, and pushed a plastic tube into his windpipe. After he received oxygen from a respirator, his complexion changed from blue to pink, and he regained consciousness. He had nearly died again and this time had been saved only by the close care he was receiving from the I.C.U. nurses.

Two weeks later his breathing had improved enough so that he could be weaned from the respirator. Six more weeks of physical therapy followed to strengthen the arm and leg muscles that had temporarily been paralyzed. After he promised me he would continue his therapy as an outpatient, I discharged him from the hospital. He walked stiffly to the elevator, and I headed back to the ward thinking about the ancient Chinese proverb: "Medicine heals those who are fated not to die."

Ward work occupied six to eight hours a day and surgery ten to twelve hours a day. Each Thursday I operated with Dr. Harkness. He was a skilled surgeon but short-tempered and impatient. His tirades, cursing, accusations, harangues, and blasts of ill temper were always directed at his surgical assistant —the senior resident.

After two years in the residency, I was accustomed to barbs from neurosurgeons. As a first-year resident, I had saved a patient's life in the E.R. by performing an emergency tracheostomy. The staff neurosurgeon, Dr. Paxton, leaned his head in the door, grinned, and asked, "Always lose this much blood doing a trach?" The day I did my first lumbar laminectomy to remove a ruptured disc in the back, Dr. Wright looked at the length of my incision and asked: "Was this patient in a car wreck?" When I finished the operation in an hour, as fast as

153

staff surgeons, Dr. Wright returned to the operating room as I was putting in the skin stitches to drawl wryly, "Is this the same case?"

Their jests were made lightly and pushed the resident to improve his surgical skills. It wasn't barbs I experienced operating with Dr. Harkness, it was verbalized anger.

Dr. Harkness first spoke to me in the operating room on the third Thursday we operated together. He had spent eight hours that morning removing a spinal cord tumor from a doctor's daughter. The microscopic work was exhausting, the danger of paralyzing the girl present every second of every minute for eight hours. My job during the operation was to suck blood away from the tumor without touching the spinal cord and paralyzing the patient. Although I wasn't removing the tumor, I had more chance to injure the girl than Dr. Harkness did. For hours I steadied my hands against her spine and kept the operative field clear of blood so Dr. Harkness could remove the tumor. My feet ached, my fingers felt numb, my joints were stiff, and I had sweated through my scrub shirt. When Dr. Harkness completed the operation, I went to the recovery room with the patient to write the postoperative orders and check to make sure her arms and legs weren't paralyzed. She awoke from the operation without any weakness in her extremities, a superb surgical result and a tribute to Dr. Harkness' skill as a surgeon. I was sitting in the recovery room drinking a Coke, with my feet propped up on the edge of a desk, when Dr. Harkness stormed in to check on her postoperative condition. He checked his patient, then turned to me and said, "I don't know why you're acting tired. You didn't do a goddamn thing in the O.R. except make a shadow!"

Each Thursday with Dr. Harkness was the same. With his

special interest in stroke, he was referred many patients with atherosclerotic narrowing of the carotid artery in the neck requiring carotid surgery. Clamping the carotid artery during the operation deprived the brain of blood for a few minutes and risked causing a stroke. Consequently Dr. Harkness was anxious for the operation to proceed smoothly, and his outbursts increased as the critical portion of the operation approached. Occasionally it was necessary to tie, and then cut, the large facial vein to provide better exposure of the carotid artery. During one operation Dr. Harkness passed a clamp under the vein, then handed me a silk suture to tie on my side of the vein. He tied the suture on his side before cutting the vein between the two knots. Ten minutes after we had tied and cut the facial vein, while Dr. Harkness was preparing to open the wall of the carotid artery, the entire neck filled up with blood as the patient hemorrhaged from the facial vein where a silk tie had slipped off. Blood poured out of the neck and splashed on the floor.

"Goddamn!" Dr. Harkness shouted across the table at me. "You're killing my patient! She's bleeding to death."

I took a clamp, reached across to the vein stump on his side and clamped it with the instrument. Immediately the bleeding stopped.

"Give me the silk this time," he instructed the nurse. "I'll tie the knot so it won't slip off the vein again."

When he finished tying the silk around the vein, I held up my side of the vein, with its knot still securely tied.

"Want to tie this knot again, too?" I asked.

"No, goddammit!" he yelled. "My tie won't slip!"

It was important that the resident avoid critical remarks concerning Dr. Harkness' surgical complications. At the end of one spinal case, when Dr. Harkness broke off a needle in

155

the thick spinal muscles and couldn't find it, I asked him how he would like me to dictate the loss of the needle in the operative report.

He glared at me across the table, and said, "Dictate that you found the needle!"

He peeled off his gloves, ripped off his surgical mask and threw it into the corner of the operating room, and marched out of the room. I stared at the operating doors as they whistled shut behind him, hardly believing he would instruct me to lie in the medical record. Then I realized what he meant. I was to stay in the O.R. and search for the needle until it was found, doing whatever was required: X rays, hooking it with a magnet, or further dissection.

Thirty minutes later, with the help of a sharp-eyed scrub nurse, we found the needle and closed the patient's incision. I took the needle into the surgeon's lounge to show Dr. Harkness that it had been found. He flicked the needle and his cigarette into the wastebasket and stood up to go back to the operating room.

"Why aren't you getting the next patient positioned on the operating table?" he growled.

While the twelve hours spent operating each Thursday with Dr. Harkness were painful, the one hour spent with him at the Monday night conference was worse. Sometimes called the senior conference, it was a weekly one-hour review of every operative case the senior resident had done. From 5 to 6 P.M. every Monday, the senior stood in front of view boxes on the Baptist Hospital auditorium stage and defended his management of charity patients. It was the most popular conference in the medical center. Physicians, surgeons, residents, medical students, and nurses relaxed in the blue theater seats and drank coffee while they enjoyed the sharp interchange between Dr. Harkness and the senior resident. Staff neurosurgeons remained neutral in the arguments and offered constructive comments. Chief residents, attending from other hospitals, always vigorously supported the senior resident's position. Junior residents, medical students, and nurses observed but didn't talk. Successful senior residents remained unflustered and defended their treatments with reams of surgical literature. Residents bending to the pressure of Dr. Harkness' searing criticism were delayed in receiving appointments as chief resident or labeled, by innuendo, a marginal neurosurgical resident.

My first three Monday night conferences as the Baptist senior were uneventful as I discussed the follow-up care of patients operated on by the previous resident. But in the fourth conference Dr. Harkness turned up the heat.

The first ten rows of the thirty-row auditorium were packed with observers. Several staff surgeons were telling jokes and smoking cigars while they waited for the conference to begin. Most residents were drinking coffee, a few were flirting with nurses and trying to line up dates with them for off-duty hours. Medical students sat flipping through books, apprehensive that Dr. Harkness might ask them a question. The laughter and murmur of conversation ceased immediately when Dr. Harkness knocked the swinging doors open and paced into the room, his long white coat flapping behind him as he marched to the front row. The complete silence was interrupted only by the creaking of his chair as he pulled it down and fell into it.

"Go ahead," he ordered.

I looked at the attentive audience and took a sip of coffee to wet my dry mouth. My face and stomach burned, and I had a headache. Raoul's smile encouraged me and reminded me of his comment after his last senior conference: "Only Mexican diarrhea for me now!" I understood his comment exactly as my intestines began dancing to their own music.

I took a deep breath and presented the first case. "Willie Lee is twenty-four years old and was shot in the back of the head Saturday."

"Be more specific," Dr. Harkness snapped. "Where was he shot, what kind of gun was used, what time did it happen?"

"Yes, sir," I replied. "I was coming to that." I had already decided to swing back when Dr. Harkness began attacking.

"Willie Lee was shot by his girlfriend with a thirty-two-caliber pistol when she came into his house and caught him making love to his wife."

The auditorium erupted in laughter, and Raoul continued chuckling as I clipped the X rays onto the view boxes. Only Dr. Harkness' scowl silenced him.

"The entrance wound is in the right occipital lobe, just behind his right ear," I explained, pointing to the X rays. "The missile crossed through the center of the brain and exited the right frontal lobe just above the right eye. He was shot about two P.M. I saw him in the E.R. at three."

"What's he doing making love at two in the afternoon?" Dr. Harkness asked. "Doesn't he work?"

"Yes, sir," I answered. "He works midnight to eight A.M. as a security guard at the Memphis Pink Palace Museum. His wife said they always make love in the afternoon, so they'll have time to finish before he goes to work."

"Get on with the case," Dr. Harkness demanded.

"I got an emergency CT scan of Willie Lee's head and took him immediately to the operating room."

"Why did you waste time getting a CT scan? You knew he needed surgery," Dr. Harkness said. "Patients with blood clots in their brain can die while you're screwing around getting unnecessary tests."

"Well, Willie Lee was stable," I answered. "He was awake, talking, and not paralyzed. He had severe headache and some visual loss, but he wasn't in immediate danger of dying. Also, I wanted to know the course of the bullet, the location of the blood clots, and the amount of missile fragmentation. Besides, it takes thirty minutes for the O.R. to set up for a craniotomy. I decided to put the time to good use." Dr. Harkness said nothing. I continued.

"I did a right occipital craniotomy and a right frontal craniotomy and cleaned all debris out of the brain throughout the entire course of the missile. I evacuated the blood clots, removed the bone and missile fragments, and stopped all arteries and veins that were bleeding. While I was closing his head, he developed severe brain swelling, so I had to leave the bone flap out and just close the scalp over his brain."

"Goddammit!" Dr. Harkness exploded. "You're telling me you had an open, contaminated wound, and all you did was close the skin? That's malpractice! Everyone knows you must do a careful layer closure to prevent infections in contaminated wounds. You must close the dura, replace the bone flap, close the muscle, galea, and skin. A one-layer closure is inadequate. You have just ignored the most basic principle every surgeon since Halsted has followed! You have totally mismanaged this case. The operation you did is a disgrace!"

Dr. Harkness was now red-faced and pounding the stage floor in front of him. He continued his tirade as he paced in front of the audience. "All you can do is explain to his wife you didn't do the operation right and then take him back to the O.R. and close all layers of the wound."

"Wait a minute," one of the chief residents spoke up. "How is the patient doing post-op?"

"He's doing fine," I said. "His incisions are healing well without infection. He doesn't have any fever. He's eating and walking in the hall and is scheduled to go home Friday."

"It's hard to criticize success," a staff surgeon added.

Dr. Harkness sat down. "Next case," he bellowed.

The next patient had severe back pain and difficulty urinating. I put the myelogram on the X-ray boxes and pointed to the blockage of dye in his spine, which showed a mass at the disc-space level between the fourth and fifth lumbar vertebrae.

"The preoperative diagnosis was nerve root tumor," I said.

"No, he doesn't have a tumor; he has a ruptured disc," Dr. Harkness interjected. "Ruptured discs are much more common than spinal tumors, especially in that area. Did you take off extra bone in preparation for removing a tumor?" Dr. Harkness asked.

"Yes, sir," I answered.

"That's wrong," Dr. Harkness said. "You removed too much bone and weakened his spine unnecessarily, and put him through a more extensive operation than he needed. Didn't you learn anything the first two years in the residency?"

"Let him finish," one of the staff surgeons said, trying to moderate Dr. Harkness's criticism. "What did you find at surgery?"

"A ruptured disc," I answered.

"Next case," Dr. Harkness shouted.

"Sadie Watson is a seventy-six-year-old white female who has been confined in Oakview Nursing Home for twelve years with a diagnosis of Alzheimer's disease. She fell on the wheelchair ramp and then had a grand mal seizure. The nursing home doctor told the nurses to send her to Baptist for a CT

160

scan to rule out the possibility of a blood clot in her brain. She didn't have a blood clot, but the CT showed a huge benign tumor in her left hemisphere. I talked to her son and daughter, and they wanted the tumor removed if there was any chance it might make their mother better. She's been confused for twelve years and hasn't talked in the last six years, but she still walks by herself and recognizes her children. I operated on her yesterday, and she's doing fine after surgery. She isn't talking, but she seems less confused."

Dr. Harkness walked up on stage and studied the X rays for a few minutes, then thumbed through the arteriogram. "How long did it take you to remove this tumor?" he asked.

"Three hours," I said quickly, pleased at the opportunity to reveal my surgical ability.

"Then you didn't get it all out!" Dr. Harkness said.

The room was deathly silent as Dr. Harkness faced me on stage and glared. "No one can take this large a tumor out in three hours. Get a postoperative CT scan on this patient, and don't discharge her from the hospital until I see the scan. I won't allow my residents to put an old woman to sleep, risk her life under general anesthesia, and then not even do the operation completely. That is unacceptable treatment from a senior resident!"

The audience remained quiet, squirming as Dr. Harkness continued to criticize me on stage. When he finished talking, he marched out of the auditorium without speaking to anyone. I gathered up the X rays as Raoul and the other residents walked up on the stage.

"Great job!" one of the chief residents said, patting me on the shoulder. "You hung in there great today. He won't be as tough on you in the other conferences. He has to get it out of his system at least once."

"Yeah," Raoul agreed. "He ate me out for a wound infection on a back operation. Told everyone in the auditorium I didn't wash my hair thoroughly. Don't worry about it."

"But you were there, Raoul. I got all of that tumor out," I said.

"I know," Raoul said. "Just play it cool. Get the CT scan, show him the tumor's out, then drop it."

"Don't you think he should apologize to me next Monday night?" I asked.

"Don't mention it again. Just forget about it," Raoul repeated.

"That's hard to do after he embarrassed me in front of every resident, medical student, nurse, and neurosurgeon in Baptist Hospital," I said.

"No one else will remember this tomorrow. It's no big deal. Come on," Raoul said. "Let's go get some supper."

"No, thanks," I said. "I've lost my appetite. I'm going to the charity ward and take Sadie down for her CT scan tonight. I'll show him on rounds tomorrow morning that the tumor's out."

"Well, I'm going to eat dinner," Raoul said. "I'll stop by X ray after I finish and look at the scan with you."

I walked up six flights to the charity ward instead of taking the elevator so I could avoid Dr. Harkness. I found Sadie sitting on the side of the bed sipping soup as her daughter steadied the spoon. Her son was stirring her iced tea. I said hello to her children and then explained to them Dr. Harkness wanted a postoperative CT scan to make sure all the tumor had been removed.

The son and daughter helped me slide Sadie from her bed to a stretcher, and I pulled the sheet up to her shoulders to keep her warm. I pushed the stretcher down the hall to a service elevator which served the kitchen but could be stopped near the CT scanner on the first floor. Once the X-ray technician and I positioned Sadie in the CT scanner, I started an IV on her and began infusing iodine into her vein for the highest-resolution scan possible. While the technician performed the CT, I stretched out on Sadie's stretcher for a twenty-minute nap.

"All through," the X-ray technician said to me as she shook my shoulder. "The scan's on the view box."

"Thanks," I said as I sat up, rubbing my eyes.

I walked back into the scan room to look at the X ray and flipped on the view box lights. I was startled by the CT and sat down in a chair to study it further. A wave of nausea flooded me, and my legs felt rubbery. Much of the tumor was still in Sadie's brain, exactly as Dr. Harkness had predicted. I had removed about half of it, but another portion of the tumor, at least as big as a baseball, had burrowed into another lobe of the brain. The tumor, instead of being one large sphere, had really been shaped like a dumbbell, and I had stopped the tumor resection at the neck connecting the two tumor balls. I rested my chin on my palm and stared at the CT, wishing I could think of some other explanation for the circular white ball shining against the gray brain on the X ray.

"Jesus!" I turned around to see Raoul looking at the scan. "I thought we got all the tumor out."

"I did too, Raoul. But some of it extended into the parietal lobe, and it looks like it's eroded into the ventricular system in the center of the brain. There's no way I would have known to look for it there."

"What are you going to do now?" Raoul asked.

"I'm going to take out the rest of the tumor," I answered.

"When?"

"Tonight."

"It's eight P.M. now," Raoul reminded me. "That's a six-hour operation you're looking at. You haven't been home in a week, you're tired, and you've got a full day of surgery ahead of you tomorrow. Why don't you just schedule it later in the week?"

"Because I'm not going to give Dr. Harkness another shot at me on this case. The only way to stop his criticism is to get this tumor out," I said.

"Do you think the family will let you take Sadie back to the O.R.?" Raoul asked.

"I don't know."

"Well," Raoul said, "if you're going to do it tonight, I'll stay and help you. A lot of that tumor is in the ventricle. You'll need an extra pair of hands when you get down that deep in the brain."

"I sure will. Thanks, Raoul."

I pushed Sadie's stretcher back to her room and showed her son and daughter a copy of the CT scan.

"There's tumor left," I explained. "I'll have to take your mother back to the O.R. and take the rest of it out."

"But you said you took it all out in the first operation," the son said.

"I thought I did. But I was wrong."

"Are you sure you're qualified to do this operation?" the son asked.

"Yes, I am. I would never do an operation I wasn't qualified to do. I just missed part of the tumor last time," I answered.

"When will you operate?" the daughter asked.

"Tonight."

"Why tonight?" the son asked. "Won't that make it harder

on Mother with you and the operating team tired? Why don't you wait until the morning?"

"It's going to be tough on your mother whether we operate at eight tonight or eight in the morning," I said. "As for me, if I didn't operate when I was tired, I'd never finish my work."

At 8:30, Raoul reopened the craniotomy flap while I rested my hands for the dissection ahead. A crater in the left frontal lobe was still indented where I had removed a portion of the tumor. A small pencil of gray tumor was burrowed into the brain, camouflaged by the grayish-yellow brain convolutions surrounding it. I pulled the microscope in and, with more careful inspection this time, tracked the tumor through a tunnel it had formed as it grew into the brain. Four inches deeper into the brain, the thin neck of tumor mushroomed out of the tunnel into a second, massive ball of tumor. The tumor had eroded the wall of the ventricular system, and part of the tumor was floating in spinal fluid, in the hollow cavity in the very center of the brain. Arteries fed the remaining tumor from all directions, causing it to pulsate and beat in a tangle of vessels like a trapped insect surrounded by a spiderweb. My job was to remove the tumor without tearing the web of arteries, since sacrificing arteries to remove the tumor would kill Sadie as vital brain was deprived of blood. From 9:30 P.M. until 2 A.M. Raoul and I carefully teased arteries off the surface of the tumor before delivering the mass from the center of the brain. At 2:15 I lifted the meningioma out of the brain. It was the weight and size of a peach, and produced a "thud" when I dropped it on the Mayo stand.

"Nice job," Raoul said. "There's no doubt it's all out now."

"Yeah, that's right," I said. "I just hope she wakes up."

Raoul closed the head, and I left the O.R. to speak to Sadie's children. I told them the surgery had gone well and I would know more about Sadie's condition in a few hours. I walked back to the recovery room and took an hour's nap on an empty hospital bed while I waited for Sadie to recover from the anesthetic. At 4 A.M. a nurse woke me up to tell me Sadie was awake. I walked over to her bedside and told her the operation was over.

"You're in the recovery room doing fine, Sadie," I said.

"I'm cold," she whispered.

It was the first time she had spoken in six years.

I hurried back to the sleeping room, shaved and showered, then walked through the cafeteria for some fresh coffee before meeting Dr. Harkness for morning rounds. At 5 A.M. I saw Dr. Harkness heading down the hall to begin rounds. I caught up with him outside Mary Hurst's room. He was arguing in the hall with her father.

"Your daughter had a benign tumor of the pituitary gland. I removed it totally, and she's free of disease," Dr. Harkness told her father. "That's all you need to know. That's enough questions."

"You better answer my questions," Mary's father said, "or you can answer them in court! Now I want to know exactly what type of tumor it was, what's the chance of recurrence, what activities she should limit, when she can go back to work, and whether or not these tumors run in families."

"I've been over all of this with your daughter," Dr. Harkness replied sharply.

"I'm not through talking to you," Mary's father yelled at Dr. Harkness, who was walking away to see another patient.

Dr. Harkness didn't stop and continued his rounds, walking into another patient's room.

166

"That conversation isn't going to help your image with lawyers much," I said to Dr. Harkness.

"A winner doesn't have to worry about his image," he replied.

We continued making rounds, and several minutes later Dr. Harkness abruptly asked me, "What did the post-op CT scan show on your patient with the brain tumor?"

"It showed a large portion of the tumor wasn't removed," I answered. "Interestingly, much of the tumor was in the ventricular system."

"When are you going to reoperate her?" Dr. Harkness asked.

"Raoul and I operated on her last night. All the tumor's out," I replied.

"And she's talking now?" Dr. Harkness asked.

"Yes, sir."

"Good," Dr. Harkness said.

He never mentioned the case again.

In October I had my first patient with a pituitary tumor and scheduled her for surgery on Thursday, so Dr. Harkness would be available to help me if necessary. Like Mary, she had been unable to get pregnant and had been referred by a gynecologist. I was anxious to remove her tumor and see how long it would take her to get pregnant. Mary Hurst had gotten pregnant two months after her surgery and had written Dr. Harkness a nice note thanking him for his participation in her pregnancy.

"While the work you did was more complicated, although less exciting, than my husband's contribution," Mary had written, "it still must be a thrill for you to be responsible for more babies than any man alive!" Dr. Harkness showed the note to the residents but not to his wife.

The seniors operated in the room next to Dr. Harkness, since he was responsible for overseeing their surgery. Dr. Harkness had too many cases of his own, so he couldn't possibly scrub on every charity case, but he was always available to help when needed. I positioned my patient with the pituitary tumor and began the operation after I instructed the circulating nurse to turn on my tape player loaded with Simon and Garfunkel's *Greatest Hits*.

Three minutes later Dr. Harkness screamed from the next room, "Goddammit, turn that music off! This is a goddamn operating room, not a rock concert!"

The nurse had forgotten to shut the door to his operating room.

I exposed the pituitary gland without difficulty through a transsphenoidal approach but was unable to locate the tumor. Finally, after searching for forty-five minutes, I requested the nurse to ask Dr. Harkness to come in and help me. He stopped in the middle of his operation and walked into my room fully gloved and gowned. I expected a sarcastic remark or burning criticism, but instead he looked through the microscope and said, "These damn tumors are hard to find sometimes."

His skilled hands manipulated the pituitary gland until he found the tumor, atypically located behind the gland. He showed me the tumor, then returned to finish his own operation.

He paused at the door and said, "That's the hardest tumor to find I've ever seen."

It wasn't, but he never belittled any surgeon honest enough to ask for help.

On Thursdays, during the routine portion of operations, such as opening or closing the head, Dr. Harkness reviewed the progress of junior residents by discussing their work with

168

the senior. He would inquire about their workups, diagnostic accuracy, attitude, and surgical technique, including their ability to perform arteriograms and myelograms. The senior was his conduit to the other residents, since Dr. Harkness had little interaction with junior residents or the chief residents. Consequently, the senior assigned to Dr. Harkness became the resident leader. Orders from Dr. Harkness were carried out by the senior, and residents brought complaints to the senior, since he had the most access to Dr. Harkness.

The senior was also important because he handled administrative scheduling of vacations, night duty, and the selection of residents to attend medical meetings. Although never writing a resident evaluation, the senior's thoughts in surgery influenced Dr. Harkness' opinion of junior residents as much as the formal report submitted by their attending neurosurgeons. Staff surgeon reviews were submitted to Dr. Harkness every six months, giving a broad overview and rating of each resident's performance. But the senior's weekly comments provided specific anecdotal incidents which painted a fresher, more detailed picture of the resident.

After I had been the senior for about two months, Dr. Harkness began asking my opinion of other residents. One Thursday morning as we were beginning an extracranial-intracranial bypass, he blurted, "What do you think of Daniels, the first-year resident from Florida?"

"He's smart, has good hands, but is very insecure about everything he does," I answered. "I've taught him to open backs and heads, but he slows me down too much in the operating room. He's so precise and compulsive that he wastes time controlling bleeding, and it takes him an hour instead of ten minutes to expose a disc."

"I want you to spend more time with him in the O.R.," Dr.

Harkness ordered. "Make sure his operative time is down to where it should be by Christmas. If it's not, tell me, and I'll keep him at Baptist six more months."

"Yes, sir," I answered.

"What about Jackson?" Dr. Harkness asked. "His attending's evaluation said he was lazy. Said he never saw him on the ward after nine P.M. If that's true, I may fire him. I won't have a lazy resident."

"He's not lazy at all," I answered. "In fact, he's one of the hardest-working residents here. He's spending his evenings with his twenty-five-year-old cousin, who's dying of a malignant brain tumor. His parents brought him to Memphis from Georgia because Jackson's a resident here. Surgery and cobalt radiation didn't help, and his cousin is going downhill fast. Jackson sits with him every night for a few hours while his aunt and uncle get some rest, then he does his ward work after midnight. That's why the staff neurosurgeons don't see him as much as the other residents."

For the next two hours Dr. Harkness didn't say anything as he sewed two arteries together on the surface of the brain. When he finished and began closing the head, he said, "The junior residents are having too many complications from their arteriograms. In the last one hundred arteriograms they've had four strokes and ten blood clots in the neck and ruined two arteries in the arm they injected dye through. That complication rate of sixteen percent is a disgrace. Take care of it."

"Yes, sir."

"You have one month. Then I want a report from you on their next one hundred arteriograms," Dr. Harkness added.

"Yes, sir."

That evening at eight, I met with the junior residents in the cafeteria to discuss the arteriogram problem. I outlined the complications and asked them if they had received proper instruction on how to do the test. All three replied "No." Two of the three had come to Memphis from medical schools where all arteriograms were done by radiologists through a different approach, passing a catheter into the femoral artery in the groin and up the aorta and selectively studying each artery supplying the brain. They were unfamiliar with our arteriograms, where needles were stuck through the skin into the left carotid artery and right brachial artery without making an incision. This procedure was harder to do since the femoral artery in the groin was larger and easier to hit. But it was much safer, as I showed them with statistics comparing the neurosurgeons' arteriograms with the radiologists' arteriograms over a twelve-month period citywide. The complication rate from neurosurgeons performing arteriograms was less than 1 percent. The complication rate of the radiologists' arteriograms was 4 percent.

"You have no option in your residency," I told them. "You must learn to do arteriograms correctly. Your complication rate must be less than one percent. Starting this week, schedule your arteriograms on Sunday. That's the day I have the most free time to help you. We'll line up eight or ten arteriograms every Sunday this month, until you've learned how to do this procedure."

"But Sunday's the quietest day in the hospital and the best chance to go home and see our families," one resident protested.

"You're right," I agreed. "That's when I get to see Julie most often, too.. But learning this procedure takes precedence. How much do you think those four patients you stroked out during arteriograms are enjoying their families now?"

Three days later, we had our first session on arteriograms. We started at 8 A.M. and finished the eighth arteriogram at 5 P.M. I could have finished them all by noon, and it annoyed me to spend a Sunday doing arteriograms, but, as I explained the procedure to them, it was obvious they had not received adequate instruction. By the end of the day they were already much improved. They were bright and well coordinated and just needed training. No one had shown them technical tricks like sticking one wall of the carotid artery instead of both walls, or how to thread the needle into the artery to avoid breaking off cholesterol plaques and causing a stroke. The next Sunday we finished the arteriograms at four in the afternoon. By the end of the month their time was down to thirty minutes per arteriogram, and we finished at 2 P.M.

In November Dr. Harkness required the junior residents to keep a log of every arteriogram they did. In sixty-four arteriograms they didn't have a single complication. The attending staff had one complication that month and the radiology staff several, but they declined to participate in the review.

Later that month Dr. Harkness allowed me to operate on some of his private patients. He assisted me on several brain tumors and a dozen back operations. I thought he had finally accepted me as a surgeon, but when I mentioned the change to a chief resident, he commented dryly, "He's only seeing if you can operate well enough to be a chief."

In January I switched hospitals with Raoul. He returned to Baptist for a second rotation as senior, and I moved to Methodist. On New Year's Eve, Raoul and I met at Baptist to go over our charity patient lists, so that there would be no confusion as their care was assumed by another doctor. We were sitting in the E.R. talking as the junior residents triaged the injuries resulting from the holiday drinking. At midnight an

172

internal medicine resident tapped me on the shoulder and asked me to see one of his patients, who was to be discharged in the morning.

"He told me on rounds tonight that he wanted to have his back pain checked before he went home," the medicine resident explained to me. "He's a good patient and never complains much, so I told him I'd talk to you. I know you're busy, but would you mind checking him?"

"Sure," I said. "Raoul and I are changing hospitals tomorrow morning, so I'll see him tonight."

"I'll be happy to see him," Raoul said. "I left you a couple of patients to see at Methodist," he chuckled.

"Okay, thanks, Raoul. I'll go on over to Methodist and see if the junior residents need any help with all the drunks coming into the E.R. tonight."

The next afternoon Raoul called me at Methodist while I was watching the Orange Bowl football game in the residents' quarters.

"What did you think of the two patients I left for you at Methodist?" he asked.

"They were the most interesting, fantastic neurosurgical problems I've ever seen," I answered sarcastically. "One patient had a seizure because he ran out of Bacardi rum, and the other patient was complaining of a numb dick and the goddamn internal medicine service wanted neurosurgery to see the patient to rule out multiple sclerosis. Those guys are so compulsive, they probably examine their bowel movements each morning to see if they're eating right!"

Raoul snickered a minute and then said, "I saw the patient with back pain that you left for me."

"Thanks, Raoul. What did he have—a ruptured disc?" I asked.

"No," Raoul replied. "He has a spinal cord tumor. I did a myelogram this morning, and I'm going to operate on him tomorrow. It's a great case, and I wanted to thank you for leaving it for me."

"Dammit!" I shouted. "You leave me two crocks to see and then find a spinal cord tumor to do. Are you sure you're telling me the truth?"

"Yes, I am," Raoul answered. "Why don't you come over to Baptist about noon tomorrow and help me take it out?"

"I sure will, Raoul. I won't get to do anything in the operation except hold a sucker while you have all the fun removing the tumor, but it sure beats holding this guy's numb dick in my hand while he tells me it's beginning to feel better!"

January 1, 1979, marked the beginning of my six-month rotation as senior resident at Methodist Hospital. The 1000-bed Methodist was slightly smaller than the 1500-bed Baptist Hospital, so Dr. Harkness assigned only one senior and one junior resident there. The workload was about the same since fifteen staff neurosurgeons admitted patients, but Methodist had a major advantage over Baptist in that the atmosphere was more relaxed. With Dr. Harkness and the medical school primarily affiliated with Baptist, much of the academic pressure was diluted in Methodist. Consequently, staff surgeons felt more comfortable allowing residents to operate on private patients. Residents gained more surgical skill operating at Methodist, but more confidence operating under the intense pressure at Baptist. Methodist was considered the outland, Baptist the Mecca.

Rotating back to Methodist was like returning home for me, since I had spent my first twelve months in the residency there. The staff surgeons knew me much better than the ones at Baptist did, so I operated on more major cases than I had at

Baptist. After my six months at Methodist I had operated on more aneurysms than any previous resident in the program. After three years I was the primary surgeon on twenty-two aneurysm cases. However, other residents were quick to point out that seven of the aneurysms had been in one patient.

John Kirk Williams was the most famous patient in Memphis for the first six months of 1979. He was an unemployed automobile mechanic and had come to the Methodist emergency room following a severe headache that was diagnosed by the junior resident as a brain hemorrhage from an aneurysm. His diagnosis was exactly right, but, in addition, John Kirk had six other aneurysms and an arteriovenous malformation, or A.V.M., of the left parietal lobe. The A.V.M., an abnormal collection of dilated arteries and veins which may bleed or cause seizures, was the size of a silver dollar and located near the speech area. John Kirk was fifty-four years old and otherwise in good health. After neurosurgeons at Baptist and Methodist viewed his arteriogram, the decision was made to treat him surgically. John Kirk was ambivalent, but his wife readily agreed to sign the operative permit, so I scheduled him for surgery.

I planned to operate the three aneurysms in his right brain first and then, in a second craniotomy, clip the four aneurysms in his left hemisphere and remove the A.V.M. The first operation went very smoothly, with no hemorrhage from any of the three aneurysms I clipped. However, postoperatively John Kirk was unexpectedly paralyzed in his left arm and leg, so I was forced to cancel the second craniotomy and discharge him from the hospital to the Lamar Unit, a stroke rehabilitation hospital in Memphis.

I thought I wouldn't see John Kirk again, but six weeks later his wife brought him back to the E.R. to show me that his paralysis had completely resolved. "I want him to have the other operation now, Doc," his wife said.

"What do you think, John Kirk?" I asked.

"Doesn't matter to me, Doc," he answered, shrugging his shoulders.

With that vote of confidence, I admitted John Kirk to the charity ward and scheduled him for an arteriogram the next day. The X rays showed that all three aneurysms in the right hemisphere were perfectly clipped, and that the other four aneurysms and A.V.M. were unchanged. The next morning I took him to the O.R. and performed a second craniotomy, in preparation for clipping the other four aneurysms. The first three aneurysms were easily clipped, although it took me six hours. As I approached the fourth aneurysm, it ruptured and was difficult to clip. When I finally controlled the hemorrhage and clipped the aneurysm, the brain was too swollen to continue operating, so I closed his head without excising the A.V.M. Postoperatively John Kirk was paralyzed on the right side of his body, and once again I discharged him to the Lamar Unit for more physical therapy.

Three months later, in the spring, John Kirk and his wife returned to the E.R. Once again his strength had returned.

"I want him to get that A.V.M. out of his head now," his wife said.

"John Kirk, do you want to have a third operation on your brain?" I asked.

"Don't matter," he said.

I admitted him to the hospital and scheduled his third operation for the following morning. The A.V.M. was removed in four hours, and a week later he was ready to be discharged. The postoperative arteriogram showed that all seven aneurysms had been clipped and the entire A.V.M. had been

176

removed. John Kirk had normal speech and no paralysis in his arms or legs. His thinking, always a bit slow, was unchanged. On his last morning in the hospital I presented him on grand rounds, and all the physicians marveled that he had withstood three major brain operations. His wife dressed him as the physicians, nurses, residents, and medical students discussed his case.

"Time to get you home, John Kirk," his wife said. "You've been off work long enough!"

She pushed his wheelchair through the circle of doctors and mumbled "Thank you" to me as she turned the corner. As our group walked down the hall to see other patients, Raoul remarked, "John Kirk made one basic mistake in his life."

"What's that?" I asked. "Marrying that woman?"

"No," Raoul answered. "I think he bought too much life insurance!"

In June, Dr. Harkness informed the residents that Dr. Walters would be visiting Memphis as a visiting professor. He was a highly respected neurosurgeon at the Mayo Clinic and a member of the American Board of Neurological Surgery. Dr. Harkness planned to make rounds with Dr. Walters at Baptist and John Gaston on June 28, at Methodist and the V.A. on June 29, and to have a joint conference on June 30 for all Memphis neurosurgeons. Chief residents and senior residents were expected to present difficult surgical problems for Dr. Walters to explain his ideas concerning management.

My presentation was last and began at 9:30 A.M. There were over a hundred people in the auditorium, and Dr. Walters was seated on the stage beside the view boxes to review the X rays. Dr. Harkness was seated in the front row of the audience, chain-smoking and listening intently as Dr. Walters grilled the residents.

"Mr. Hoyt is a forty-eight-year-old white male who presented with a two-year history of dizziness and difficulty hearing out of his left ear," I began. "His neurological exam was normal except for decreased function in the left fifth, seventh, and eighth cranial nerves. CT scanning demonstrated a large posterior fossa tumor compressing the cerebellum and brain stem and extending up into the middle fossa. Differential diagnosis was acoustic neuroma versus meningioma."

"When did your patient experience facial nerve dysfunction?" Dr. Walters asked.

"Sometime in the last two years," I answered.

"You should take a closer history," Dr. Walters admonished. "Meningiomas tend to knock out the facial nerve early, and acoustics tend to spare it until late in the course of the illness. Why is it important to have a good idea about what type of tumor it is before the operation?" Dr. Walters asked.

"I don't know," I answered. "Both are benign tumors and should be completely removed. A biopsy at the time of surgery can establish the diagnosis definitively."

"Then I don't want you operating on my brain," Dr. Walters snapped. "The facial nerve tends to lie in front of a meningioma and behind an acoustic neuroma. That's important to know, because if you think you've got a meningioma, then you'll come across the facial nerve much quicker than if it's an acoustic. That one fact might make you more cautious and avoid cutting the nerve by accident, leaving your patient with a paralyzed face."

"Yes, sir," I answered.

"Has the patient been operated?" Dr. Walters asked.

"Yes, sir. The tumor was a meningioma," I said.

"Did you cut the facial nerve?"

"No, sir."

178

"How long did it take you to remove the tumor?"

"Eight hours," I answered.

"Did you totally remove it?"

"Yes, sir."

"I don't think anyone can totally remove that tumor. It involves too much brain," Dr. Walters argued. Dr. Harkness remained quiet.

"I opened the middle fossa and the posterior fossa and removed the tumor from two different directions," I explained.

"I still can't believe you took it all out," Dr. Walters continued. "We require our residents to back up statements like that with a postoperative CT scan."

"I have a post-op scan," I said as I hung it up on the view box.

Dr. Walters stood up and studied the scan in detail, then said, "You're right. It is all out. That's a nice job."

"I'm surprised you questioned this resident," Dr. Harkness said to Dr. Walters. "He's one of next year's chief residents."

I beamed at the announcement but controlled my excitement so Dr. Harkness wouldn't think I hadn't been confident about receiving a chief resident appointment. Several residents waited for me in the lobby and passed out cigars when I walked out of the auditorium. I shook hands with each of them and with Raoul, who had also just been notified of his chief's appointment.

"Congratulations!" they shouted in unison.

"Thanks," I answered. "But it's not that big of a deal."

"Yes, it is," Raoul said, smiling. "You have an eight-and-a-half-pound son!"

Julie had just delivered our second child, John Kenyon, Jr. Raoul lit my cigar and I puffed it furiously for a few minutes while the other four residents lit theirs. The lobby filled up quickly with smoke. Dr. Harkness and Dr. Walters came out of the auditorium a few minutes later. Both glared at us as they edged around our circle. Raoul grinned, held his arm out toward me, and turned his palm up. I slapped my beeper in his hand, rushed to the elevator, and headed for the obstetrical hospital.

CHAPTER 7

CHIEF RESIDENT—1979

THE JOHN GASTON Charity Hospital, run entirely by chief residents, was 523 beds of misery: patients suffering gunshot wounds, stab wounds, car wrecks, pneumonia, kidney failure, psychiatric disease, complicated obstetrical problems, tuberculosis, syphilis, and cancer. The patients lay in open twenty-bed wards, with no privacy except for curtains drawn on metal runners between the beds. The red brick exterior was weathered; the concrete block wall interior, peeling and moldy. In the main walkways the checkered brown and gray linoleum floors were chipped and faded. Roaches scurried along the baseboards. The sick moaned and often turned to face the window at the end of each ward. Blood oozed and trickled through their bandages, and vomit, urine, and feces fermented in containers surrounding their beds. Only the nurses' dresses and the bed linens were clean.

The John Gaston Hospital, called "The John" by residents, was an inefficient inner-city hospital that was underfunded and understaffed, with outdated equipment and too many patients. City leaders had upgraded its name to City of Memphis Hospi-

181

tal and given its facade a face lift, but the core remained obsolete. Community leaders complimented each other in the paper and at civic meetings, while we struggled through surgery without power drills to open the head, operated without standard X rays because machines were broken, and transported patients all over the city to other hospitals for CT scans because the John Gaston scanner was outdated and often broken. City officials were impressed by their changes in the hospital; residents and patients weren't. But city officials were never in the emergency room at 2 A.M. caring for a patient bleeding to death from a gunshot wound to the neck, while the blood bank announced it was out of type-specific blood.

I began each day at John Gaston by making rounds on A and B Ward, to which most neurosurgical patients were admitted. After ward rounds I checked the patients in the surgical intensive care unit on the fifth floor and then walked down to the ground floor near the main entrance of the hospital and bought a ten-cent cup of coffee at the blind man's stand. Residents milled around his wooden hut in the hospital lobby, drinking coffee and eating doughnuts while requesting advice from other doctors on difficult cases. Internists thought the surgeons were too quick to operate; surgeons thought the internal medicine residents were more interested in naming a disease than curing it. But we all recognized that help from other specialists was invaluable, so we politely listened to dozens of case histories each morning as we tried to wake up in the warm sunlight flooding through the large glass-front door of the hospital.

Much of my first week was spent in the emergency room. The ninety-degree summer evenings and lack of air conditioning for many poor Memphians encouraged them to stay outside at night, leading to more accidents. People on the streets at night were often drinking, which led to car wrecks, fights, and gunshot wounds. Major trauma training for residents is usually learned by treating indigent patients in large city hospitals, such as Charity Hospital in New Orleans, Grady Hospital in Atlanta, or Bellevue Hospital in New York. The John Gaston Hospital was Memphis' war zone.

One Saturday night at eleven, I was called to the E.R. to see a forty-nine-year-old man who had been shot in the head during a robbery at a convenience store. I hustled down the back stairs from my call room, dodged two ambulances as I ran across the parking lot behind the hospital, and then bounded through the metal swinging doors into the E.R. The intern was waiting at the entrance and walked down the hall with me to watch me examine the patient in the trauma room.

"Another drunk shot in the head," I grumbled.

"Not exactly," the intern answered. "This man's sober. He was working a cash register in the store. The robber shot him six times in the head."

"What kind of shape is he in?" I asked.

"He's conscious," the intern answered.

The intern pushed the trauma room door open for me, and I walked to the patient's bedside. He was thin and looked much older than forty-nine. His black hair was combed straight back. He was unshaven. He lay flat on the stretcher, with his head resting on his arm. Bloodstains covered his blue jeans, high-top sneakers, and Elvis Presley tee shirt. His face was puffy, and there were four bullet holes under his right eye that were dribbling blood. The other two bullet holes were in his hair, above the right side of his forehead. He was awake, alert, and not complaining of headache or double vision. The intern held up his skull X rays. All six bullets had lodged outside the skull and had not penetrated the brain. Six bullets to the head, yet no major, permanent injuries. I closed the lacerations under his eye with nylon stitches, gave him a tetanus shot, and then started him on antibiotics to prevent infection.

"You'll be fine," I assured him.

While the intern finished bandaging his face, I went to the waiting room to talk to his wife. Two previous wives and his current girl friend were waiting for me. Two of the women sat smoking cigarettes and flicking ashes onto the floor. They wore sleeveless white blouses and jeans and smelled like beer. The third woman, who identified herself as his girl friend, sat quietly by herself in the corner. Her white cook's uniform was spattered with grease spots, but her shoes had been rubbed clean and her hair was pulled neatly into a bun.

"Goddamn! What took you so long?" one of the women asked.

"He's okay." I spoke to them all, ignoring her comment. "He'll be in the hospital for a few days, and then he can go home."

"When can the son of a bitch work again?" rasped the first wife. "He owes me fifty dollars a month to feed my kid."

"In about a week," I said.

"Good!" the second wife said. "I've got two of his kids. He better keep sending my money, too."

"Does anyone want to see him?" I asked.

The girl friend nodded and stood up. I looked at her lined face and rough skin. She had on no makeup and wore no jewelry except a cheap heart-shaped locket around her neck. There was little expression on her face, but as she looked at me the worry in her eyes was obvious. I led her back to see him.

As we walked down the hall she told me that she and her

boy friend, Danny, were alcoholics, and that they had met at an Alcoholics Anonymous meeting two years ago. They had shared an efficiency apartment for the last eighteen months, and neither one had drunk any alcohol since they moved in together. Neither had finished high school. They had joined a church, and every Sunday they spent the day with his three children. She pulled out her billfold and showed me a picture of the five of them at the zoo. She told me Danny was working two jobs now and had saved twelve hundred dollars to send his older son to trade school.

"I wish the other women didn't hate him so much," she told me. "He's no angel, but if they just knew him now."

We walked into the trauma room and she stood at his bedside looking into his swollen eyes. They didn't talk; there were no tears. She held his right hand and rubbed his fingers, and touched his forehead with her left hand. A moment later he sat up, and they knelt down together beside the bed. They were a rough-looking couple kneeling on a dirty floor. But as they held hands and prayed together, they were the eye of a hurricane with life swirling furiously around them.

The next morning was Sunday, so instead of going to sleep at 3 A.M., when I finished admitting Danny to A and B Ward, I drank a cup of coffee, completed my medical records, then started morning rounds early so I could get out of the hospital for a few hours. However, at nine, I was called to the E.R. to see a gunshot wound to the neck.

"Goddammit," I muttered to myself as I walked down to the E.R. "How can you get shot on Sunday morning?"

The patient was lying on a stretcher in the hallway of the emergency room. He looked about thirty years old and was fully conscious, with no paralysis in his arms or legs. The right side of his neck, where the bullet had entered, was powder burned and swollen, indicating the gun had been held against his neck when the shot was fired. His blood pressure was stable and he wasn't in shock from blood loss, so I began asking him questions.

"Where were you robbed?" I asked.

"I wasn't robbed," he answered. "I was shot at home."

"Who shot you?"

"My wife," he said.

"Your wife?"

"Yes," he repeated. "I was lying in bed half asleep when she shot me. Usually on Sunday morning she brings me coffee in bed. I heard her come back into the bedroom and I could smell the coffee. She straddled me in bed like she always does to crawl over to get back to her side of the bed. I felt something cold on my neck and then heard an explosion. My neck burned. I heard my wife call me a son of a bitch, then I heard five clicks right in a row. The police who brought me in told me the gun misfired the next five shots."

"Where is your wife now?" I asked nervously, wanting to make sure she wasn't wandering around the E.R.

"In jail," a policeman who was standing behind me answered.

I finished examining the patient and then X-rayed his neck, chest, and skull. The radiology resident was called in from home to do a barium swallow to rule out injury to the esophagus. Next I did an arteriogram to make sure the carotid arteries and jugular veins weren't injured. An ear, nose, and throat resident performed a laryngoscopy to check for tracheal injury. Finally I did a cervical myelogram to evaluate possible injury to the spinal cord. By 2 P.M. the workup was complete and the tests showed no major injuries.

The bullet had missed the esophagus and trachea. The arteriogram showed that the carotid artery was open, which had protected him from a stroke. The arteriogram showed no injury to the jugular vein, explaining why he hadn't bled more from the bullet wound and why he wasn't in shock. X rays of the neck showed that the bullet was lodged in the fifth vertebral body, ten millimeters from the spinal cord. A half inch deeper, and he would have been quadriplegic. Somehow the bullet had missed every major structure in the neck, preventing his death or paralysis. The .22 caliber bullet itself was so firmly lodged in the bone that surgery to remove it wasn't even necessary. I admitted him to the ward, still amazed that he had required no surgery and no medication, and had no serious injury.

I left the hospital, disappointed that I had lost most of the day. I thought about how close the man had come to dying, and how Goethe was right to say, "Nothing should be more highly prized than the value of each day." At 4 P.M. I pulled into the driveway, determined to get home more often.

Laura was now seventeen months old, John two months. I loaded Laura into her red wagon and pulled her down the sidewalk while Julie pushed John's stroller. After a walk to the park, Julie fed and bathed the children while I cooked hamburgers outside on the grill. By 8 P.M. I had fallen asleep in the den with my plate still on my lap. Julie guided me to the bedroom, helped me undress, and tucked me into bed. She kissed me on the cheek and whispered, "Thank you for a wonderful day." Four hours, I thought to myself as I drifted off to sleep. She doesn't ask for much.

Mondays were usually quiet at John Gaston because most of the people we treated had run out of money after the weekend and couldn't afford any more booze or bullets. It was standard practice on the neurosurgical service to visit the psychiatric wards whenever there was a lull in the action and look for patients with diseases such as brain tumors or blood clots in the brain that were filed away in locked-up rooms with misdiagnoses such as schizophrenia. An energetic resident could easily find two or three brain tumors a month on the psychiatric service. Neurosurgery residents in the past had gone from room to room and examined each patient to find those who had been diagnosed incorrectly. But I devised a shortcut. I simply waited until new residents were scheduled to rotate onto Psychiatry, and the night before they switched I ordered CT scans on all the patients on the ward. In the confusion of new residents on the service, no one realized I had ordered the tests.

I took the elevator up to the eighth floor, where the psychiatric ward was located. It had been a week since I had ordered ten CT scans on their patients, and I was now ready to see what my trout line had caught. I punched the buzzer on the outside steel door, and about five minutes later a heavy nurse waddled to the door, swinging a large key ring. She unlocked the door, and together we walked to a second steel door. The first door had locked behind us before the second door was opened from the inside. Inside the second locked door, each patient room was also locked. Only the nurses, orderlies, and residents were free to walk in the halls.

The back door of each patient room opened onto a hall that led to a recreation room at the end of the ward. By making this hall the only route to this room, the number of escapes had dropped dramatically in the last two years. Steel bars on all outside windows had eliminated suicide jumps. By 9 A.M. most of the patients were in the recreation room, so I walked down to the end of the ward and entered from the medical side after a nurse unlocked the door. The clang of the metal door slamming behind me and the click of the key turning in the lock always made me uneasy. I never enjoyed visiting the psychiatric ward, but I needed to find brain tumors for more surgical practice, so I ignored my fear and walked through the room.

It was a thirty-foot-square area, with a TV mounted nine feet up on one wall. There was a Ping-Pong table, a pool table, card tables, and a bookcase with magazines and paperbacks. There was a Coke machine that worked without money and a shuffleboard design painted on the concrete floor. Most of the thirty patients in the room were oblivious to all this, and to me.

The mental patients wandered aimlessly throughout the room looking at the floor or at imagined objects in their hands. They didn't walk, they strayed; they didn't talk, they digressed; they didn't eat, they foraged. But as I looked closer I heard sparks of intelligence in their conversations and saw flecks of expressions on their sedated, masked faces. I buried my biases and kept in mind that these patients had organic, not psychosomatic, illnesses. I constantly reminded myself that insanity is only one disordered emotion beyond genius.

I leafed through the charts and read the X-ray reports while constantly watching the patients' movements out of the corner of my eye. Of the ten CT scans I had ordered, one was positive. A fifty-five-year-old white female, Mildred Farmer, had a large meningioma, a highly treatable brain tumor. I looked for her admitting diagnosis, knowing what I would read. Like so many patients misdiagnosed on psychiatric services, she had been admitted with the diagnosis of Alzheimer's disease.

The cause of Alzheimer's disease, a common type of insanity, is unknown. The disease occurs with equal frequency in men and women. The early symptoms of withdrawal, depression, and deterioration in work performance are often missed. Eventually, deterioration in judgment or memory loss leads to diagnosis. Most patients die of pneumonia or kidney infection five to six years after the onset of the disease.

When I found Mildred Farmer, she was sitting slumped over in a wheelchair by the water fountain. She was rubbing her head with both hands. Although she didn't talk, it was obvious her head was hurting, a key differential between brain tumor patients and those with Alzheimer's disease, who don't have headache. She had pressure in her eyegrounds, papilledema, that I could see with my ophthalmoscope. Alzheimer's does not cause a buildup of pressure in the brain. I called the chief resident in psychiatry and told him the patient's correct diagnosis, confirmed by her CT scan. He was embarrassed but helpful and came immediately to the psychiatric floor and helped me transfer Mildred to A and B Ward.

That night I started Mildred on Decadron, a powerful cortisone medication, to reduce the brain swelling. I typed and cross-matched her for six units of blood in preparation for surgery and checked her bleeding time to make sure that her blood clotted normally and that she wasn't a free bleeder. I asked the internal medicine service to examine her heart, lung, and kidney function thoroughly. There was no family to discuss the surgery with, so I took her to the operating room on Wednesday morning.

Her tumor was located in the ventricular system, the hollow cavity in the center of the brain which contains spinal fluid. It was best approached by opening the top of her head and splitting the two hemispheres. By pulling the two halves of the brain apart, I was able to open the roof of the ventricular system and begin removing the tumor. For eight hours I chipped away at the tumor. With electrical forceps in my left

190

hand, I cauterized arteries feeding the tumor and then sucked or cut chunks of tumor away with my right hand. The tumor was gray and, with its puffy capsule, looked like a boxer's cauliflower ear. Its surface was the size of an ear, but below it mushroomed into a larger tumor the size of a fist. After my experience as senior resident at Baptist Hospital, I knew to look for the characteristic mushroom and had no difficulty locating the bulk of tumor.

Finally I came to the last, marble-sized portion of tumor. It had eroded through the back of the ventricular system and was stuck to the brain stem. I knew no one would fault me for leaving a small amount of tumor attached to the brain stem because of the high risk of death from removing it. But now was the only chance for a total tumor removal and a cure. To quit would compromise my patient's chance for a normal life, while being too aggressive and trying to remove the entire tumor could kill Mildred. I had already removed 95 percent of the tumor and she was fifty-five years old. I had probably given her ten additional years of life before the tumor would recur. If only I could get the last tumor fragments off the brain stem, she might live twenty-five or thirty years. Ten years or thirty years; I considered my options and rested my hands.

I decided to remove the remaining tumor and slowly, delicately, began stripping flecks of tumor off the brain stem. Suddenly, without warning, the brain began swelling so violently that I had to hold it with the palm of my hand to keep it inside her head. The cause of the swelling was unclear. The most common cause, a massive hemorrhage resulting from a torn artery, was obviously not occurring, because I could see the brain was dry; there was no bleeding. The brain continued to swell so rapidly that it was clear to everyone in the O.R. that Mildred would die in three or four minutes if the process were

191

not reversed. I knew of a dozen causes of acute, massive brain swelling, but there wasn't time to work through the different causes systematically to solve the problem and save her life. If death were to be averted, I had to find a single remedial cause and correct it. I felt nauseated as I watched the brain swell as it continued its course toward explosion. So many causes to consider and correct, and so little time.

"Get her blood pressure down, quickly," I shouted to the anesthesiologist. "Her brain's falling out of her head. I can't hold it in much longer."

"Her pressure won't come down. It's still 200/100, and I've given her every drug I can think of," the anesthesiologist answered.

"Raise her head, then. Maybe that will relieve some of the pressure in the brain."

The anesthesiologist reached under the surgical drapes and grasped Mildred's head, pulled it up, and put two pillows under her neck. Still the brain continued to swell like a balloon filling under a faucet.

"I've got about three more minutes," I said to the anesthesiologist. "Then this brain is going to explode onto the floor. Check all your tubes and IVs. Make sure she's getting the right drugs, and check her catheter to see if we're draining her bladder adequately."

"All the tubes are in place."

"Then why is her brain still swelling?" I asked.

"Is she bleeding from the tumor?"

"No, goddammit! Don't you think I'd see blood pouring out of her brain if she were bleeding?"

"She's losing her heartbeat," the anesthesiologist reported. "She's fibrillating. She's going to die."

192

"Don't give up. We can still get her through this. Give her more oxygen!"

"I can't."

"Why?"

"I'm squeezing the bag as hard as I can, but the air won't go into her lungs."

"Check the tube in her windpipe. Is it still in proper position?" I asked.

While the anesthesiologist checked the tube, I put both my palms on the surface of the brain and pushed it back into the head. Despite my efforts, bits of brain squeezed between my fingers, oozed over the skull, and began dripping onto the floor.

"My God!" the anesthesiology resident shouted. "The tube is kinked in her windpipe!"

"Straighten it out! We've still got a chance to save this brain!"

Thirty seconds later the brain swelling began to subside. I continued pushing against the brain to keep it inside the skull until it had shrunk down to its normal size and retreated inside the head. Only several small bits of brain had been lost and were lying like wood chips on the operating room floor.

With the brain again pulsating, no longer swollen, and resting inside the skull, I removed the remaining tumor. I closed Mildred's head and waited at her bedside in the recovery room while she awoke from surgery. She regained consciousness promptly and had clear speech, normal mentation, and no paralysis, having survived the most major of brain tumor surgery. I understood, then, Dr. Wright's remark three years earlier: "Good surgeons know how to get out of trouble; better surgeons know how to avoid it."

On Friday mornings Dr. Harkness made rounds with the John Gaston chief resident. If Dr. Harkness was out of town, a neurosurgeon from the Semmes-Murphey Clinic took his place. Usually his replacement was Dr. Fleckman, a Mayo-trained surgeon, long on book knowledge and short on personality. His main interest in life was practicing brain bypass operations on rats in the Cerebrovascular Research Laboratory. To his credit, Dr. Fleckman had an enthusiastic interest in neurosurgery and a specific fascination with pain relief operations. Many patients, and all residents, had heard his famous saying, "There is no pain I can't relieve."

Dr. Fleckman spoke confidently to patients dying from cancer who were in severe pain. Many of these patients with lung, breast, and prostate cancer had disseminated disease with metastases to bone and could no longer be relieved of their pain with morphine. Dr. Fleckman's confidence that he could relieve their pain by cutting nerve fibers in the brain or spinal cord convinced many patients to opt for surgery rather than take more narcotics, which led to constipation, loss of appetite, mental confusion, disorientation, and eventually difficulty breathing and death. Dr. Fleckman's indications for surgical relief of pain included a failure to respond to milder narcotics such as codeine or Percodan, a life expectancy of more than six months, and an overall general medical condition that permitted a safe general anesthetic. For those patients who could not tolerate a general anesthetic, such as those with lungs full of cancer, he introduced a needle through the skin into the spinal cord and destroyed the pain fibers without making a surgical incision.

"I can make you pain-free," Dr. Fleckman told patients who were often balled up and squirming or too sedated to even

194

talk. "And then you can enjoy your life again," he added. And he did.

I was impressed by Dr. Fleckman's ability to relieve pain by destroying certain areas of the brain or spinal cord. Although there were a few mortalities from surgery due to the poor medical condition of patients dying from cancer, only about 10 percent of patients had complications such as weakness or paralysis in their arms or legs. The complications resulted from damage to the nerve fibers that provide movement to the extremities, which anatomically lie next to the nerve fibers that conduct pain impulses.

I studied Dr. Fleckman's surgical technique carefully whenever he performed a pain operation. In August I had a chance to help a terminally ill patient. I was asked by the chief resident in medicine to see a twenty-six-year-old black woman, Jo Williams, who was dying from a sarcoma in her left leg. The highly malignant, basketball-size tumor was growing in her left thigh and had already spread to her lungs. Amputation of her leg and pelvis would not cure her, and morphine was not relieving her pain. The massive, rock-hard tumor had stretched the skin of her thigh, turned her foot out to one side, and left her crippled and unable to walk. I had first met her on E and F Ward sitting in a wheelchair, talking to her four- and six-year-old daughters. She wasn't married.

I introduced myself and explained to her that I could relieve her pain by performing a cordotomy, an operation to cut the pain fibers in her spinal cord.

"I'll wake up from the operation without any pain?" she asked.

"That's right," I answered.

She bent her head and cried with relief. Her daughters sat

beside her without talking. They didn't understand what I had said, or that their mother was dying.

At 7:30 the next morning I operated on Jo. With her lying on her stomach on the operating table, I made a four-inch incision between her shoulder blades over the spine. I nibbled away the spinal bone with pliers and then opened the dura covering her spinal cord. The spinal cord was pale white and about the diameter of my thumb. It is one of the most delicate tissues in the body, and even an instrument falling on it during surgery can permanently paralyze a patient. Carefully I pulled the cord to one side and, looking through the microscope, cut four millimeters into the right side of the cord to cut the pain fibers coursing from the left leg which crossed to the right in the spinal cord on their way to the brain. I was careful to avoid injuring the anterior spinal artery and the nerve fibers controlling movement in the legs, which would have paralyzed her. After I checked to make sure there was no bleeding, I closed the incision with silk stitches. The operation was over in two hours.

Jo awoke in the recovery room totally free of pain. She had no paralysis in her legs. That evening I began weaning her off morphine, and by the time she was ready to be discharged ten days later she was completely off narcotics. Her mind had cleared, her speech was no longer slurred, and her energy had improved. Each day she enjoyed her daughters more. She brushed their hair and read them stories at bedtime. And on the Saturday of her discharge she planned a picnic in Overton Park.

I saw her each month in the outpatient clinic for a checkup. Although the internists had thought she would live a year, she died four months after surgery. But in those final days she was alert and no longer sedated. She walked without pain and wasn't bedridden. She was cheerful, and not depressed from narcotics. Her final admission to the medical service was for pulmonary edema as her lungs filled with fluid from the spread of tumor. I stopped by one evening about ten to see her. She died at 3:30 the next morning. She left me with a thank-you, she left her daughters with love, and she left life with a smile.

The months before Christmas blended together in the hospital as I spent the days operating on brain tumors, aneurysms, and ruptured discs in the neck and back and worked at night elevating depressed skull fractures off the surface of the brain, removing blood clots within the brain, and cleaning up the head wounds resulting from gunshots and car wrecks. Every other night I covered the Children's and V.A. hospitals for Raoul. Whenever we could, we operated together, continuing to improve our surgical ability. We went home infrequently, usually a few hours on Sunday afternoon.

One December evening when I prepared to call Julie at home, I couldn't remember the phone number. I sat down on my cot in the drafty call room, ate a Snickers, and searched my wallet for our phone number. I found it written on the back of my driver's license. When Julie picked up the phone, her voice sounded tired, and I heard Laura or John crying in the background. I wanted to talk, but Julie was exhausted from teaching full time at Memphis State and taking care of the children. She answered my questions but wasn't concentrating on our conversation. I could tell she wanted to get the children to bed so she could get some rest before going to work in the morning. I told her good night, and as always she asked, "Is there anything I can do for you?" But she and I both knew: she couldn't help me, and I couldn't help her.

By December, with only six months left in our residency,

Raoul and I noticed we were receiving less criticism in conferences and more acceptance as peers from other surgeons. Often staff surgeons asked our advice about difficult trauma cases, because they recognized our experience from treating the large volume of trauma cases taken to the John Gaston. Occasionally we even ate dinner with a staff surgeon in the hospital cafeteria.

One night as Raoul and I were leaving Baptist Hospital after dinner, we passed through the emergency room on our way to the V.A. hospital. One of the staff surgeons was lying in an examining room, having suffered a heart attack. While we stood in the hallway watching the interns check his heart rhythm and start an IV on him, he had a cardiac arrest and quit breathing. Raoul and I pushed the interns aside, and began C.P.R. While Raoul intubated him to provide more oxygen, I pounded his chest and began cardiac massage. When his heart didn't start, I pushed harder. His ribs cracked, but eventually his heart began contracting and his blood pressure stabilized. The cardiologist arrived, thanked us, and admitted him to the coronary care unit. Two weeks later, he had recovered sufficiently to go home. On the morning of his discharge, he summoned Raoul and me to his room.

"At last, after four years, we're going to get our first compliment from a staff surgeon," I said.

"I guess so," Raoul answered. "I don't see how he can criticize us for saving his life."

We took the elevator up to the tenth floor, walked down the hall to his room, and knocked on the door.

"Come in," was the gruff reply.

We stepped inside the door and looked across the room where he was sitting beside his bed reading a newspaper. He looked up, stared as he removed his glasses, and then stood

198

up and walked toward us. He stopped a few feet away, pointed, and said, "Which one of you is the son of a bitch who broke my ribs?"

Neither of us answered in the awkward silence that followed, so he told us to go back to work.

As we hurried down the hall Raoul glanced over at me and snickered, "It's great being a resident here."

On Christmas Eve Dr. Harkness invited the neurosurgeons and residents to his home for a buffet party. Raoul and I scheduled a lengthy brain tumor operation so we would have an excuse for missing the party. We felt uneasy socializing with the neurosurgeons, who had criticized and worked us, but never thanked us, during the last four years. The next Monday after the party, at the conclusion of the Monday night conference, Dr. Harkness dismissed the staff neurosurgeons and told all the residents to stay for a meeting.

All ten of us were present, and at 6:15 Dr. Harkness stood up and shouted, "Goddammit! One resident came to my Christmas Eve party. That's rude as hell, and I won't have my wife treated that way! What in the hell has happened to you? You don't seem to have any social manners, and I understand now that eight out of ten of you are either separated or divorced. I won't stand for this. I want my residents to be good surgeons and good men. Raoul, what's happened to the residents? You seem to have the strongest marriage of the group. What are the other residents doing wrong? Are they running around with the nurses? Drinking or screwing in off hours? What in the hell has happened?"

Dr. Harkness continued to scream, but Raoul didn't answer. One by one, Dr. Harkness called each of us by name, demanded we stand up and explain why we hadn't come to the party and why we were having trouble at home. Most of the

199

answers were the same: too much work to do, too few residents, too many nights on call, and no free time.

Dr. Harkness' answer was always the same: "Learning to be a neurosurgeon isn't fun. I can't do anything about the work load."

Dr. Harkness addressed me last. "What's your excuse?"

"I was removing a brain tumor at John Gaston," I answered.

"Could the operation have been postponed until after Christmas?" he asked.

"Yes, sir," I answered.

"And when is the last time you went home?" Dr. Harkness asked me.

"Two weeks ago," I answered.

"Why haven't you been home since then?" he asked.

"The last time I went home," I replied, "everyone was asleep when I got there at eleven P.M. and still asleep the next morning when I left at four. Not much reason to go home for that."

"So what's the solution?" Dr. Harkness asked me. "Cut back on night duty? Get more residents?"

"No, sir," I answered. "There is no solution. Either you want to be a neurosurgeon, or you want a smooth home life. You can't have both."

"I don't accept that!" Dr. Harkness shouted. "Everyone get the hell out of here!"

Dr. Harkness said nothing more about the residents' social life or home life. But he informed Raoul and me that he had accepted four first-year residents for July 1, 1980. Since only Raoul and I were leaving the residency, that would spread the night work among two more residents. In addition, Dr. Harkness demanded that Raoul and I make sure that every resident take two weeks' vacation a year and attend at least one medical meeting during another week. Dr. Harkness instructed the staff neurosurgeons that they were to begin doing their own histories and physical examinations on routine admissions, perform their own myelograms, see patients themselves in the emergency room before 5 P.M., and not expect a resident to scrub with them on elective operations beginning after 5 P.M. The residents tried to pay more attention to their families, but it was obvious from conversation that most of us still didn't get home much. Most neurosurgery residents never talked of a weekend at home, only hours; and we didn't speak of seeing our families, only visiting them.

On June 27, three days before Raoul and I were scheduled to complete our residency, Dr. Harkness invited us to dinner with several other neurosurgeons and their wives at the Four Flames Restaurant on Poplar Avenue in midtown Memphis, three minutes from Baptist Hospital. Dr. Harkness was led in by his wife, a southern blond beauty with a soft drawl who told him where to sit and what to order. Dr. Fleckman's attractive wife was stunning in a low-cut black evening dress. Raoul and I both scrambled to sit opposite her. Raoul's wife had left for Mexico three days earlier; Julie was vacationing with her parents and the children in Atlanta. No one had expected a dinner invitation from Dr. Harkness.

The twelve of us were seated in a private dining room in the restored antebellum mansion and enjoyed a hearty meal of prime rib and red wine by candlelight. Dr. Harkness toasted Raoul and me individually, complimenting us on our service as residents and our bright futures as neurosurgeons. After a Bananas Foster dessert, Dr. Harkness presented each of us with a wrapped present. Raoul and I had kidded each other about receiving a $50,000 bonus when we completed

201

our training. This didn't seem excessive to us because we had calculated that we had generated about $200,000 per year for the staff surgeons by doing their workups, myelograms, arteriograms, and emergency surgery and assisting them on their operations. After four years and $800,000 of income for our professors, a 6 percent bonus seemed reasonable to us. We opened the gifts simultaneously and unwrapped a twenty-dollar navy blue tie with the Semmes-Murphey Clinic logo, SMC, on its front. I could tell Raoul was forcing back a smile, and I had to look away from him quickly to keep from laughing. Each of us thanked Dr. Harkness for the tie and made a few lame comments about how nice it would look with a blazer or dark suit. Dr. Harkness nodded, asked the waiter for the check, and then called Raoul and me to one side as we were leaving.

"I didn't know if you had the surgical ability to be neurosurgeons when I selected you for the residency four years ago," Dr. Harkness said. "But I believed you were honest men, and the years I've known you have confirmed this. Always be an honest surgeon. Admit what you don't know or can't do, and ask for help. Admit your complications, and learn from them. Remember, when a physician is honest, the quality of medicine increases; the art is achieved, and the patient benefits."

He nodded good night to us and walked away.

Three days later, our residency was over. Raoul and I felt surprisingly proud as we put on our new Semmes-Murphey ties before going to the hospital administrator's office to turn in our parking cards, beepers, and call room keys. We walked through John Gaston Hospital one last time, stopped for a cup of coffee at the blind man's stand, and laughed as the new residents grimaced as they sipped the strong coffee. Then, at

10 A.M. on July 1, we walked out the front door of the hospital and listened to it slam behind us.

"What do you want to do?" I asked Raoul.

He didn't answer, but I knew what he was thinking. We hurried across Madison Avenue to Baptist Hospital, walked up the stairs to the operating room, and stood quietly in the corner, watching as Dr. Harkness removed a rare brain tumor.

PRACTICING
THE ART

PART III

CHAPTER 8

MAKING THE LETTERHEAD

A FTER HIS RESIDENCY, Raoul and his family moved home to Mérida to join his father's practice covering the Yucatán Peninsula. I remained in Memphis and joined a group at Methodist Hospital headed by Dr. Shelton, a fifty-two-year-old neurosurgeon who had taken an active role in my residency training. He was the senior partner and autocrat of a five-man group. But because of his surgical skill and business acumen, he was well respected by his partners and physicians throughout the community. After several telephone conversations, we met in his office to work out the final details of my association with his group.

"I have discussed your joining our group with the other partners," Dr. Shelton said, as his palms rubbed the rim of grey hair surrounding his bald head. "We have all agreed to start you at $60,000 a year." He leaned back in his leather desk chair and studied my reaction.

I was surprised by the low offer. My friends had all entered private practice with salaries ranging from $90,000 to $110,000 for the first year. Even those salaries were low, considering the fact that most neurosurgeons in their first year of practice generate about $300,000 of income. Most residents finishing before me had chosen to join groups rather than start a solo practice because it was easier, even though it cost them money. An established group had the business machinery of running a medical practice in place: secretaries, nurses, X-ray technicians, and insurance clerks; equipment, furniture, and an office building; accounting and legal advisers; and the computers necessary for billing patients and recording accounts receivable. More important, a group provided additional opinions on difficult diagnoses, support during complicated operations, and an excellent opportunity to continue improving the surgical skill necessary for more complex operations.

When I didn't answer, Dr. Shelton added, "Of course, the group will provide you with a car, gasoline, and all repairs. Your family will be covered with complete medical, dental, and life insurance. We will pay your malpractice insurance premiums, which are about $15,000 a year. And you may take two weeks' vacation the first year."

"I think $60,000 is too low," I replied. "I might increase your group's overhead by $50,000, but I'm sure I'll generate at least $300,000 the first year. My salary and the increase in overhead are only $110,000 added expense for your group. If you subtract that from the $300,000 I'll bring in, that means I'll make $190,000 for the group my first year. That's a $40,000 bonus for each partner."

"That's about right," Dr. Shelton agreed. "But in return you have a guaranteed salary, experienced supervision, and none of the headache of setting up your own practice."

"Do I share in the bonus at the end of the first year?" I asked.

"No," answered Dr. Shelton. "The first year is strictly probationary. The partners see if they like you, and you see if you like us. If, at the end of the first year, you wish to join the group, and the partners vote to accept you, then your contract will change."

"How does it change?" I asked.

"First," Dr. Shelton said, "the group will put $30,000 a year into your pension plan. Second, your salary increases to sixty percent of a full partner's $250,000 salary, or about $150,000 for the second year, and to eighty percent, or about $200,000, for the third year. If you receive a unanimous vote of the partners at the end of the third year, you become a full partner at the beginning of the fourth year. After one year, you receive the same free time as the partners—six weeks a year for vacation and medical meetings. In the second year you may enter into the group's investments if you wish."

"What investments are those?" I asked.

"The office building is one," Dr. Shelton answered. "You can buy a one-sixth share for $60,000."

"What happens to my $60,000?" I asked.

"It's split among the partners who own the building," he answered.

"And the other investments?"

"You can buy into the condominium several of the partners own in Florida, and you may choose to join our partnership that owns two CT scanners. It will probably cost you about $100,000 to get in that investment."

"Well, thanks for outlining everything for me," I said. "I respect you and the other partners, and I'd like to join your group. But I'm worth more than $60,000 a year."

"All right," Dr. Shelton said. "I'll tell the partners we agreed on $75,000 for the first year and the sixty, eighty percentages for the second and third years. Is that okay with you?"

"Yes, sir," I answered.

"Okay," Dr. Shelton said, "why don't you start September first?"

"Fine, I'll see you then," I answered.

We shook hands, and Dr. Shelton walked me out of his office. I paused to admire his medical paintings, certificate of appreciation from St. Jude's Research Hospital, and a letter signed by Harvey Cushing, America's first neurosurgeon, written to a publisher complaining about the condition of a book's binding that he had received. Dr. Shelton had found the letter in an obscure bookshop in London and purchased it from a proprietor who did not know its value. He paused in front of the framed letter, faced me and said, "Other residents have told me you're a writer and you've kept a journal of your patients throughout your residency."

"Yes, sir, that's right," I answered.

He tapped the glass covering the framed letter and said, "You have a rich heritage in Harvey Cushing. The biography he wrote of an English physician, *The Life of Sir William Osler,* was awarded a Pulitzer Prize in 1926. Would you like to read it?"

"Yes, sir, I would."

Dr. Shelton unlocked the glass bookcase, retrieved his copy of the biography, and then said, "Dr. Cushing's medical writing proves he was a skilled neurosurgeon, but this book shows Dr. Cushing was a compassionate physician. You should emulate him, and when you are eligible apply for membership in the Harvey Cushing Society."

Dr. Shelton handed me the biography, said good-bye to me, and returned to the clinic to see his patients. He had encouraged my interest in writing but also focused my attention on the importance of being a physician who cared more about the ill and injured than about income.

From the first day I worked with Dr. Shelton's group, I was amazed by the pace of their practice. Each surgeon kept approximately twenty-five patients in the hospital, saw five or six clinics of fifteen to twenty patients each week, operated on eight to ten cases per week, took calls one or two nights a week and one weekend a month, and made rounds in three or four hospitals each day. Each physician was serious about providing the highest-quality surgical care and consulted freely with other members of the group and other neurosurgeons in Memphis. In addition, most had committee responsibilities in the different hospitals, with early morning and evening meetings to attend. Not only did Dr. Shelton's responsibilities include teaching residents, with all the conferences this required, but also, as president of the medical staff at Methodist Hospital, his attendance was required in countless meetings. He never complained of his extra work load, and he shouldered his share of the group's practice with equanimity. He started his day at 6 A.M., earlier than most, and finished later at night. My day started earlier than his, but I usually finished my work around 7 P.M. Dr. Shelton's car was always in the parking lot when I left to go home.

I applied for, and was granted, attending staff status with major surgical privileges in six hospitals: Methodist Central, Methodist North, St. Francis, Eastwood, Crittendon Memorial, and St. Jude's. I had courtesy staff privileges at Baptist and Methodist South but didn't admit patients there. I started morning rounds at Methodist Central Hospital in midtown Memphis about 5 A.M., headed north to Methodist North, then east to St. Francis and Eastwood, then back downtown to

211

St. Jude's before completing the sixty-five-mile round trip and returning to Methodist Central, where most of my patients were admitted, for evening rounds. During the day I saw clinic patients and operated at the various hospitals, always hoping that a postoperative patient would not develop a complication such as bleeding or a cardiac arrythmia while I was en route to another hospital. It would have been easier to have practiced at one hospital and spent the entire day there, but because of the referral nature of neurosurgery we had to go where other physicians needed us.

The entire group had over a hundred patients spread out in six hospitals, so each surgeon needed a nurse to organize his day's work. Usually my nurse, Janet, made rounds while I was in surgery and handled routine problems that would have slowed me down, such as changing bandages, taking out stitches, filling out disability forms, and dictating medical records. Janet was thorough and well liked by patients. I received more compliments on her than on the results of my operations.

Weekends were the most difficult workdays. The other five physicians signed out to one man, who took all phone calls, saw the emergencies, and made rounds on all the patients from Friday at 5 P.M. to Monday morning. It was unpleasant making rounds on the group's entire practice. Even if you started fresh at six Saturday morning (which often wasn't the case, since many emergencies required lengthy surgery on Friday night), rounds usually lasted until 5 P.M. Interspersed with rounds were emergencies in hospitals all over Memphis, patients calling requesting prescriptions, and occasionally surgery. It was only one weekend a month, and the other three weekends were free. But it was sixty hours of nonstop work that ruined the entire preceding week as it loomed closer.

Early on in my association with the group, I recommended we each make our own weekend rounds as other groups in the city did. But the other members liked the free weekends to travel or spend with their families, and they seemed oblivious to the fact that we were delivering superb medical care during the week but hurried medical care on weekends. One surgeon could not possibly listen to the complaints of one hundred people on rounds, then care for or accurately act on the problems the patients mentioned. After two nights without sleep from answering patient calls and emergency room calls, it was difficult to maintain the same keenness on Sunday. Weekend medicine was a finger in the dike, with the surgeon on call holding off a flood of problems until the other surgeons returned to work on Monday.

When I suggested a change in weekend call to Dr. Shelton, his response was predictable. "It's worked for fifteen years," he said. "No reason to change now."

Private practice brought a welcome increase in income over the $14,000 per year I had made as a resident. More noticeable to me than the income was the increase in freedom I now had to treat patients without the strict supervision required in a residency. Accompanying this independence was an intense pressure to dispense accurate medicine because of the constant threat of medical malpractice litigation. Consequently, the surgeons in Dr. Shelton's group consulted frequently among themselves, assisted each other in the operating room, and monitored the surgical complications within the group. No surgeon scheduled operations that he wasn't fully trained for or capable of performing. And no surgeon was reluctant to speak out when a patient had been mismanaged or an operation poorly performed. This private, constant peer review explained the quality of Dr. Shelton's group.

Soon after I entered private practice, other surgeons in the group began referring me cases because I had been trained to use the operating microscope and laser; several of the older surgeons had not. In November 1980 I was referred a patient with a spinal cord tumor.

The patient was a successful entrepreneur in Tennessee. His name was Lee Hampton, but everyone called him "Ham," a nickname based on his back-slapping, grinning, boisterous personality. He was a big man, over six feet tall and heavy. He had a broad, bright smile and a deep baritone voice. I had seen him interviewed on TV. He would have made an excellent politician.

When I first met him on the 7-Thomas neurosurgical ward at Methodist Hospital, he was sitting in the suite next to his hospital room reading *The Wall Street Journal.* He was wearing a navy blue silk bathrobe, beige pajamas buttoned to the neck, and tortoiseshell, half-rim glasses. He stood up as I introduced myself and motioned me to sit next to him but remained quiet and reserved, totally different from his normal outgoing personality. He knew he had a serious problem, and he knew I had come to talk with him about it.

"Mr. Hampton," I said, "the myelogram test you had yesterday shows that you have a spinal cord tumor in your neck. One of my associates asked me to examine you and talk to you about surgery."

"Do you want me to take off my robe?" he asked.

"Yes, sir, please."

He slipped off his bathrobe but then had difficulty unbuttoning his pajamas. I watched as he fumbled with the buttons, and it was obvious he had lost the ability to use his hands and arms well. I leaned over and helped him out of his pajama shirt and pulled his pants down. The horror of his disease struck me as

214

I stared at his withered arms and legs protruding like tooth-picks from his flabby trunk. The muscles in his arms and legs had wasted away because of the tumor in his spine, and only skin seemed to cover his knobby bones. It was an odd sight; a healthy head on a body that looked like it was starving to death.

I was surprised he had hidden his disease so long. He wore only long-sleeved shirts and had stopped wearing shorts around his friends. Unfortunately, he had been told by another doctor several years ago that he had untreatable muscle weakness and atrophy secondary to alcoholism, which had been a problem for him ten years ago. He had accepted the diagnosis and had not asked for another opinion. The doctor had not performed a myelogram, so the correct diagnosis of spinal cord tumor had been missed for three years, making it larger and more difficult to remove now.

"Hell, Doc," Ham said, "why didn't my doctor do a myelo-gram three years ago?"

"I don't know," I answered. "I didn't examine you then. Perhaps the diagnosis wasn't as clear."

"I think it's malpractice and you're covering up for him," Ham said.

"No, I'm not," I answered. "It's just that I don't know what happened three years ago. All I can do is help you with the problem now."

"Okay, tell me about the tumor."

"It's located high up in your neck, at the base of your skull." I talked slowly and pointed to the area of his neck, just below the hairline where the tumor was. "It's large, about the size of a Vienna sausage, and it's pressing on the spinal cord, which carries the nerves to your arms and legs. The tumor must be removed if there is to be any chance of your regaining strength and walking again."

"How risky is the surgery?" he asked.

"You could be paralyzed from the neck down following surgery." I watched his face cloud. "You could become quadriplegic, unable to do anything except blink your eyes."

"Quadriplegic? You mean like a football player who breaks his neck?"

"Yes."

"Could I die from surgery?" he asked, lowering his voice.

"Yes."

"Then why didn't you mention that as a risk of surgery?"

"The risk of surgery is becoming quadriplegic," I answered. "Death is a gift compared to quadriplegia."

"What happens if I refuse surgery?"

"You'll die," I said, "but only after you've lain in bed for months after the tumor has paralyzed you from the neck down."

"Not much choice, is there?"

I didn't answer.

"That son-of-a-bitch doctor should have found this tumor three years ago," Ham grumbled.

"That doctor didn't give you this tumor," I reminded him.

"Yeah, maybe not, but I hope that bastard enjoyed spending the money I paid him for giving me the wrong information."

I remained silent.

"How much does this operation cost?" Ham asked.

"The surgeon's fee for removing a spinal cord tumor is thirty-five hundred dollars. The hospital bill, however, will probably be over fifteen thousand dollars," I answered.

"You doctors have it made," he muttered.

216

"What do you mean?" I asked.

"You get paid whether you make a mistake or not."

I didn't pursue the conversation. "Your surgery is scheduled for seven-thirty tomorrow morning. I'll see you then." I told his wife good-bye. She thanked me for coming in.

"Wait a minute," Ham called to me as I walked to the door. "Tomorrow's Sunday. You're not going to operate on Sunday, are you?"

"Yes," I answered. "There's no other choice. The tumor's putting so much pressure on your spinal cord that it may completely destroy the nerves unless we go ahead and operate soon. We only have a window of about twenty-four hours. After that it may be too late to operate and repair the damage."

The operation began at four the next morning. Ham worsened during the night and developed more weakness in his legs and lost his bladder function, forcing immediate surgery. The operation began smoothly. The twelve-inch incision over the base of his skull and down the back of his neck did not bleed much. After I peeled the muscle back from each side of the spine, removed the bone covering the spinal cord and opened the dura, the tumor was clearly visible. However, instead of lying next to the spinal cord, it was growing inside the cord and had burrowed a tunnel into it like a mole.

The tumor was rubbery and would not suck away from the spinal cord and nerves. Biopsy of the tumor confirmed it was benign and that total removal was necessary. I pulled in the microscope, and by noon, eight hours into the operation, I had disintegrated about seventy-five percent of the tumor by burning it with the laser. I leaned back in my chair and took a few minutes to rest. A nurse held a straw under my mask so I could sip some Coke while she held the cup. My hands, gloved and

217

sterile, remained folded over Ham's open spinal cord as a protection against anyone else accidently hitting the nerves with their hands or instruments and paralyzing him. After a nurse put a few M&M's in my mouth, I resumed work. By four o'clock that afternoon I had the entire tumor out. The precise, tedious work had exhausted me. It was like being asked to remove all the seeds from a watermelon without touching the red fruit. The spinal cord was pale and flattened by the tumor but had not been injured during its removal. I was confident that there would be no complications and that Ham would make a full recovery.

A month later I was proven right. Ham made an excellent recovery and was ready to be discharged from the hospital.

"Doc," he said, smiling and patting me on the back, "you've got it made. Thirty-five hundred dollars for one day's work. No one else does that good!"

I looked at Ham, now restored to health. I started to tell him about all the weekends away from home because of emergencies and how little time I spent with my children. But it was easier just to shake his hand and wish him well.

On Christmas Eve, as I was preparing to leave Memphis for a week's vacation, a patient I had never met was admitted to Methodist Hospital with a brain hemorrhage. He asked his family doctor to call me to take care of him. I was surprised when his doctor called about ten o'clock that night and asked me to come to the emergency room. I wasn't on call and had purposely cut back on my surgery and hospital admissions during the week in preparation for the trip home. Since the patient had asked for me, I dressed and drove to the hospital.

Charlie Landon was a pleasant, portly Englishman with thinning white hair and a gray moustache. He said he was seventy years old, but he had an energy and vitality that made him seem younger. He told me I had operated on a friend of his for a ruptured disc in the neck and relieved his pain. "Please do the same thing for my head," he said. "This headache is terrible."

He reminded me of a grown-up leprechaun with a wry smile, yet an intuitive understanding was hidden behind the furrows on his brow. It was clear that he had experienced a brain hemorrhage from a ruptured aneurysm that would require surgery. It was also clear that he understood the seriousness of his illness. But he approached it with the confidence common to a generation who had grown up believing in doctors. He listened carefully as I explained the brain surgery that would be necessary, but he wasn't afraid. He held out his hand to me, and said simply, "Whatever you say." We shook hands and our eyes fixed. It was a contract signed by us both, more binding than any legal document.

I felt uncomfortable as I drove home at midnight. In a few hours, about 7:30 the next morning, I would begin Charlie's operation. If surgery went smoothly and his postoperative course was stable, I would leave Memphis on Friday for a Christmas vacation. It didn't seem right to leave him in the care of another surgeon, but it also didn't seem right to miss the Christmas holiday with my family. Either way seemed wrong, but I placed the thoughts out of my mind as I reached home, knowing I had only four hours to sleep before surgery.

The operation was straightforward and the aneurysm was easily clipped, but Charlie was slow to wake up after surgery. By late in the afternoon on Thursday, he was mumbling a few words and squeezing his wife's hand, but he wasn't as alert as he should have been. A CT scan showed no postoperative blood clot, just brain swelling. This confirmed my own opinion that he would make a full recovery from the aneurysm hemorrhage, but only with very thorough medical care.

That evening after dinner, I settled in front of the fire and read several journal articles on other surgeons' treatment of this potentially fatal brain swelling. My son, John, was already asleep when Laura came downstairs to kiss me good night about 9 P.M. The heat from the fire was all that warmed the cold den. She snuggled next to me and held my hand, placing her palm against my palm, comparing our hands.

"Good night, Daddy," Laura whispered as she crawled out of my lap.

I didn't answer; my mind was still on the man recovering from surgery. As we walked upstairs to her bedroom, she reached for my hand again. I looked at her and thought that this too was a contract; a contract of love between a daughter and her father.

Early the next morning, before anyone was awake at home, I was in the intensive care unit at Charlie's bedside. He was still stable but not yet out of danger. I had two decisions to make. First, his further treatment, and second, whether or not I would leave town for the Christmas vacation. I gave the necessary medication orders to the nurse and then went to the prayer room to speak with his wife. It was clear from the look in her eyes that she wanted me to stay and take care of her husband. But I also knew my family was looking forward to spending the Christmas holiday with me. The decision flowed naturally as I touched his wife's arm, reassured her he would recover, and told her I would see her in the morning.

"See you in the morning." Words of reassurance to her but words, I knew, which closed the door on the holiday trip. I offered several excuses for missing the vacation, but the children couldn't hide their disappointment. I helped Julie pack and continued to wave long after the car had rounded the corner. I went back into the house, ate a sandwich, showered, and went to bed early.

As I turned back the covers, I found a letter on my pillow. It was a Christmas wish from everyone. In addition, Laura had folded up a drawing and placed it in the card. I unfolded it and found a tracing of her hand. Underneath the drawing had been written, "This is to remind my Daddy, When I've grown so big and tall, That once I was a little girl, And my hands were very small."

Holding the drawing, I tried to sleep but couldn't. I wondered if years from now I would think my life worthwhile if all I could recall were the hundreds of patients whose lives my surgery had saved, but I couldn't remember the touch of Laura's hand.

Within a week Charlie Landon's brain swelling had subsided, and he was again alert and anxious to go home. That night Julie called from Atlanta to tell me Laura was sick.

"She's coughing and running a fever, and is short of breath," Julie explained.

"Probably just a virus," I said. "I think you can wait until the morning to see a pediatrician. Just give her some Tylenol tonight for the fever."

The next day at noon, an operating room nurse called me out in the middle of surgery to come to the phone. "An emergency," the nurse said quietly. One of my partners scrubbed in and finished the operation for me while I took the call from Julie.

"The pediatrician said Laura's in pulmonary edema," Julie said, her voice quavering. "She has a heart murmur, and he thinks she has an atrial septal defect. He recommended I take her immediately by ambulance to University Hospital in Birmingham. What's wrong with her?"

"It sounds like he thinks she has a hole between the right and left sides of her heart, and fluid is backing up into her lungs, causing her to be short of breath," I explained.

"Does that mean she needs surgery?" Julie asked.

"It might," I answered. "Let's worry about that after we get her to someone who knows. You take her immediately to the University Hospital emergency room in Birmingham, and I'll make all the arrangements over the phone. I'll have a cardiac surgeon waiting for you when you get there."

"When will you come?" Julie asked.

"Tonight."

I canceled the rest of my surgical schedule, asked one of my partners to see my patients in the hospital, and, after calling a friend, Dr. Welch, who was a cardiac surgeon on staff at University Hospital, I left immediately. I arrived about 10 P.M., went straight to the cardiac I.C.U., and found Dr. Welch explaining the seriousness of Laura's illness to Julie. There was a large hole in her heart which was preventing blood from circulating normally. In addition, the veins draining into the heart were affected and would have to be repaired as well. Emergency surgery would be necessary to close the opening in the heart and reroute the blood flowing through it.

"There are no other options," Dr. Welch said.

I didn't question Dr. Welch's advice. I had complete confidence in him and knew little about cardiac surgery myself.

"Why didn't the pediatrician hear a heart murmur and find this before Laura got so sick?" I snapped.

"I don't know. I wasn't there," Dr. Welch answered quietly.

At six the next morning, a nurse stepped into the waiting

222

room and told Julie and me we could see Laura briefly before she was taken to surgery. We got to her bedside in the intensive care unit just as a nurse was folding back the oxygen tent to give her a pain shot in preparation for taking her to the operating room. I kissed Laura and held her for a minute until she stopped crying from the shot. Then Julie leaned over the rails and hugged her for several minutes until Laura fell asleep from the medication. The nurses asked us to leave. We went back to the waiting room, but I was unable to forget the confused look on Laura's face as she hurt and struggled to breathe. And all we could do was hold her because, at age two and a half, she was too young to understand what was wrong.

Julie and I sat in the surgery waiting room with dozens of other people as we waited to hear from Dr. Welch. Julie fought back her tears and bravely tried to read a magazine while I drank coffee. She didn't say a word to me and didn't hold my hand. It was the moment I realized how distant we had become. Unconsciously, Julie was calling on her own inner strength rather than looking to me for support, as she undoubtedly had been forced to do through four and a half years of marriage when I had not been home to share her life.

"Laura will be fine," I reassured her. "Dr. Welch is the best."

She nodded but didn't look up.

At noon the hostess motioned for us to come to her desk. She told us Laura's surgery was over and a doctor would be down in a minute to talk with us. Several minutes later, Dr. Welch's chief resident came in and told us the surgery had been successful and Laura was fine.

"Where is Dr. Welch?" I asked. "Is he coming down to see us, too?"

I wanted to hear from the surgeon in charge, not his resident. I wanted to touch Dr. Welch, read his eyes, and be told by him that Laura was okay.

"No, sir," the resident answered. "He's into his second operation now and has four more to do after this. But I assure you, your daughter's fine."

"Thank you," I mumbled.

I thought about the hundreds of times I had called the families of patients I had operated on and told them over the phone, just to save a few minutes in a busy day, that surgery was over and everything had gone smoothly. Never again, I promised. From now on, whatever time it took, I decided I would speak to every family myself.

While Laura recovered in Birmingham, I returned to Memphis and increased my work load to fill up my time. I actively sought head cases, and several of the older surgeons in the group were happy to refer tedious, lengthy cranial cases to me while they concentrated on the easier spinal cases. I had a particular interest in brain tumors, aneurysms, and brain bypasses, and after six months in practice I was averaging five craniotomies a week. Some neurosurgeons were doing only five brain operations a month. I became one of six neurosurgeons in Memphis performing the delicate brain bypass operation, microscopically sewing tiny arteries together on the brain's surface to deliver blood around atherosclerotic narrowing of cerebral arteries. My practice and surgical skill continued to increase from the large volume of surgery I was doing. By 1982, when I became eligible to take the oral examination of the American Board of Neurological Surgery, my application included over four hundred spinal cases and two hundred cranial cases.

Board certification is the final hurdle for any specialist. It represents a quality education, a lengthy residency, passage of difficult written and oral examinations, and acceptance as a peer by the American medical establishment. Board certification is so prestigious that most attorneys require no other confirmation of a physician's competence when taking his expert testimony during depositions.

Requirements for board certification in neurosurgery included graduation from an A.M.A.-approved medical school, a year of general surgery training, originally four but later five years of neurosurgical residency, passage of the written examination, the recommendation of the residency's chief of neurosurgery, two years of documented neurosurgical practice, including the number and results of surgical cases operated, and then passage of the oral examination. By the fall of 1982 I had met all the preliminary criteria and was eligible to take the oral examination.

Each morning for three months prior to the exam, I got up at 4 A.M. and pored through the six-volume, 4,000-page textbook *Youman's Neurological Surgery.* Each night after dinner I studied until midnight. At the end of my studies I made an appointment with Dr. Harkness, who was still on the board, and for three hours one Saturday morning I met with him and two neurologists from the Semmes-Murphey Clinic who asked me mock oral questions. In the session they identified five or six rare diseases I needed to study more, but otherwise they felt I was ready for the examination.

On Sunday evening I left Memphis for the flight to the Mayo Clinic in Rochester, Minnesota. My exam was on Tuesday morning, but I went a day early to settle down and find out the location of the exam.

At 7:30 Tuesday morning I dressed and walked over to the Mayo Clinic and took the elevator to the neurosurgery floor. When all twelve candidates had arrived, we were led into the neurosurgery library and seated around a conference table. A few minutes before eight, Dr. Harkness walked in and explained the examination to us.

"The test will be three hours," he said. "You will have one hour of questioning on cranial surgery, one hour on spinal surgery, and one hour on neurology. Following the examination you are to return here and wait for me to talk to you before you leave."

He passed out three-by-five cards listing the examining room for each hour and the two examiners that would question us on each section.

"The test will begin at eight-thirty, so you have a few more minutes if you want a cup of coffee," he said.

There were no takers; coffee was the last thing we wanted.

At 8:30, the twelve of us filed out of the library to begin our exam. My card read Neurology—Room 2, Cranial Surgery—Room 4, and Spinal Surgery—Room 3. Neurology was the hardest section since neurosurgeons spend so little time with medical diseases because they are boring, difficult to treat, and often impossible to cure. I was glad to get it out of the way first and walked down the hall with thoughts of Alzheimer's dementia, Parkinson's disease, multiple sclerosis, epilepsy, and meningitis racing through my brain.

I walked into the neurology examination room, and two neatly dressed men with white hair and bow ties stood up, introduced themselves and shook hands with me. Both looked like neurologists: rumpled clothes, thick glasses, and intelligent demeanors with arms folded across their chests. I was sure they were really nuclear physicists masquerading as physicians. But as they began examining me I was shocked. They asked me basic questions about stroke, epilepsy, and brain infections and offered their own experience to answer questions I couldn't. They didn't try to trick me or ask difficult questions. Instead, they seemed to envision the hour more as a conversation than a test, and their questions simply a chance to see how neurological diseases were treated in Memphis. At the end of the hour they thanked me for coming. I left the room, bewildered that my examiners had been such gentlemen. I walked down the hall for the cranial examination, praying my luck would hold out.

The cranial hour was the heart of the oral board examination. Orthopedic surgeons perform spinal surgery, but only neurosurgeons perform brain surgery. So it was an intense hour of questioning on aneurysms, head injuries, and brain tumors to see if the candidate deserved to be called a neurosurgeon. The first forty-five minutes of the questioning passed without incident, and then one of the neurosurgeons asked me how I treated trigeminal neuralgia, a condition of severe face pain. I explained the medical treatment with Dilantin and Tegretol, nerve blocks over the affected portion of the face, exploration of the posterior fossa with decompression of the nerve, and, finally, cutting the nerve permanently if all other treatments failed. I concluded my answer with a brief review of the history of trigeminal neuralgia, remembering the talk I had given during my residency.

"What about the operation through the middle fossa, under the temporal lobe?" one of the examiners asked. "Isn't that safer than the posterior fossa approach?"

"The middle fossa approach used to be the preferred operation in the old days," I answered. "But no one does that operation now. It's outdated and has fallen into disrepute."

The bell rang in the hallway to announce that the second hour of questioning was over, and I stood up to leave. I shook hands with each examiner and thanked them both.

227

"By the way," one of the neurosurgeons told me, "I just want you to know I did fifty middle fossa operations last year."

I didn't answer, and I staggered to the door. I headed for my final examination in spinal surgery, wondering how I would explain failing my strongest suit, cranial surgery.

The final hour in spinal surgery was uneventful. My examiners recognized I was shaken from the previous hour and spent much of the time complimenting my answers and restoring my confidence. At the completion of their questions they told me I had done the best job of any candidate answering questions on disc surgery.

"You must be from Memphis," one examiner said.

"Yes, sir," I answered. "How did you know that?"

"Memphis neurosurgeons are always strong on disc surgery," he replied. "You can thank Dr. Semmes and Dr. Murphey for that. They kept orthopedic surgeons from doing disc surgery there and mucking things up."

"Yes, sir, I'll tell them," I said, turning to leave.

One of the neurosurgeons stopped me and said, "I have one more question."

"Yes, sir."

"Dr. Semmes is ninety-one years old now, and one of the first four neurosurgeons in the United States. He's one of the historic figures in the history of neurosurgery, and you should be proud to have spent time learning from him. Tell me one thing Dr. Semmes taught you."

"He taught me the proper indications for taking out a ruptured disc in the back," I answered.

"What did he teach?" the neurosurgeon asked. "Severe sciatic leg pain unrelieved by medication, paralysis in the leg, or loss of bladder function?"

"No, sir," I answered. "He said when a patient comes to

228

your clinic with severe back pain, tell him to go home. If he won't go home, take his ruptured disc out."

"He's right, you know," the neurosurgeon agreed. "These days we get too fancy in medicine. The old doctors knew which patients were sick."

I walked back to the library and sat down with the other twelve candidates, whose clothes and expressions were in various stages of disarray. Some still appeared confident, but most looked shell-shocked. I could only imagine what awaited us now.

At 12:15, Dr. Harkness walked into the room and said, "Gentlemen, your exams are over and the board thanks you for coming today. Most of you did very well on the orals. However, three of you didn't and I need to see you after the other nine leave."

Dr. Harkness reached inside his coat pocket and pulled out a three-by-five card with three names written on the back. We all just stared at him, praying our names wouldn't be called. He read out the three names, and the rest of us filed out of the library. Not a word was spoken, and no one looked at the three men still sitting at the conference table. But out of the corners of our eyes we could see their heads bent, their eyes staring straight down at the table.

I rushed back to the hotel, grabbed my bags, and took a cab with three of the other neurosurgeons who had been tested with me. We were all anxious to catch the 2 P.M. flight to Atlanta, which provided connections that would get us all home by 5 P.M. We urged the cabbie to drive faster and ran into the small Rochester airport, only to find our flight delayed and not leaving until 3 P.M. We checked our bags, headed for the airport café, and ordered a pitcher of Budweiser. After the second pitcher fifteen minutes later, we loosened up from our ordeal and began asking each other the answers to some of the questions we had been asked. The conversation quieted as each of us spent more time drinking beer than talking. I related my faux pas when I told one of the neurosurgeons that the middle fossa operation to relieve the pain of trigeminal neuralgia was outdated and in disrepute. Everyone laughed uproariously and wondered why my name hadn't been called out in the library after the exam.

"Hell," New Yorker Mike Canton said as he sucked down more beer, "that bastard asked me the same question."

"How did you answer it?" I asked.

"The same way you did," Mike said. "The posterior fossa approach is far superior to the middle fossa operation."

"What did you say when the examiner told you he had done fifty middle fossa operations last year?" I asked.

"I told him that was bullshit!" Mike answered. "I told him no one had done that operation in fifteen years and it would be ridiculous to do it now."

"Jesus!" I said. "What did the examiner say?"

"He laughed and put his arm around me," Mike said, "and then he whispered that I was the only son of a bitch who had answered the question honestly without backtracking!"

Two months later I was formally notified that I had passed the oral board examination. I opened the letter and read the good news alone. Julie and I had separated, ending our six-year marriage. I had not provided what she wanted most—a home and a family. She had accepted a job teaching in Atlanta and moved that winter.

I remembered the last morning before they moved. I was leaving for the hospital at 4 A.M. Laura and John were huddled in sleeping bags on the den floor in front of the fireplace. All the furniture had been loaded into the moving truck, and Julie had planned an early start that day for the seven-hour drive to Atlanta. I bent down beside Laura and John and kissed each on the forehead.

John stirred, but remained asleep. His brown hair and pointed chin already hinted he would look like me. We had only one outing together—a trip to the grocery store on a cool fall Saturday afternoon. Not much to remember, and just as well that he wouldn't. I laid his blue flannel bathrobe over his shoulders and turned away quickly.

Laura woke up and said, "Daddy, we're moving to Atlanta. When are you coming?"

Laura was four, John three. They didn't know what was happening; to them it was an adventure.

"I don't know, darling," I answered. "But I'll come visit you soon."

I worked late that day but finally had to go home. The house was cold, the rooms empty, sounds echoing. I searched Laura's room and finally found a jack in the corner of her closet. In John's room I found a tennis ball and a tinker toy. I put the jack and tinker toy on top of the TV and rolled the tennis ball into the middle of the room so it would look like the children were still there playing when I came home again. I stretched out on the bed, exhausted, but couldn't sleep.

In the months that followed, work occupied most of my time. After I passed the oral examination, I was certified by the American Board of Neurological Surgery. I was elected to the Congress of Neurological Surgeons and the Harvey Cushing Society. A year later I was elected to fellowship in the American College of Surgeons and the International College of Surgeons. In the fall of 1983 my partners unanimously voted me a full partner in the group. Finally, after long years of training and work, my name made it to the letterhead next to the surgeons I respected so much. Unfortunately, I had no one to tell.

CHAPTER 9

THE COST OF DOING BUSINESS

O N   T H E   A F T E R N O O N of September 22, 1983, a
nurse at the St. Francis Hospital emergency room called
our main office at Methodist Hospital and asked for the surgeon on call for Dr. Shelton's group. Since it was my day to
see new consultations, my secretary called me to the phone.
The nurse told me Dr. Wingate, a cardiologist, had requested
that a neurosurgeon see his patient, Barry Linder, who had
just had a transient ischemic attack, or T.I.A. This interruption
of blood flow to the brain, caused by heart disease or atherosclerotic narrowing of the arteries supplying the brain, results
in temporary stroke symptoms, such as numbness or weakness
in the arms, legs, or face, difficulty talking, confusion, and loss
of vision. T.I.A.s are called warning strokes because 67 percent of patients suffering permanent strokes have temporary
symptoms first. Consequently, a T.I.A. is a true emergency, so
I left the office immediately and drove to St. Francis Hospital
to see Mr. Linder.

Barry was sitting on a stretcher, opening a fresh pack of
Camels, when I walked into the emergency room. He was a

thirty-eight-year-old electrician, married, with three children. He was of average height and overweight and wheezed between puffs on his cigarette. After introducing myself, I sat down in a chair next to his wife and listened to his history.

That morning he had experienced numbness on the left side of his face, then numbness in his left arm and leg. For twenty minutes he had felt weak and his vision was blurred. He had lain down on a couch, and when he had awakened from a nap thirty minutes later the numbness was gone. His arm and leg felt normal again, and he was able to walk without stumbling. He had a mild headache but otherwise no persistent symptoms.

"I called Dr. Wingate," Barry explained. "He said it sounded like a T.I.A. and told me to come to the emergency room so a neurosurgeon could check me."

"That's right," I said. "It was a T.I.A. How's your general health?"

"I have high blood pressure sometimes, but the doctors say I don't need medication yet," Barry answered. "Five months ago I had a triple vessel coronary artery bypass graft for angina because of the hardening in my coronary arteries. I have diabetes but don't like to take insulin, so they give me a pill called Tolinase to keep my blood sugar down."

"How much do you smoke?" I asked.

"Not much. About two packs a day."

"For how long?"

"I started in high school. I guess I've been smoking twenty years."

"Do you know smoking leads to heart attacks and strokes, as well as lung cancer and emphysema?" I asked.

"Sure do, Doc," Barry chuckled as he looked at his wife,

who was also grinning. "We've been told that before, but I can't break the habit. Got to die from something, don't you?"

"Do you have any family history of atherosclerosis?" I asked.

"One of my brothers has angina, too, and had the same heart operation I did. My other brother and my sister died of heart trouble. My brother was thirty-seven, Sis was thirty-nine. My mother died at forty-two. She had hardening of the arteries in her heart, too," Barry added.

"You've got every major risk factor for a stroke, Barry," I said. "You have hypertension, diabetes, a strongly positive family history, and documented atherosclerosis already in your coronary arteries. And if that's not enough risk factors, you laugh about smoking, which is the only risk you can control."

"I know, Doc. I've heard all this before," Barry repeated.

"Okay," I said. "I'll get you admitted to the hospital, and tomorrow I'll do an arteriogram to see how much hardening of the arteries you have in your neck and brain."

The next morning, after I finished the arteriogram, I explained to Barry and his wife that the test had shown narrowing and irregularities in the wall of the right carotid artery in his neck. The same atherosclerotic disease that had caused his heart trouble was beginning to block the arteries supplying his brain. Fortunately, the warning stroke had called attention to the clogged artery in his neck. As the blood to the right side of the brain had been cut off by the blockage, the left side of his body had been affected by weakness and numbness. I recommended an operation, a carotid endarterectomy, to prevent a permanent stroke. I planned to open the artery and clean it out by removing the cholesterol plaques blocking blood flow to the brain.

"Can you promise me I won't have a stroke if I have the operation, Doc?" Barry asked.

"No. I can't, Barry. You have severe atherosclerosis, made worse by your genetics, hypertension, diabetes, and smoking. The operation does nothing for the underlying disease. All it does is unblock an artery supplying your brain."

"What's the risk of surgery?" Barry asked.

"The main risk is that you could have a stroke during the operation," I explained. "The carotid artery has to be clamped for a few minutes so the cholesterol can be cleaned out of the inside. You could have a stroke when the artery is clamped off, or a piece of cholesterol could break free and go to the brain and cause a stroke. In addition, the operation carries the same risk as all major operations: cardiac arrythmias or heart attacks from the general anesthesia, wound infections, bleeding, pneumonia, phlebitis from lying in bed, and, of course, there is always a chance you can die from any operation."

"Well, I sure don't want to have an artery stop up and cause a stroke," Barry said. "I want you to clean it out, Doc. When can you do it?"

"Probably in two days," I answered. "As soon as Dr. Wingate evaluates your medical condition and makes sure your blood pressure, diabetes, and heart are in good enough condition for you to have surgery."

The next morning Barry's EKG was reported as abnormal with an irregular heartbeat. I postponed surgery until Dr. Wingate obtained several EKGs to be sure Barry's heart was stable before he underwent a general anesthetic and carotid endarterectomy. On Monday, four days after his admission, his EKG had normalized and Dr. Wingate gave the okay for surgery.

The two-hour operation was uncomplicated. I opened the

carotid artery and found it full of chunks of cholesterol and small blood clots. The normally smooth inside wall of the artery was rough and filled with sandy debris resembling gravel. I removed the inside lining of the arterial wall to relieve the obstruction to the blood flow and carefully irrigated the artery clean to prevent the cholesterol debris from breaking free and lodging in the brain. After I closed the carotid artery and neck incision, the anesthesiologist turned off the anesthetic gases. Within minutes Barry awoke on the operating table. He was fully alert, with normal speech and mentation. There had been no paralysis. The operation had been highly successful.

The next morning I moved Barry out of the intensive care unit, and that afternoon on evening rounds he was up in a chair watching TV and smoking a Camel. Again I advised him to quit smoking, but Barry just grinned and said, "It's safe now, Doc. You've cleaned out my artery."

Two days after surgery Barry complained of blurred vision, and examination by an ophthalmologist demonstrated a 25 percent loss of the visual field in each eye, the result of a stroke in the occipital lobe, an area of brain not supplied by the carotid artery I had operated on. He had no other symptoms; no weakness or numbness in his arms or legs, no speech loss, and no confusion, since the area of brain supplied by the carotid artery was not involved by the stroke and was functioning normally. But his hypertension, diabetes, genetics, atherosclerosis, and smoking had caught up with him, producing a small stroke in the occipital lobe which controls vision. Only a successful operation had prevented his entire brain from being affected by the stroke.

"Barry," I pleaded. "You've got to start taking care of

yourself or you're going to have more strokes. It's suicide to continue smoking and refusing insulin for your diabetes."

"Everybody in my family has hardening of the arteries," Barry answered. "There's nothing I can do about it, so why should I care?"

A CT scan of Barry's brain was normal, confirming that the stroke in his occipital lobe was minor, too small even to show on X rays. I encouraged him to pay more attention to his health. A week after his operation, I discharged him from the hospital.

Barry returned to the office for routine postoperative visits in November and December and remained stable, without any further strokes or heart attacks. In March, six months after his carotid endarterectomy, he had a T.I.A. involving the other side of his brain. I admitted him to St. Francis Hospital and performed a second arteriogram. The previously operated-on right carotid artery was smooth and wide open, without any blockages, and adequately protected his right brain from strokes. The left carotid artery was also open, without obstruction or debris, indicating his T.I.A. this time was from narrowing and hardening of the small arteries deep within the brain, which cannot be operated on and cleaned out with surgery. I continued to thin his blood with aspirin to help the circulation in his brain and discharged him from the hospital after several days of observation.

In May, Barry returned to the office and said, "Doc, I need your help."

"What is it?" I asked.

"I want you to write a letter for me to help me get disability," Barry explained. "I've had a stroke and lost some vision. I've got high blood pressure, diabetes, and hardening of the arteries everywhere in my body. Everybody in my

238

family dies young from atherosclerosis, and I just don't think I can work anymore."

"You're just thirty-eight," I said. "Are you sure you don't want to keep working? Maybe if you would take better care of yourself . . ."

"I haven't worked for two years, since I had my heart bypass operation. With all my problems no one will hire me. Just help me get disability, will you, Doc?" Barry said.

"Okay. I'll write the letter today and send you a copy," I answered. "And let me see you in a month, or sooner if you have any trouble."

"Sure will. Thanks, Doc."

That afternoon I wrote to the Social Security Administration, requesting permanent, total disability for Barry, but I never saw him again. He didn't return for his monthly check-ups and stopped calling the office for medication. Two months later I found out why when I received a call from my attorney, Bill Wright. Barry Linder's lawyer had filed a medical malpractice lawsuit against me.

"I'd like to discuss the complaint with you," Bill said.

"Fine," I answered. "But this is the craziest thing I've ever heard. I'm the only reason Barry is still alive and not lying around paralyzed and speechless from a stroke!"

The lawsuit alleged that I had "carelessly" performed surgery on Barry Linder's right carotid artery, and I had been "negligent" in not performing surgery on his left carotid artery. From the legal complaint, it appeared that Barry's symptoms of numbness on the left side of his body and his visual loss when he looked to the left had prompted his lawyer, A. K. Upton, to mistakenly think the wrong artery had been operated on. The lawyer apparently didn't know that the right side of the brain controls the left side of the body. In addition, he didn't seem to understand that Barry's visual loss, resulting from a stroke in the occipital lobe, was unrelated to the carotid arteries. Barry's arteriogram showed that the occipital lobe was supplied not by the carotid artery but rather by the posterior cerebral artery, which branched from arteries in the back of the brain unrelated to the carotid artery in the front of the brain.

The lawsuit claimed that Barry was blind in both eyes, suffered severe headaches, and had lost his ability to work. Barry and his lawyer were suing for $3 million in damages.

"This is ridiculous!" I exclaimed. "I've never heard such lies in my entire life."

"I agree this is awfully insulting to listen to," Bill replied. "But we have to defend every suit. How much malpractice insurance do you carry?"

"One million dollars," I answered.

"Then we better prepare carefully," Bill cautioned.

"This doesn't seem right," I sighed. "There's no malpractice here. Barry had an excellent surgical result from the carotid endarterectomy, and he knows it. Why should I be held responsible for a stroke that was caused by his diabetes, hypertension, atherosclerosis, smoking, and genetics? The stroke wasn't even in a part of the brain supplied by the carotid artery. It had nothing to do with the operation."

"I suspect Barry Linder still believes you're a good doctor," Bill replied. "Some lawyer found out that he had a stroke and suggested a lawsuit. Some lawyers think that any personal injury should be blamed on someone else, so they can ask for damages. It's the way lawyers make a living."

"Doctors shouldn't have to defend frivolous suits like these," I complained.

"You've just got to look at it as the cost of doing business,"

240

Bill answered. "The more money you make, the more risk you take, and the more people take shots at you."

In the months that followed I prepared my defense. I went to the medical school library and reviewed the literature on carotid artery surgery. I researched the operating room records and obtained the names of the last one hundred patients I had performed a carotid endarterectomy on. My complication rate was less than 1 percent, well below that of other surgeons and in line with the standard of medical care. I contacted Dr. Harkness, who had written the chapter on carotid surgery in the textbook *Youman's Neurological Surgery.* He reviewed the case, agreed it was frivolous, and agreed to be an expert witness on my behalf.

My anxiety over preparing a defense gradually dissipated as I watched older surgeons, who had been sued before, defending lawsuits. They remained relaxed, although they, too, spent evenings carefully directing the defense attorney's preparation.

One surgeon was sued following the death of a child who was in a car wreck with his parents. The child, who suffered a massive head injury, died in the emergency room following unsuccessful cardiopulmonary resuscitation. It seemed ironic that a physician who had nothing to do with the accident and had rushed to the emergency room to try everything possible to save the child's life should have to defend his actions in court.

Another surgeon was sued following a brain tumor biopsy. The pathologist had studied the frozen section slides under the microscope and reported brain tissue next to the tumor, but no definite tumor. Other neurosurgeons in the operating room at the time had agreed with the operating surgeon. It was riskier to continue trying to obtain tumor tissue since the tumor was located in the speech area of the brain. Further attempts at biopsy would have resulted in damage to this area and loss of the patient's speech. The lawyer contended the surgeon had injured the patient by removing normal brain.

The lawsuits were eventually dismissed by the court, but both had required time and money to defend.

More distressing than the lawsuits was the attitude of doctors. They no longer enjoyed medicine. Lawyers had made physicians afraid of their patients. Doctors compulsively documented in the chart every conversation with family members, every option discussed, every family decision. The explosion of malpractice suits had merged the adversarial nature of law into medicine. The trust between a physician and his patient was gone. The conversation in the surgeon's lounge was the same every morning: What can we do about all these lawsuits?

One Monday morning the lounge was full of fifteen or twenty surgeons drinking coffee and waiting for their operations to begin. Two surgeons were outraged over a lawsuit that had been filed against them the week before. A man had been brought to the emergency room dead on arrival, following a fight and a stab wound to his abdomen. The two surgeons had resuscitated him, rushed him to the operating room, and sewn up the bleeding artery in his stomach. The patient never regained consciousness and died two days later of complications from prolonged shock. The surgeons were being sued for his death. The other doctors listening to the story were bewildered and angry. Finally, one of the surgeons asked Dr. Morris, who was sitting quietly in the corner by himself, what he thought about the suit.

Dr. Morris was eighty-two years old, a smallish, bald-headed man who had practiced medicine, obstetrics, and surgery for fifty years. He had delivered some of the surgeons in the room. He took his glasses off, cleaned them with his handkerchief, then rubbed the top of his head as he considered his answer. The room remained quiet. He stood up, poured another cup of coffee, and shuffled toward the door, shaking his head. He opened the door to leave. Without turning around, he said sadly, "It's just no fun anymore."

Under Tennessee law, plaintiffs must obtain an expert witness who will testify that malpractice has occurred. Barry Linder's lawyer, Mr. Upton, had been unable to find an expert witness for his lawsuit against me. Bill Wright asked the judge for a summary judgment, a dismissal of the suit. Mr. Upton requested a voluntary nonsuit, which the judge granted. Since Mr. Upton had voluntarily withdrawn his suit against me, the law allowed the suit to be refiled anytime in the next twelve months.

"Why did Barry's lawyer do that?" I asked Bill Wright when he notified me of the decision.

"Maybe Upton's looking for a hired gun," Bill suggested.

"What do you mean?" I asked.

"Some doctors advertise as professional expert witnesses in legal journals. For fifteen hundred dollars a day plus expenses, they will fly into Memphis and testify against you. They're paid by the plaintiff's attorney. Sometimes it's the only way a plaintiff's lawyer can get a doctor to give expert testimony against another doctor."

"What a mess," I said, then returned to the hospital to make rounds.

In 1979, one out of every twelve physicians was named in a medical malpractice suit. In 1984 a claim was filed against one out of every five physicians. Seventy-five percent of malpractice suits are dismissed by a judge before they reach a jury. Of the 25 percent that go to trial, physicians win 70 percent.

In 1975 the average settlement in malpractice actions was $48,500. Now it is $338,000. American physicians are in the odd position of providing the best medical care in the world, yet defending the greatest number of lawsuits. The reason is simple: there are more lawyers in the United States than in the rest of the world combined.

The effect of excessive lawsuits is staggering. Defensive medicine—unnecessary tests ordered by physicians to document diagnoses—costs the nation $52 billion a year. Malpractice premiums have risen 400 to 600 percent in the last ten years. In New York, on Long Island, $1 million of malpractice coverage now costs neurosurgeons $101,000 a year. The cost of higher premiums has added $3.6 billion to the nation's health care bill, and if the trend continues the AMA predicts it could reach $7 billion within three years.

"What's your answer to malpractice litigation?" Bill Wright asked when I was voicing my frustrations to him. He had called to tell me my malpractice suit had finally been dismissed. After searching for a year Mr. Upton had been unable to find, or hire, an expert witness.

"There should be a cap on the amount of money juries can award for pain and suffering and other noneconomic damages," I answered. "There should be limitations on punitive damages. There should be a limit on attorney's fees and a penalty paid by lawyers who file nuisance lawsuits that are dismissed without even going to trial."

"Maybe lawyers will strengthen medicine by suing doctors," Bill said.

"And maybe lawyers will take American medicine, the best medical care system in the world, and destroy it," I replied.

"A change in medicine doesn't necessarily mean it will get worse," Bill argued.

244

"Did the change in A.T. and T. help phone service?" I asked.

Bill didn't answer. He knew malpractice litigation would continue. Defense attorneys didn't want to lose the business. Plaintiff attorneys wanted to continue the tort lottery. For them each win meant hundreds of thousands of dollars in attorney's fees. The real reason malpractice lawsuits continue is obvious. Lawyers make the laws.

CHAPTER 10

THE CONSTANT COMPANION

IN AUGUST 1982, I was called to the Methodist Hospital emergency room to see a teenager, Jack Cawthon, who had been flown in by helicopter from northern Alabama. While canoeing on a river, he had dived out of his canoe into the water to cool off. When he didn't surface, friends had jumped in and pulled him up from the muddy river bottom. They had dragged him to the bank and wrapped his head with their shirts to stop the blood pouring out of a gash across his forehead. The Air National Guard had answered their radio call for help and dispatched a helicopter to fly Jack to a hospital. When he arrived three hours later in Memphis, the gaping wound across his forehead was no longer bleeding and he was not in shock. Jack was awake and talking but unable to move his arms or legs. His neck was broken and he was quadriplegic.

I moved Jack off the wooden board the paramedics had strapped him to for the flight to Memphis and onto a stretcher in the E.R. trauma room.

"That should feel better," his father said to him. But Jack

didn't reply and stared blankly at the ceiling. Mr. Cawthon continued to rub his son's hand to comfort him, but Jack didn't respond. I reached for Mr. Cawthon's hand and moved it up to his son's temple.

"Rub here," I whispered to Mr. Cawthon. "He can't feel anything from the neck down."

While I sewed up the ten-inch forehead laceration, Mr. Cawthon told me about his son. He was seventeen years old and about to start his senior year in high school. He had several girlfriends, wasn't much of a student, and wanted to be a National Park Service Ranger when he finished school. He was physically fit and had been on a two-month wilderness canoe trip through the southeast.

"I've never hunted or fished much," Mr. Cawthon explained, "so Jack takes two or three backpacking trips a year with his friends. They're all very experienced campers."

When I finished suturing the laceration, I screwed tongs into Jack's skull. The tongs were strong steel pins hooked to weights which pulled the fractured spine back into proper alignment. Sometimes when a broken neck is straightened out, enough pressure is removed from the spinal cord to allow recovery from paralysis. But Jack wasn't so lucky. I straightened the fracture out easily with forty pounds of weight, but there was no change in his condition.

By the next morning he was worse. In addition to the paralysis, he was now losing the ability to breathe on his own. Only a respirator would prevent him from dying. I asked the hospital administrator, another physician, and two nurses to join me and then walked to the dayroom at the end of the ward to talk with Jack's parents. "Your son is permanently and totally paralyzed from the neck down. He will never recover." I was blunt but I wanted to be sure they understood what I was

247

saying. "Jack has now lost the ability to breathe on his own," I continued. "He will die within the hour unless he is connected to a respirator.

"I recommend you don't put him on a respirator."

The silence in the room was oppressive as my words sank in on the parents. At first they just stared at me and then seemed bewildered as they looked at each other and the other family members present. Then Mr. Cawthon's face tightened and he trembled with anger.

With his voice shaking, he said, "I thought you were a doctor. And all you have to tell me is to let my son die. Hell no. Do everything possible to save my son!" He shoved away the card table at which he was sitting and rushed out of the room.

I returned to Jack's room, performed a tracheostomy, and connected him to a respirator. Five minutes later he was fully alert again after receiving oxygen from the machine. I explained to Jack that his breathing muscles were weak from the accident, and that he required a tube in his windpipe and a breathing machine to provide him with enough air. He didn't understand all that I was saying, but he did understand that he had lost something else, his ability to talk.

Once connected to the respirator as his father had wished, Jack became a full recipient of all that modern medical science had to offer. He lay naked, his head shaved, steel pins protruding from his skull hooked to weights, tubes in his nose, trachea, veins, and penis, feeding nutrients and flushing waste products. A large hole in the center of the bed collected his bowel movements. Except for the smell, he never knew when his bowels were moving. Every two hours nurses turned his bed, moving Jack from his back to his stomach to prevent pressure sores from developing on his skin. Bright heat lamps shone on him to keep his skin dry, preventing rashes and sores. All the time he lay there helpless, unable to even say hello or cover his body when someone walked into the room. For two hours he looked at the ceiling; for two hours he looked at the floor. His whole world became three by five feet. He cried continuously, except for the brief periods of mercy when he was asleep. His tears were not of pain, not of self-pity; they were the tears of anguish, the excrement of suffering. He was alive, but not living; imprisoned in a corpse.

In the weeks that followed, I watched his parents. I wondered when they would realize that their decision to put their son on a respirator to prolong his life had treated their souls humanely, but not his. They kept a steady vigil at his bedside for the first month. Friends came daily, and Jack's girlfriends sat and talked to him for hours. They brought him cakes he couldn't eat, books he didn't want to read, and albums he couldn't put on a record player. But as the months passed his friends had other activities, his mother had other children to care for, and his father had to return to work. Gradually the visitors dropped off, leaving him more and more alone.

Despite our efforts, Jack's body deteriorated. Pressure sores developed on his buttocks, his ankles, the back of his head. His urine became infected, as did the sputum erupting from his tracheostomy whenever he coughed. By six months his torture would have been complete had he not been so young and healthy when the accident occurred. He had lost thirty pounds, his whole body smelled of pus, and only his eyes acknowledged the presence of life.

Nine months after the accident Jack died. He suffocated from the overwhelming infection and pneumonia in his lungs. His parents sat expressionless by the bedside as orderlies removed his withered corpse from the room. I thought about our conversation nine months earlier and wondered if they understood that their son had become not a recipient but rather a victim of medical care. I hoped they would realize there was a difference between a physician and a technician of medical science; the difference being that to the physician, the greatest enemy is not death, it is suffering.

Neurosurgeons have no more constant companion than death. Strokes, brain tumors, aneurysms, hemorrhages and blood clots continuously challenge the surgeon's ability to preserve life, defeat death. But death is never really defeated, only avoided. For in the end, even though medicine has increased man's life span from sixty to seventy and soon to eighty years, the mortality rate has never changed—it remains one per person. The oddity of death, therefore, is not that it occurs, but that it is inconsistent and unpredictable. Why does the child die in a car wreck while the eighty-year-old languishes with Alzheimer's disease, or the teenager from a brain hemorrhage while an adult lingers from repeated strokes? There is no answer. Death can't be understood, only observed.

On a sunny Saturday afternoon in April 1981, I was called to the Methodist Hospital emergency room to see a nine-year-old girl who had collapsed on the school playground following a massive brain hemorrhage. She lay unconscious on a stretcher gasping for air. Her dark hair, which matched her dark eyes, was pulled back from her face with bright barrettes. She was wearing a plaid skirt, knee socks, and black and white saddle oxfords. Her name was Jell, a family name, but her friends called her Jell-O.

I intubated her to give her 100 percent oxygen and started IVs to give her medications that would lower her blood pressure and reduce the pressure in her brain. An arteriogram outlined an arteriovenous malformation involving the left hemisphere. The malformation had ruptured, causing the hemorrhage.

I scheduled an emergency craniotomy to remove the abnormal blood vessels. The enlarged arteries and veins lay on the surface of her brain like writhing worms, wiggling with each beat of her heart. One by one I freed the pulsating arteries from the surrounding normal brain. Then, with the blood supply to the malformation eliminated, the veins peeled away from the brain easily. I tugged the baseball-sized blood clot beneath the malformation out of the brain, relieving more pressure and relaxing the brain further. After ten hours of tedious work, the malformation was totally out. All that remained was the cavity left by the blood clot and indentations on the brain's surface where the tangle of blood vessels had been removed.

Two weeks later Jell-O regained consciousness, and three months later, after intensive speech and physical therapy, she was discharged from the hospital. Always she had believed in her ability to recover, and her positive attitude translated into health.

Once a month for the next year I saw Jell-O in my office. Each Friday morning we sat in my office for an hour, and I encouraged her to talk and move her weak right arm and leg. Gradually Jell-O improved. At first there were only a few words and a twitch of her arm, but eventually full speech and movement in her arms and legs returned. She blossomed more each time I saw her, and I looked forward to her cheery visits.

I saw Jell-O frequently during the next two years. She no longer came to my office as a patient but periodically dropped by with her parents to visit. Often she brought me a surprise, such as a pumpkin at Thanksgiving or a pine cone sprayed silver at Christmas.

One morning as she was leaving the office, she told me she was going back into the hospital. "Why?" I asked. Although thin, she looked healthy.

"Something's wrong with my kidneys," she answered.

"Fibrocystic disease," her father explained.

"Oh," I mumbled. "Well, I'll come see you every day in the hospital, Jell-O."

"You won't cut my hair off again, will you?" she asked.

"No, I won't," I answered. "I'll just be coming by to say hello while the other doctors take care of you." I tickled her stomach and laughed at her giggles as she got into her car. But inside the office I slumped into my chair, dismayed by the bad news.

Two months later the extent of her kidney disease was recognized. Jell-O needed a kidney transplant; without it, she would die. She was maintained on dialysis as an interim solution, but with each passing month she grew weaker. Her healthy color gave way to a pale, yellowish shade; dark circles surrounded her eyes; her bones stuck out everywhere as she continued to lose weight. But always her smile remained.

For the first time in my medical practice, I diligently tried to find organ donors. Every week I saw patients with massive head injuries from car wrecks. With renewed vigor, I approached the parents of these young, previously healthy victims who had sustained brain death following these accidents. "Please," I would plead with the parents, "even though we can't save your child, please allow us to transplant his organs to save another child's life." Usually the response was the same, totally negative. Often the parents became angry and

252

criticized me for being callous and asking for an organ dona-
tion at such a grievous time. Most didn't understand how I
could ask for their child's kidneys, lungs, eyes, liver, or heart
while their child was still alive. I couldn't make them understand that even though their child's heart was beating brain
death had occurred, and, in fact, their child was gone. And
each time parents said no, I lost a another chance to save
Jell-O.

I wanted to help all those waiting for organs, but I thought
most about Jell-O. She had suffered enough in her twelve
years, and she didn't deserve to die. "Please, God," I said,
"leave her alone." But she continued to worsen. A proper
tissue match had not been found for her, and a kidney transplant from her father was unsuccessful. One morning her
doctor told me she would die within the next twenty-four
hours.

That night about eight, after visiting hours were over, I
went in to see Jell-O. Her exhausted parents sat beside her,
holding her hand and brushing her wet hair back from her
face. Her mother wiped her forehead with a cool, wet cloth
and pulled the covers up to her chin as Jell-O shook with chills
from her high fever. The sheets seemed gray, the air stale,
expressions frozen. Jell-O opened her glazed eyes briefly,
worked hard to focus until she recognized me, then faintly
smiled but didn't speak. In a few minutes she was asleep again.
I stood up to leave, then leaned over the bed rail, kissed her
forehead, and said good night; I could not bear to say good-
bye. She died that night, several hours before I returned for
morning rounds.

Through the years there have been other patients whose
premature deaths seemed unfair. One twenty-seven-year-old
man, Bobby Hopper, was at first just another patient, but over

the two years I knew him he became a friend. He was a soft-spoken man, short and muscular, who unloaded freight for independent truckers. He had finished high school, spent two years in the army, and still wore his black hair short, shaved on the sides around his ears like white sidewalls.

It may have been a mistake to become friends since he was dying from the moment I first met him. Physicians train themselves to remain aloof and detached from the emotions of those for whom they care. During those times of intense grief and sadness, the physician must remain stoic to provide the foundation, the safe harbor, for those suffering the loss of a loved one. Emotional restraint is a necessity when attending the terminally ill. But as I treated Bobby, my guard slipped and my principles became more compromised with each day our friendship grew.

Bobby's severe headaches and difficulty with coordination were diagnosed as resulting from a malignant brain tumor in the cerebellum. The malignancy was growing rapidly and exerting pressure on the back of his brain, resulting in difficulty walking and maintaining balance. When informed of his diagnosis, his first reaction was concern for the welfare of his wife after he died, rather than his own chance for life. He took the news well, and never was there a hint of self-pity; either then, when I first told him about the tumor, or at any time during the ordeal of the next eighteen months that he would live.

Perhaps our friendship began because of his love for chess. At first I felt I was humoring him, playing chess to help him pass some time while he was recovering from his first operation. But as the games went by, I found myself concentrating harder to maintain an edge over him. Gradually, as his mind cleared following the brain surgery, his victories became more regular. I caught him studying books, then trying new openings and gambits on me. I began spending more time with him and studied my moves longer. What had begun as short games now stretched into thirty-, forty-five-minute, then one-hour games. It was during those times that I began to listen to the thoughts of a young man dying from cancer.

He spoke often of his parents and his wife. He had relatively few friends, which may have explained the depth of his feelings toward his family. He spoke a lot about the ability of physicians, with the help of God, to heal. We laughed a long time one night when he presented me with a plaque which read, "God heals, the physician takes the fee."

But he believed in doctors. My very presence seemed to give him hope and strength. He believed that the doctors, nurses, and hospital would make him well. He believed that with all his heart. But it was still early in his illness.

His first operation went well: I removed approximately 75 percent of the tumor located in the cerebellum. But some of the tumor had spread into the brain stem, an area of brain inaccessible to the surgeon because of its critical functions of maintaining blood pressure, respiration, cardiac rhythm, and temperature control. Pulling on tumor stuck to the brain stem often causes the patient to lose respirations and blood pressure, followed by abnormal heartbeats, then cardiac arrest. It was my hope that cobalt X-ray treatments would shrink the tumor remaining on the brain stem, allowing him more time to live.

Seven weeks after the initial surgery, I discharged Bobby from the hospital. He had lost weight, but his mind was clear and his coordination had temporarily improved. He was anxious to return to work; he hadn't yet realized that his life would never be normal again.

After a few months at work, he was unable to continue. I

readmitted him to Methodist Hospital on a Sunday afternoon because of worsening headaches. Now the headaches were accompanied by vomiting, and a CT scan confirmed a buildup of spinal fluid in the brain, hydrocephalus, which would require drainage. The next day I shunted the spinal fluid from the cerebral ventricles to his abdomen, where the body could reabsorb the necessary nutrients in the fluid. Once again his symptoms improved. We talked more now, and in greater depth. He talked of dying but viewed it only as an extension of living. It saddened him only in the fact that he would be separated for a while from his family. He considered death a gift, given to those who had fulfilled a good life, and he had absolutely no fear of it.

His disease progressed as the months passed. He experienced daily nausea, weight loss, double vision, and headaches. His coordination continued to fail, so he dictated his chess moves to me, since he could no longer move one piece without knocking over the other ones.

One day while I was studying the chessboard, he began to cry. He had never felt sorry for himself, so it puzzled me to see him upset. "What's wrong?" I asked.

"I'm going to miss my family so much," he said. "Look what I saw in the newspaper today."

He pushed a crumpled sheet of paper toward me across the table. It was torn, and it looked like it had been very difficult for him to tear out of the paper because of his poor coordination. It was a quotation credited to Walter Rinder, a writer and photographer, who wrote in 1971, "We arrive upon this earth alone, we depart alone, this time called life was meant to share."

Bobby looked at me and said, "I wish I had shared more."

I stared out the hospital window thinking of Laura and John, now living in Atlanta. I saw them one Saturday a month and always drove back to Memphis wishing I had more time with them. One weekend I had taken pictures of Laura on her first bicycle, complete with training wheels, balancing carefully on the sloping driveway. The next time I saw her she was riding a bike without help, without training wheels, and wasn't even interested in showing me her new skill. It was second nature to her by then. On one visit John had asked me to take him to a baseball game, but the Atlanta Braves were playing out of town that Saturday. On my next trip John had a baseball cap and glove, provided by a father next door who had taken John, with his own son, to a baseball game.

I turned away from the window and looked again at Bobby. Although I remained silent, he knew I understood his comment.

The third operation was necessary twelve months after the initial surgery. The tumor mass had regrown sufficiently to require further removal, and it was again exerting too much pressure on the brain. This time I was more aggressive in removing tumor and spent longer during the operation. Somehow I wanted to believe I could alter the natural history of this disease. If only I could take out more tumor, I thought, I could prolong his life.

I gave Bobby three more months of life, but it wasn't good life. He remained alert but was confined to bed and had increasing difficulty talking, moving, and eating. He couldn't read or play chess. He couldn't even watch TV as his vision worsened. But he seemed to enjoy our conversations; I hoped so, since I had given him nothing else from the last operation.

One Thursday evening I stopped by his room before going home. He was clearly dying now. He couldn't focus his eyes; his mouth was dry, his breathing labored and noisy. I told him

I was there and squeezed his hand. His family had gathered at his bedside. As I surveyed the room I could still see a flicker of hope on their faces that I could do something that would make him well. The battle was lost now, and I thought it best to discuss this with the family to help them prepare for his death.

"Would you step outside with me for a moment?" I asked them.

We gathered in the hall outside his room and I told them he would die soon. As we stood in silence outside the room, I heard Bobby's weak voice call for me. I went back in the room by myself and sat on the edge of the bed.

"This is my last day, isn't it?" he asked me.

I knew he didn't want lies. "Yes," I said.

"I knew it was bad this time," he said, his voice failing.

"Why do you say that?" I asked.

"Because you never asked to talk to my family out in the hall before."

I returned to the hospital early the next morning. As I stood at the foot of Bobby's bed, I knew these were his last minutes. I thought of sticking a needle into his brain, draining more fluid to relieve the pressure, giving him another few days to live. But I knew that was wrong. There was no longer any reason to prolong the inevitable. I thought of the words of Stewart Alsop, who wrote in *Stay of Execution* as he was dying of leukemia in 1973, "A dying man needs to die, as a sleepy man needs to sleep, and there comes a time when it is wrong, as well as useless, to resist." I watched Bobby's last breath shortly before dawn, and, fifteen minutes later, his last heartbeat. I was glad Bobby's wife and parents were with him that Friday morning. Even though the pain of family members is

258

intense, the dying are comforted by their presence, and it becomes a grief worth suffering.

I was afraid that one of my patients, Cooper Long, would die alone. Divorced nearly twenty-five years before, he had chosen to remain alone, devoting his life to genetic research on inherited diseases and limiting contact with his son and two daughters. When his death approached in 1983 from leukemic infiltration of his brain, it saddened me to see him unable to say good-bye to his children. He wasn't even sure where they lived now, but as he grew weaker he tried harder to find them. The telephone calls became more frequent, the conversations more intense, as he struggled from his bed to locate his children. As he realized his strength was failing too fast for him to complete his search, his despair became obvious. After all these years, he realized he was dying as he had lived, alone. He didn't want much from his children, just a hand on his shoulder, a daughter's smile and the smell of her perfume, and words of reassurance that he had once been loved and would always be missed. But I was afraid these were beyond his reach because his illness was aggressive and swift, and oblivious to the emotions of a dying man.

Finally, by good luck and the hard work of hospital pastors, Cooper's son was located in Orlando, Florida, and flown to the hospital. His daughters, former wife, and other relatives declined. Only his son, Chuck, wished to see him again. Just eight hours after Chuck was informed of his father's condition he reached Methodist Hospital. It was nine o'clock on a biting winter's night when I first saw Chuck outside the doors of the intensive care unit. He was a handsome, thirty-five-year-old man with a firm handshake. I remember his thick dark hair still had snow in it when I met him. He stood erect and well groomed in his suit and topcoat. His eyes were intense, his mind crisp, his manner direct. We sat down in a small room outside the I.C.U. and drank some coffee while I explained his father's illness. I thanked him for coming and told him he had arrived just in time; tonight would be his father's last. As I spoke affectionately of the time I had spent with his father through the years, Chuck relaxed and talked about his childhood. He opened a door to his father's life I had never seen, for Cooper had never confided the pain of his past to me.

Chuck dated his life from the time of his parents' divorce, when he was eight years old. Gone were the happy memories of a father, son, and family during the eight years they had been together. He didn't mention a Christmas, a vacation, or a birthday. He talked about the fights and the tears, on both his parents' and his sisters' faces. He spoke of his fear that the noises would come into his room, and he recalled his sisters crawling into his bed to hide under the covers. He told me of the three of them crying under the blanket so their parents wouldn't hear them. He recalled trying to figure out what was happening, but not understanding why two people he loved so much couldn't love each other. He told me of waving good-bye to his father as he drove away and asking his mother if his father would be home for supper. Later, he said, as the days went by, he asked his mother if his father was coming home for Christmas. When the first Christmas came and his father didn't return, he thought he had forgotten it. But when the second and the third Christmases passed without his father, he gave up on ever seeing him again. As he gave up, Chuck said, he grew to hate his father because he wanted so much to see him, but his father didn't call or visit. He grew up constantly hearing his mother curse his father and his many faults, and he grew to believe it. Chuck admitted he had seen his father only three times in the last twenty-five years. He didn't want to see the man, or be the son of a man, who he had heard was so bad. So he had spent only three brief weekends with his father since he was eight years old.

"Ironically, though," Chuck said, "each time I saw my father he spoke highly of Mother and complimented her. He spoke of Mother's smile, her soft hands, and her devotion to the children. Each time he talked to me about Mother, he told me to obey her, love her, and believe in her, because she represented all of what is good in life." Chuck paused a minute, then continued, "When I returned home after visiting my father, I was confused by my mother's hatred and my father's kindness. I grew up hating my father and loving Mother, but now I love my father for helping me to love my mother, and I'm bitter toward Mother for stealing my chance to love my father. If only I had these twenty-five years back, I'd tell my father, and show him, how much I love him."

"Why don't you tell him now?" I suggested.

"What should I say?" Chuck asked. "Father, I miss you? Father, I love you?"

"You'll find the right words," I said. "Come on, let's go see your father."

We walked back into the I.C.U. to Cooper's bedside, and Chuck reached over and touched his father's shoulder. Cooper was quite weak now, and looked up through sunken eyes and smiled faintly on the outside, but joyously, I'm sure, on the inside to see his tall, handsome son standing beside him. I watched the two men look at each other and the tears form in their eyes. Chuck knelt down, put his arm across his father's chest, and laid his head on his shoulder. I drew the curtains around the bed and stepped out to the nurses' station to leave them alone. In a few minutes I motioned Chuck to leave. He leaned over to his father's ear and whispered, "Good night,

Dad." A smile formed at the corner of Cooper's mouth as he closed his eyes.

As I watched Cooper die that night I wondered why he must die so young. He was sixty-five, but except for the leukemia which had silently ravaged his body for six weeks before it was diagnosed, he had no other diseases. Yet a fluke disease he couldn't prevent claimed his life. Death's movements certainly seem random, its decisions without a motive.

That same winter I was called to the emergency room to see Eula Jones, a maid who had worked in Methodist Hospital for twenty years. I had known her for six years, since my first days as a neurosurgery resident. She was a tall, broad-shouldered, bulky black woman, weighing 290 pounds and always dressed in an immaculate white, starched uniform. She suffered from hypertension, diabetes, angina, and gout, necessitating slow movements with frequent stops to catch her breath as she worked on the wards changing beds and cleaning bathrooms. She always had a bright smile and a cheerful hello for everyone, and patients and hospital staff alike looked forward to seeing her each morning ambling down the hall singing "How Great Thou Art."

I found Eula unconscious in the E.R. following a brain hemorrhage from a ruptured intracranial aneurysm. I admitted her to the intensive care unit and began the long, careful process to stabilize her before she could undergo craniotomy and clipping of the aneurysm. While examining her heart and lungs, I discovered a mass in her right breast which was clearly cancer, adding another problem to the many she already had. I began Eula on Amicar to prevent breakdown of the blood clot surrounding the aneurysm, which was acting like a scab covering the hole in the aneurysm dome and preventing its rebleeding. I gave her mannitol, Lasix, and Decadron to lower

her intracranial pressure. I began her on Dilantin and phenobarbital to prevent seizures and carefully lowered her blood
pressure with Nipride to prevent the aneurysm from exploding and hemorrhaging again. I fed her intravenously and
brought her electrolytes back to the normal range by supple-
menting her with potassium. Her cardiac arrythmias were
controlled with lidocaine, and her hematocrit, renal function,
liver enzymes, and bleeding studies all normalized. A week
later she had regained consciousness, and her medical condition was optimal for surgery. I met her in the operating room
at 6:30 that morning and spoke to her briefly before the
anesthesiologist put her to sleep. After discussions with general surgeons, I had decided to proceed with the aneurysm
surgery first, since the aneurysm hemorrhage was more life-
threatening than the cancer. In the recovery phase following
her craniotomy, general surgeons planned to perform a mas-
tectomy for the breast cancer.

I had asked Dr. Karpik, an experienced neuroanesthesiolo-
gist, to put Eula to sleep for the craniotomy. He carefully
checked her pulse, cardiac rhythm, and blood pressure before
injecting the pentothal into her IV. "You'll be getting sleepy
in about ten seconds," he said to Eula in his low, reassuring
voice. "And you may taste some garlic in the back of your
throat. That's just the medicine, so don't worry about it." Eula
fell asleep quickly, her deep, snoring breaths puffing her
cheeks until Dr. Karpik injected Pavulon to stop her respirations entirely so he could intubate her. Seconds later, with a
tube in her windpipe and connected to a respirator, he nodded
to me that I could position her head for the operation. As I
shaved Eula's head and chatted with the scrub nurse about the
rain and sleet outside, Dr. Karpik suddenly interrupted and
said, "Her blood pressure's falling." Immediately I turned off

the barber clippers and felt Eula's carotid pulse in her neck. I could barely palpate it, and her pulse was slowing.

"What's the matter?" I asked Dr. Karpik.

"I don't know," he answered. "I can't keep her blood pressure up. I've turned off all anesthetics and she's on one hundred percent oxygen now. But her pressure's still dropping!"

"What is it now?" I asked.

"60/40," he answered. "I'm starting dopamine to try to get it up."

Her pressure continued to fall until it could no longer be heard with the Doppler stethoscope. Next she had a cardiac arrest, and I began pressing her chest to keep her heart contracting. Five minutes later the dopamine began working and her blood pressure increased to 80/60. Her heart began beating again in a normal sinus rhythm. She was stable, but I decided to cancel the operation since I didn't know what had caused the sudden drop in blood pressure and cardiac arrest. It might have been a reaction to the anesthetic, but I wanted to be sure she had not had a heart attack or pulmonary embolism. I took her back to the I.C.U. and called an internist to see what he thought had happened to Eula on the operating table.

Eula's aneurysm had not hemorrhaged in the week since her admission to the hospital, but I had limited time in which to repair the ruptured artery in her brain. It was risky to postpone the surgery because a rebleed from the aneurysm might cause a severe stroke or death. The internist and I worked all day to determine the cause of Eula's hypotension and cardiac arrest. She had not suffered a heart attack or thrown a pulmonary embolus to her lungs from a blood clot in her legs. The internist concluded that certain substances being released into Eula's bloodstream from the breast cancer had adversely

264

affected her blood pressure, making it labile and difficult to control. By 5 P.M. her blood pressure was stable, and I rescheduled the operation for 7:30 the next morning. I left the hospital about 10 P.M., tired but convinced I had made the right decision to postpone Eula's surgery until the next morning.

At midnight I received a call from the intensive care unit. The neurosurgery resident told me he had seen Eula sit up in bed, grab the side of her head, and scream, "It's hurting." She had then collapsed backward, unconscious. C.P.R. was unsuccessful, and Eula had died at 11:30 P.M.

I dressed and drove to the hospital and talked at length to the family about Eula's many medical problems and the necessity of postponing her surgery. They thanked me, kissed Eula good-bye, then left. After signing the death certificate, I left about 2 A.M. It was just five hours before I was scheduled to operate on Eula's brain and repair the ruptured aneurysm. If only I had started the operation a few hours earlier, I might have prevented the rebleeding which killed her. I wondered if her death had come five hours too soon; was I five hours too late in operating; or did she die at her appointed time?

The answer remains elusive. Eula's medical treatment was carefully planned, meticulously delivered; a product of scientific thinking and medical technology. Yet she had died. I had balanced proper treatment and proper timing, but in the end it was the disease, not I, that determined the length of her life.

My observations of death included several patients who, having been resuscitated, recounted afterlife experiences. Their stories of the afterlife provided a calming balance and a different perspective on the unfairness and undirected harshness of death. After experiencing death and returning to life, patients seemed to view death more as a change rather than an end. W. J. Larkin, a seventy-year-old retired electrical engineer, provided me with the first of several afterlife experiences in my practice.

Mr. Larkin was brought to the office by his wife, who said he had rapidly deteriorated mentally in the last three months and their family doctor had diagnosed him as having senile dementia. "I just want another opinion," Mrs. Larkin said, "to make sure there isn't something that can be done for him."

I examined Mr. Larkin, who looked pathetic. He sat expressionless with his shoulders slumped forward. He was unshaven and dirty and smelled of urine. Saliva drooled from the corner of his mouth, and he licked his lips continuously as he slobbered.

"He hasn't always been like this," Mrs. Larkin said. "Only for the last three months. For no reason, he sold his business, began drinking heavily, and his personality changed. He became withdrawn from our family and began spending hours lying in bed." She tried to continue but couldn't as she began crying.

I looked back at Mr. Larkin. He wasn't paralyzed, and he could talk and answer questions. But he seemed totally unconcerned about continuing any conversation. I walked to the CT scanner with him and waited fifteen minutes until the brain scan was completed. As I had suspected, he had a large, malignant brain tumor, a glioblastoma multiforme, invading the left hemisphere and extending up into the frontal lobe, which controls emotions.

I knew from experience what I would have to tell Mrs. Larkin. First a craniotomy to remove as much as possible of the tumor, then six weeks of cobalt X-ray therapy to kill more of the malignant cells. Next, three to six months of relatively

266

normal life. Finally, a progressive deterioration with death about one year after the diagnosis.

After I had finished explaining the problem to Mrs. Larkin, she replied, "I think he knew something serious was wrong. We didn't understand why he sold his business, but I believe now he was putting his affairs in order. He was trying to clean things up while he still could."

I shook my head noncommitally, but I agreed with her. Many patients sense their death and prepare for it. I wished Mr. Larkin could tell me why he had sold his business, but he was too ill to answer my questions.

At surgery the tumor was found to have spread extensively throughout the brain and could not be removed. As expected, Mr. Larkin lived nine months. Several months after his death, Mrs. Larkin stopped by the office to see me.

"Do you know what he said just before he died?" she asked me.

I shook my head no.

" 'I'm leaving now. It's all so beautiful, and they are calling me.' "

I shivered, thinking his words referred not to his death, but to an afterlife.

A similar experience occurred when a teenager who had been killed in a head-on car wreck was brought to Methodist Hospital dead on arrival. Because he was young and healthy, I began cardiopulmonary resuscitation. Once blood began perfusing his brain and body, he regained consciousness. After I pumped blood into his drained body through four IVs I rushed him to the operating room, where general surgeons were waiting to control the hemorrhage in his abdomen. On the way to the O.R. he mumbled, "Why did you bring me back?"

"Bring you back?" I repeated his phrase. "What do you mean?"

"You put me back inside my body," he said. "I was happy where I was. I saw my family, and I was comfortable and not afraid. I watched you squeeze my heart. It was odd. Each time you squeezed the heart, I was drawn closer to the body and further from my family. I wanted to stay with them, but they kept drifting away from me. For a while I willed myself to stay out of the body as I watched you. I closed my eyes as if to blink, but when I opened them, I was looking out of the body's eyes again. You put me back inside."

The teenager fell asleep as the anesthesiologist administered the pentothal. He awoke in the recovery room following the successful surgery, complaining of severe abdominal pain. The long incision in his abdomen to stop the hemorrhaging was clearly painful, and a nurse gave him a shot of Demerol. He was, however, no longer speaking of his body with the detachment he had before surgery. It was not his body that was hurting; he was hurting.

I leaned over his bed and asked him, "Do you remember what you said on the way to the operating room?"

"Sort of," he answered. "I remember talking to you about starting my heart again and putting me back inside my body. I don't know; I feel foggy, like I just came out of a dream."

"Well, just rest now," I said. "We can talk more later." I left his bedside to tell his family he would live.

Another afterlife experience occurred when a patient in the cardiac intensive care unit had a second massive heart attack while his wife was feeding him during visiting hours. Immediately doctors responded to the "Code Blue" paged throughout the hospital, and the man's wife was pushed outside into the hall as we thumped his chest, defibrillated his heart, and started IVs to inject bicarbonate, calcium, and epinephrine into his veins. Thirty minutes later we revived his heart, and he regained consciousness. Wearily, the man whispered, "Let me be. I want to be with my wife."

"Your wife's right here," I answered.

"No, she's not," he said. "She's waiting for me elsewhere."

"I'll go get her," I reassured him. He relaxed a bit as he watched me walk through the crowd of doctors and nurses surrounding his bed and out into the hall to get his wife. I found her slumped forward against a desk, dead, the apparent victim of a heart attack from the terror of seeing her husband dying. No one in the room had noticed her. All attention had been directed to the man we were resuscitating. Yet he had known.

Stunned, I walked back to his bedside and said, "You're right. Your wife has passed away."

"I know," he answered. His face untensed, he closed his eyes, his breathing became more shallow, and in a few minutes he, too, was gone.

Despite the hope provided by patients who describe an afterlife, death remains frightening, difficult to confront. Each time I face death, I hope it will be easier. But each time seems to be the first. A palpable sadness always accompanies the physician at the bedside as he tells a patient he is to die. Sometimes it is easier, as with the elderly, who have had a full life but are now suffering and view death only as a chance to rest and renew their lives. As Jonathan Swift wrote, "It is impossible that anything so natural, so necessary and so universal as death should ever have been designed as an evil to mankind." As an extrapolation, this seems to be true; as a specific, it often is not.

Chester Clements was no different. He was young, twenty-five, and had been admitted to St. Francis Hospital for evaluation of severe headaches. CT scanning showed a massive, deep-seated, malignant glioblastoma multiforme in the dominant hemisphere. After surgical biopsy confirmed the diagnosis, I walked to his room prepared to tell him and his family, if they should ask, that he would die within the year. Like most patients, he did ask, "How long do I have?"

"About one year," I answered.

As I talked to him I watched him flush, until finally the bitterness burned in his eyes. He had been an All-American football player in college. He was married, and a child was on the way. As I watched his anguish, I knew he wanted to ask, "Why me?" but he didn't. He knew no one could answer.

The months passed, and his body wearied, stumbled, and then fell beneath the onslaught of the malignancy. But he remained confident in his own beliefs and cheerful about the future. He spent his last six months enjoying his family. He painted watercolors in soft pastels, not in deep, gloomy colors suggesting despair and self-pity. And, at the end, the telltale sign: he thanked us all for caring for him and helping him through his illness. It was this sign, this acknowledgment, that confirmed to us all he wasn't afraid of his future.

As I watched him die that night, I was surprised by the peacefulness of the process. He didn't struggle, choke, or seem to be in pain. Although I had experienced it before, it was an odd moment when he died and his body became a corpse. For a few minutes after his death there was an aura in the room, as if he were lingering to say good-bye to his family gathered at the bedside.

The young person informed of impending death does not accept it with the same equanimity as the elderly. The young fight the thought of death and object, even, to its very mention. They are unprepared to die, for they have not yet lived. As you talk to them about death, a shower of disbelief, then anger, and finally the unfairness of it all cascades across their face. The weeks pass and the deeds of the disease transform the smooth faces of the young into the wrinkled, tested faces of the old and finally into the drawn mask of the dying. The image of the transformation surfaces in your mind from hundreds of previous patients, as you begin the long walk to the bedside to tell yet another patient words you have spoken before and are condemned to speak again.

CHAPTER 11

FINISHING A ROUGH DRAFT

D EATH, DISEASE, and illness are good teachers. Rarely are their lessons lost on the pupil. Profound changes often occur in patients surviving a major illness, such as an alcoholic reforming after nearly dying from pancreatitis or a man returning to his wife after being shot during an extramarital affair. Most changes, however, are more subtle: an indifferent spouse becomes more attentive, an absent parent more available. If disease has a positive aspect, it is its constant, forceful reminder of the brief prelude prior to death.

During the flu epidemic in the winter of 1981, a six-year-old, redheaded boy named Stetson Roberts was admitted to the pediatric service at Methodist Hospital with a temperature of 104 degrees. His illness began with flulike symptoms, including nausea, vomiting, aching muscles, fever, and diarrhea. Over forty-eight hours he rapidly worsened and developed severe headaches and double vision, then he became unconscious. The pediatrician attending Stetson called me, and I ordered an emergency CT scan. It was normal and gave no clue as to the cause of the increased pressure building up

272

inside Stetson's head. There was no brain tumor, blood clot, or abnormally large collection of spinal fluid in the brain causing hydrocephalus. I began Stetson on medication to lower the pressure in his brain and screwed a bolt through his skull onto the surface of the brain so that I could measure his brain pressure accurately. Over the next five days he grew worse, and I was no closer to a diagnosis. I presented the case to the citywide neurosurgical grand rounds conference. Every neurosurgeon agreed with my treatment, but no one was able to offer a diagnosis.

As Stetson's death approached, I spent more time with his parents. His father had not even taken time off from farming during the first four days of Stetson's hospitalization. But when he realized his son's condition was terminal, he remained at Stetson's bedside continuously.

On the eighth hospital day, I found Stetson completely unresponsive, with one pupil fully dilated, unreactive to light, and much larger than the other pupil. This sign, an omen of impending death, indicated he had only hours to live. I decided to operate on Stetson's brain—exploratory surgery to relieve the pressure inside his head. The very strict indications for brain surgery are so well known to all surgeons that exploratory surgery on the brain is very rare. Opening a head without proper indications is tantamount to malpractice. As I stood at the foot of Stetson's bed pondering my decision to operate without a specific diagnosis, I reflected on a comment made to me by a professor of surgery, Dr. Freeman Carter, when I was in medical school.

"The decision to operate," he once said, "is like any decision. You look at what you've got to lose and at what you've got to win. One of the things you've got to lose is a life—so what you've got to win had better be pretty good."

By deciding to operate on Stetson, I was now accepting full responsibility for any outcome. If he died, the parents would believe it was due to the surgery; they would quickly forget the underlying disease that had prompted the operation.

I took Stetson to the operating room, shaved his head, and then drilled a hole in the right side of his skull. I gently pushed a hollow plastic tube into a cerebral ventricle in the center of his brain. A stream of spinal fluid shot through the tube like a kettle exploding on a stove. I shunted the fluid into Stetson's abdomen so it could be reabsorbed into his body and then sewed up the incisions. The whole operation was over in an hour. It was a complete surprise to me that the spinal fluid was under pressure, since the CT scan had shown no enlargement of the ventricles or other signs of hydrocephalus. Stetson had subependymal fibrosis, a rare inflammatory condition in which the ventricles do not enlarge in response to increasing pressure inside them, leading to a falsely negative CT scan.

Within minutes following the operation Stetson regained consciousness. By the next morning he recognized his mother, and ten days later he was well and ready for discharge from the hospital.

Two weeks later I reported the diagnosis and result of Stetson's surgery to the grand rounds conference. One of the pediatric neurosurgeons replied, "Of course, everyone knows about subependymal fibrosis. I've had two cases this year." Why, I wondered, hadn't he offered that insight weeks ago when I needed help on Stetson's diagnosis?

I saw Stetson in the office for a checkup every month for a year following his surgery. Each time his father showered me with thank-you's. On his last visit Stetson came in eating some McDonald's french fries. I asked him for one but he said,

"No." His father was embarrassed, and told him to share his french fries with me. But Stetson still refused. I just laughed as I told Stetson and his father good-bye. Thank-you's only go so far.

I often thought of Stetson when confronted with other children who were dying, and it encouraged me to continue fighting for their health since I had learned from Stetson's surprising recovery that death is sometimes difficult to predict. The return to health of a child is always a treasure since they have so many more years to live and enjoy life, as well as contribute to it.

One steamy July morning I was called to the emergency room to see a ten-year-old boy, Jed Simpson, who was lying unconscious on a stretcher. The father, sitting beside his dying son, was pushing Jed's sweaty, sandy hair away from a large bruise on his forehead. Jed's right eye was swollen shut, and blood trickled from his right nostril. A CT scan was hanging on a view box over the bed and showed a large blood clot inside the right frontal lobe which would require surgery. As the interns made the final preparations, I asked Jed's father to follow me out of the room so I could explain the operation to him.

When we entered the waiting room, the father introduced me to Jed's identical twin. It was an odd feeling to see Jed dying a few feet down the hall, and then see what he must have looked and talked like before he was hurt. The father put his arm around the other twin, and we sat down to talk. The father explained that he was divorced and had custody of the two boys. Jed's mother and sister lived an hour and a half away in Jackson, Tennessee. They didn't know Jed had been hurt.

"What happened to him?" I asked the father.

"We were playing baseball," he answered. "I hit a line drive. Jed misjudged the ball and the baseball hit him in the forehead."

"Did it knock him out?"

"No," he said. "But he was dazed for a few minutes. We went home and he seemed to be doing all right. Jed didn't want any supper and went to bed early. I put some ice on his black eye and tucked him in. Early this morning I woke up when I heard him vomiting in his bed. I couldn't wake him up and rushed him here. If only I had watched him more closely or taken him to a doctor sooner."

I tried to reassure the father and ease his guilt but I couldn't, so I told him I would be back to talk to him as soon as I finished removing the blood clot from Jed's brain.

Ten minutes later I had Jed on the operating table and began opening his head. The scalp was mushy from the large bruise over his right eye and forehead, but he had the thin skull of a child and his head opened easily. Inside, there was very little normal, yellow brain. Most of the brain was blue and purple, discolored by the intense hemorrhage and blood clot from the blow. Delicately I removed the blood clot, avoiding injury to all normal brain that was possible. Once the grapefruit-sized clot had been removed, Jed's breathing became less labored and more regular. The brain began to pulsate and stopped swelling out of his head. No brain had to be removed, only the massive blood clot that had filled his right frontal lobe. I closed Jed's head, optimistic that I had helped him.

Jed regained consciousness in the recovery room and within minutes was asking for his father. I brought his father and twin to his bedside and allowed them a few moments together. Their mutual affection was good medicine for all three.

Within a week, Jed had recovered sufficiently to leave the hospital. Although a bit withdrawn and still frightened by all that had happened to him, he was, in every other way, a normal ten-year-old. He left the hospital with his father and twin, and his mother and sister, who had come to Memphis immediately when they learned Jed was sick.

I saw Jed each month following the hospitalization. His health was fine; he had no paralysis from the brain injury, no seizures, no headaches. Yet he seemed slightly afraid to get out and do much. He walked to school instead of riding his bike, he played more inside and less outside, and he was reluctant to get involved in school activities. Perhaps the pressure of the blood clot on his brain had injured the frontal lobe, which controls emotion. Or maybe he was still shaken by the accident and his operation. I wasn't sure, but about three months after the injury, during one of his regular office visits, Jed's father said his son had something to tell me.

"What is it?" I asked Jed.

"I made the baseball team!" he answered with a wide grin.

I realized then the operation had been successful, his recovery complete. I returned to the clinic, my spirits high, and spent much of the afternoon with one patient, Harvey Johnson.

Mr. Johnson was fifty-eight years old and had been operated on for a brain abscess in 1954, when he was twenty-seven. Brain abscesses were almost invariably fatal then, with mortality rates greater than 90 percent. But a collection of pus in his temporal lobe resulting from mastoiditis had been successfully drained by a neurosurgeon. Mr. Johnson was a medical fluke; he should have been dead. He had been left paralyzed in his right arm and leg and unable to talk, but he had lived. Gradually, through the years, he had regained much of his speech and was able to walk on his weakened leg. He had not been to a doctor in twenty years and had returned only because the Social Security Administration required him to have a neurological examination to document his need for continued disability insurance payments. It was a unique opportunity for me to talk to someone who knew he should have died, and talk to him about life.

"Have you had a good life?" I asked Mr. Johnson.

"Oh, yes," he answered emphatically. He had no self-pity over the illness which had leveled him when he was a young man.

"We've raised three sons," his wife added. "One son teaches high school, one son is in the army, and our youngest son runs our chicken farm."

"Did you know the surgeon who operated on me?" Mr. Johnson stammered.

"Yes, I did," I answered, "but he's dead now."

"I know," he replied. "And he'll never know how much he gave me. I have a wonderful family. No one can ask for more than that. Don't you agree?"

"You're right," I said as I glanced at the picture of Laura and John on the corner of my desk.

Quickly I refocused my thoughts on medicine to avoid dwelling on the past. I reminded myself of the constructive ways I had used the increased free time that I now had living alone. For years I had written an hour or two each day and had accumulated over five hundred essays on patients and medicine. I had organized my journal into broad sections, including a study on death, surgical complications, surgical successes, patterns of disease within families, and long-term effects of disabling disease on marriages and children. I had completed

278

my first novel and enrolled in the night law school at Memphis State University, scheduled to begin in September 1984.

I didn't think much more about starting law school until March, about six months before I was scheduled to begin. One Monday afternoon I was leaving the office about five to return to Methodist Hospital to make evening rounds. Dr. Shelton stopped me outside the office and said, "I heard you're planning on going to law school."

"Yes, sir, that's right," I replied.

"What do you want with a law degree?" Dr. Shelton asked.

"It's not a degree I want," I answered, "it's the education. I just want to learn more about the law—partnerships, corporations, wills, trusts, taxes, estate planning. I think the information will be useful to me in the future."

"Do you think you have enough free time to go to law school?"

"Yes, sir, I do," I answered. "I'm enrolled in the night class —seven to ten P.M., three nights a week. The dean told me I could cut back on the number of courses I take if the reading load gets too heavy for me. Since I'm living by myself now, my evenings are free."

"I don't think it's a good idea," Dr. Shelton said. "I think you should be more committed to medicine. You're a full partner in the clinic now, and that brings additional responsibilities. You're already avoiding committee work in the hospital."

"That bores me," I interrupted.

"And you don't go to parties and journal club meetings where you would meet new doctors that could refer work to our group," Dr. Shelton continued. "Building up referrals should be a major part of what you do at night, not writing or going to law school."

"My interests are different," I answered. "What I do after work is my business, not yours."

"It becomes my business when your interests impact on my group," Dr. Shelton snapped, struggling to control his temper. "Let me remind you that you were the only partner who didn't come to the Christmas party the clinic gave for all our referring doctors. You needed to meet those doctors to ensure they continue to refer us patients. Medicine is a business, and I expect you to treat it that way."

"You know I don't like cocktail parties," I said. "And the fact that I didn't go to that party won't affect the clinic's income."

"We better have a meeting and hammer out your future," Dr. Shelton called as I walked away and got into my car.

Two days later, at 7 P.M., I met with the other five partners in the second-floor library. The paneled walls were lined with solemn prints of such pioneering physicians as Cushing, Dandy, and Salk. Their brooding faces gazed down over the oblong mahogany conference table. We pulled our leather armchairs up to the table, and Dr. Shelton presided from the end of the table framed by a bay window and twelve-foot floor-to-ceiling navy-blue drapes. I sat opposite Dr. Shelton, my back to the hundreds of leather-bound, musty medical textbooks lining one wall. After the coffeepot had been passed around the table, Dr. Shelton began.

"Tonight I want to discuss Dr. Rainer's plans for law school," Dr. Shelton said as I stared at him. The other partners sipped on their coffee and squirmed uneasily in their chairs. "It seems Dr. Rainer believes his responsibilities to the group end after his hospital work is completed." Dr. Shelton paused, but when no one else joined the conversation he continued. "Neurosurgery requires a full-time commitment, and I have always demanded that from each partner in this clinic. I don't think it wise to allow a partner to embark on something as time-consuming as law school without a vote of the group. After all, if Dr. Rainer's productivity falls off, as I suspect it will once he starts studying law, it will mean less income for all of us. Does anyone have any comments?"

There was no response from any of the other surgeons. They looked at Dr. Shelton or at the computer printout in front of them, but no one would meet my eye. It was a kangaroo court, and everyone knew it. Dr. Shelton had already made up his mind, and no one would come to my defense over the wishes of the senior partner.

"Yes," I spoke up. "I have some comments."

"Okay," Dr. Shelton mumbled.

"I call everyone's attention to the practice statistics on the computer printout in front of you. If you look at the bottom of page two, under the column marked "Total Procedures," you will see that during the last year I did more surgical procedures than anyone else in this group. I did eight hundred seventy-nine, Dr. Shelton was second at eight hundred thirty-nine, and the low man in the group only did five hundred ninety-eight. The statistics don't support Dr. Shelton's argument against my enrolling in law school. He's arguing philosophy, not facts."

"Whether it is philosophy or not," Dr. Shelton interjected, "I don't believe it's respectable for our group if one partner is living alone in an apartment, refusing to socialize and attend parties and journal club meetings, and devoting an excessive amount of time to nonmedical activities."

"Would you like me to detail how other partners are spending their evenings?" I asked.

"The other partners are not under discussion," Dr. Shelton shouted. "You are!"

"You mean they're not on trial," I replied.

"I don't want to argue with you," Dr. Shelton continued. "I simply want a vote from the group on whether or not to allow you to go to law school."

Dr. Shelton then called each partner's name, asked if he had anything to add, then requested his vote. As I expected, the other four partners voted with Dr. Shelton.

"Good," said Dr. Shelton when the final partner had voted. "Let the minutes show the vote was unanimous that Dr. Rainer not be allowed to attend law school."

"Wait a minute," I said. "The vote wasn't unanimous. I'm a full partner in this clinic and entitled to one vote. I vote that I be allowed to attend law school. That makes the vote five to one, but not unanimous."

"The vote has been recorded," Dr. Shelton replied. "If you persist with your law school plans, then we will end our association with you."

"Then that's the way it will have to be," I said. "I won't let you tell me what I can do at night."

The weeks that followed brought detailed negotiations over dissolving my association with the group. Bitter arguments arose over the amount of money I had in the pension plan, the amount of stock I owned in the corporation, and who was responsible, the corporation or me, for my final malpractice insurance premium of $21,000. The settlement negotiated by the lawyers was a compromise accepted grudgingly by Dr. Shelton and me. We both wanted the discussions behind us so we could return to practicing medicine, where there had always been respect, and never disagreement, between us.

On a summer evening in June 1984, I left Memphis, eight years after I had first moved there. I watched the lights of the city fade in my rearview mirror. A myriad of thoughts and recollections flooded my mind: successful operations and life, disease and death, the cheerful early years of my marriage, the births of Laura and John, twenty-hour days, holidays on call, divorce, surgeons who were friends, people I wished I had known better. I kept the good memories and discarded the bad, like throwing away a rough draft. I headed south for the seven-hour drive passing through Tupelo, Mississippi, Birmingham, Alabama, then Goodwater, Gold Hill and Opelika, and finally into my hometown, Auburn.

Auburn was a small town with a population of twenty thousand people. Even when the neighboring town, Opelika, was counted, the entire population in the area was only fifty thousand, a marked difference from the one million population in the Memphis area. The tallest building off the Auburn University campus, the hospital, was only four floors. There were very few traffic lights, and most intersections were four-way stops. The roads were narrow and marked on the edges for bicycle paths. Even a few dirt streets remained. The water tank in the middle of the graveyard was unchanged, except that the high school class of 1984 had painted it pink. The trailer park behind Shoney's Big Boy restaurant was still there, but the trailer Kelly and I had lived in was gone, probably condemned by the city board of health. Very little had changed since I had been home. Even the driving time from the west city limits sign to the east city limits sign was the same—five minutes.

Kelly was just getting up about 6:30 when I pulled into his driveway. He stumbled out to my car to welcome me, his thick, black hair in disarray, looking like it had survived the nuclear accident at Three Mile Island. "Come on in and help yourself to some coffee," Kelly said. "I'll take a shower and get dressed before I frighten someone else."

I poured a cup of coffee, then went back outside and walked around the yard, enjoying the morning stillness. The dew felt cool on my loafers. In Memphis I had lived in an apartment surrounded by concrete, not grass. It seemed unusually quiet for 7 A.M., but in Auburn, unlike in Memphis, there was no traffic on the streets yet.

Kelly, who was practicing dentistry in Auburn, pushed his first appointment back to ten, then took me to the Waffle House on the interstate for breakfast. We located an apartment on campus with a three-month lease, and I moved in that morning. The college students' blaring stereos introduced me to Madonna. Tanned co-eds in halter tops, preparing to go to class, mingled around the bike racks. A few girls in bikinis were already floating on rafts in the pool. The apartment was small and gloomy, but Kelly assured me he would visit me regularly.

On the way back to Kelly's office we rode by the house we had been raised in. Mother and Dad had sold it and moved to Florida. It had been fifteen years since Dad had kicked Kelly and me out of that house. We got out of the car and stood in the front yard as we reminisced about the party in 1969 that had resulted in our eviction. We both started laughing as we walked around the yard, looking at the air-conditioning unit that had been on fire, the driveway where Dad had dressed us down, our parents' bedroom where Mother had found the last couple kissing.

I looked at the brick house standing gracefully on a small knoll with its long, columned front porch framed by oak and pine trees. The house looked in good repair. The driveway was cracked but level. The shutters were still painted gray. The bumpy side yard where we had played croquet was smoother. The trees were taller and bushier and shaded the roof more now. The house looked solid. It, like myself, had weathered the years well.

CHAPTER 12

FINAL WORDS

CHARLES HENDERSON lay quietly in bed, flat on his back, his head tilted to the left as he craned his neck to look outside through the sliding glass door, its vertical blinds open widely to let more light into the small room. From his ground-floor, semiprivate room at the county nursing home in Opelika, he could only see a few pine trees, the hospital a hundred yards beyond the parking lot, and leafless hardwoods bordering the highway. The gray winter rain had convinced all but the ambulance drivers to stay inside.

Mrs. Henderson, seated in a small wicker chair next to his bed, rubbed his paralyzed left arm and leg and wiped away the saliva drooling out of the corner of his mouth from his twisted, paralyzed face. Every few minutes she paused to dab the blood still trickling down his neck from a cut beside his Adam's apple.

"She nearly cut my throat this morning shaving me," Mr. Henderson said, turning away from the window to face me and watch while I took his blood pressure.

"Charlie Henderson! You should be ashamed of yourself!"

Mrs. Henderson exclaimed with mock anger. "I've shaved you more times than you care to remember. I think I'm entitled to one little scratch."

The blood pressure cuff whistled as I pumped it up. From the corner of my eye I saw Mr. Henderson wink at his wife. I paused before reading his blood pressure to enjoy the crow's feet lighting up at the edge of each eye when Mrs. Henderson returned his wink with a broad smile.

80/50. Mr. Henderson's blood pressure was much too low. Because of his hypertension, his normal blood pressure was 150/90. Why should it be so low now? I wondered. The stroke he had suffered three weeks ago, paralyzing the left side of his body and clouding his vision, would not affect his blood pressure. Internal bleeding? Perhaps. An ulcer could cause enough blood loss to lower his blood pressure. But there should be symptoms, some hint of trouble in his abdomen.

"Do you have any stomach pain?" I asked.

"No," he answered. "Why?"

"Your blood pressure is lower than usual. I thought you might have a bleeding ulcer."

"I don't think so, Doc. I've been eating everything on my tray, and I don't feel nauseated. I even ate some banana pudding Ruth brought last night."

"I'm going to check your blood count to be sure. It won't take but a minute."

I pricked Mr. Henderson's index finger with a razor blade, squeezed a thick drop of blood out, and filled a thin glass capillary tube with the blood. I walked down to the lab at the end of the hall, placed the capillary tube in a centrifuge, and sat down to wait three minutes until the blood had been spun down, compressing the cells and measuring the exact blood count.

I propped my feet up on the countertop, leaned back in the desk chair, and thought about meeting Mr. Henderson last year, shortly after I had begun practicing in Opelika.

About 10 P.M. on a Friday I had been returning from Loachapoka, a farming community near Auburn, after visiting a friend of mine with whom I had gone to high school but had not seen in sixteen years. As I was driving down the unpainted rural county highway, I crested a hill and saw a cow directly in my path. I swerved to avoid a collision, ran my car off the shoulder of the highway down a small ravine, and stuck my front tires in a muddy creek bed. I grabbed the flashlight in the glove compartment, jumped out of the car, and scrambled up the embankment.

From the road level, ten feet above my car, I could see there wasn't a single dent in my car. Just beyond the small creek was a hard-packed dirt road which would make pulling my car out easy. I was trembling with anger but didn't have a scratch or even any torn clothing to show for the accident.

I took a few deep breaths to calm down and then flashed the light on the highway to find a safe spot to stand and flag down a passing car. Across the road I could see the rotten, weathered fencepost that had fallen, allowing the cow to wander up on the highway. About thirty feet beyond the fence, I spotted the cow that had caused all my trouble. I scrambled back down the embankment to my car, jerked my trunk open, and looked through the tools, old clothes, fishing gear, and other junk in the trunk, searching for my shotgun. I pulled the sixteen-gauge out from under the spare tire and scurried back up to the highway.

The cow continued staring peacefully at me, munching the grass alongside the road and plopping its droppings squarely in the middle of the highway.

"Dammit!" I shouted when I realized the gun wasn't loaded. "No shells!"

I ran back to the car, afraid the cow would wander off before I could find my ammunition.

"You're not going to shoot my cow, are you?"

I jumped a foot, a shiver spreading down my spine when I heard the man speak. I hadn't thought anyone lived nearby, and the unexpected voice in the dark shadows scared me.

"It's fair to shoot her if you want," the man said, stepping across the creek into the faint yellow light from the open trunk. "But Bessie's a good milk cow, and I'd appreciate it if you'd just let me take her back to the pasture."

"That damn cow nearly killed me!"

"I'll fix the fence in the morning."

"Can I use your phone to call a wrecker?" I asked.

"If you'll let me take you home, I'll know where to bring your car when I pull it out of the creek."

"Okay," I answered. "But I need my car by noon."

"It'll be there."

I followed the farmer through a large pasture and over a hill to a smaller pasture beside his small frame house. He slipped the rope off the cow's neck and closed a sturdy gate behind her. From the front porch he leaned his head inside the screen door and said, "Ruthie, I'll be back in about thirty minutes. Bessie ran a car off the road and I'm going to give the man a ride back to town."

I climbed into the pickup truck and pushed the tools on the floorboard to one side.

"I live behind Auburn High School," I said. "Do you know where it is?"

"Sure do. I had a grandson who graduated there."

Fifteen minutes later he pulled the truck into my driveway.

"I'll have your car here tomorrow morning," he said. "I'm sorry about the accident."

"That's okay. It's just an inconvenience."

"Let me give you my name and address," the farmer said. "In case you find a problem with your car later, you'll know how to get in touch with me."

"The car's okay. Just a little muddy. Thanks for the ride home."

The centrifuge bell rang, announcing the three minutes were up and the blood count was ready to be read. I popped the lid open, retrieved the capillary tube, and laid it against a chart that computed blood count. Forty! Mr. Henderson's blood count was forty—absolutely normal. He wasn't bleeding internally; there was some other reason for his low blood pressure. I returned to his room to check him more closely.

From the doorway I watched as Mrs. Henderson helped him sit up in bed. Once upright, he helped support his weight with his good arm, while his left arm lay limp at his side. Mrs. Henderson rubbed lotion on her hands and began massaging his back, gradually rubbing the red wrinkle lines from the starched sheets out of his skin.

"Thank you, Ruthie. That feels good."

"You're welcome, darling. I've got to get you stronger so I can get you home again. I don't enjoy cooking just for myself."

"I can't wait until we're having supper together again."

"What do you want for your first dinner when you come home?"

"Spaghetti. That . . ."

Mr. Henderson's voice trailed. His head dropped; he fainted; then he slumped onto the floor.

I rushed over to the bed and helped Mrs. Henderson lift

him back into bed. In a few minutes, after lying flat, Mr. Henderson woke up, asking what had happened.

"You fainted," I answered.

"Why?" he asked. "Do strokes make you faint?"

"No," I answered.

I took his blood pressure again: 70/50. Dangerously low.

I rang the nurse's button. When the nurse answered, I asked her to bring me some IV fluids and the EKG machine. Even with the IV fluids running wide open, Mr. Henderson's blood pressure rose to only 80/60.

"I still feel dizzy," he said.

"Your blood pressure's low," I answered. "As soon as I get it back up to normal you'll feel better."

I pasted the EKG electrodes onto his chest. He lay there, his pajamas unbuttoned to the waist, eyes closed, his thick white hair falling over the left side of his forehead.

As I waited for the EKG machine to finish the tracing, I thought about that Saturday morning a year before, when Mr. Henderson had returned my car. I was already awake at 6:30 when I heard his pickup truck pull up in front of the house. I peeked out of the window and saw Mrs. Henderson driving it. Minutes later Mr. Henderson arrived in my car and parked it in the driveway. It had been completely washed, and even the white sidewalls showed no hint of mud. He stepped out of the car and walked over toward the pickup. He turned and looked one more time at my car, then walked back over to it and rubbed the chrome bumper under the headlights with his handkerchief. Moments later he left with his wife in their truck.

I hadn't thought much more about the car accident in the year since it had happened until three weeks earlier, when I was called to the emergency room to see a patient with a stroke. I recognized Mr. Henderson immediately when I entered the room.

His appearance hadn't changed in the year since I had seen him. He was tall, about 6'4", and lanky, with big, muscular arms, a tanned face and bushy white hair giving him a distinguished look. The emergency room chart said he was seventy-eight years old, but he looked sixty. He lay in the E.R. vomiting, holding the right side of his head, complaining of headache, and upset that he could not move his left arm and leg. But most of all he seemed upset by his loss of vision.

"Ruthie, are you there, Ruthie?" he repeatedly asked. "I'm having trouble seeing."

Mrs. Henderson moved closer to him, held his hand, and answered softly, "I'm here, Charlie."

Tests showed a massive stroke in the right side of his brain due to atherosclerotic closure of his right carotid artery. There was no treatment for the stroke except physical therapy and control of his hypertension. After two weeks in the hospital I moved him to the nursing home. Mrs. Henderson couldn't care for him by herself at home, and she couldn't afford full-time nurse's aides to help her. We hadn't told Mr. Henderson he wasn't going home; just that he was in the nursing home temporarily. He did fine except at night, when Mrs. Henderson left to go home. After her car pulled out of the parking lot each night, he cried. But neither I, nor the nurses, had the heart to tell Mrs. Henderson.

The EKG strip flipped out of the machine onto the floor before I realized it was completed. I bent over, picked it up, and stretched it out in front of me across the machine to read it. I was shocked by the results. The EKG confirmed Mr. Henderson had suffered a massive heart attack, a peculiar silent type which wasn't accompanied by chest pain. The same atherosclerosis affecting the arteries to his brain had also affected his coronary arteries.

Now I knew his diagnosis, and why his blood pressure was so low. He was in cardiogenic shock. Much of his heart muscle had been destroyed by the heart attack and was now too weak to pump blood. Insufficient blood circulating to his brain had caused the dizziness and fainting and accounted for his low blood pressure. I also knew he would die.

"What is it?" Mr. Henderson asked me.

"The EKG shows you've had a heart attack," I answered. "Now you'll have to stay in bed more." I glanced at Mrs. Henderson, not wanting to meet Mr. Henderson's eyes.

"It's worse than that, isn't it?" he asked.

I sat down on the edge of the bed, looked directly at Mr. Henderson, and answered, "Yes."

"How long?" he asked.

"Let me take your blood pressure," I answered.

"What is it now?" Mrs. Henderson asked.

"60/40," I answered.

"How long?" Mr. Henderson asked again.

"A few hours," I said softly.

Mr. Henderson reached up with his right arm, placed it around Mrs. Henderson's neck, and pulled her to him. I injected dopamine, a medication to strengthen the heart contractions and raise the blood pressure, into the IV.

"Nothing fancy, okay?" Mr. Henderson said as he watched me put the medication into the IV.

"Yes, sir."

Mrs. Henderson continued resting her head on his shoulder, her left hand brushing his hair back from his forehead. Mr. Henderson squeezed her neck softly, then ran his gnarled, knotted fingers through her white hair. He spread his fingers wide, allowing the strands of her hair to run through his hand like a brush. He tucked her hair behind her ears and touched her cheeks and lips with his fingers. When her tears began to hit his chest he rubbed her eyes with the back of his hand. Huge, rough working man's hands, but delicately soft wherever he touched her.

"We had sixty good years together, didn't we, Ruthie?"

"We sure did."

"And you were always the prettiest girl on the block."

"In 1920, Charlie, I was the only girl on the block."

"Well, you're still the prettiest."

Mr. Henderson was shivering now, his falling blood pressure making his body cold.

"Could you bring me our blanket from home?" Mr. Henderson asked.

"Of course, darling."

Mrs. Henderson called her daughter and asked her to bring the quilt to the nursing home.

"Remember when we courted, Ruthie?"

"Yes."

"Remember your father catching us kissing on the screen porch?"

"Oh, how he screamed at me."

"I guess this heart attack means we can't fool around any more."

Mrs. Henderson hugged his neck tightly, whispering, "Just until you're stronger, darling."

For twenty minutes they lay together on the bed, saying nothing. Only the movements of Mr. Henderson's fingers through his wife's hair were noticeable, and only the soft clicking of Mrs. Henderson's kisses on his neck were audible. Otherwise the room was still.

An hour later his blood pressure had fallen to 50/40, barely enough to keep him conscious. But still he held his wife's hand and smiled each time their eyes met.

When their daughter arrived, Mrs. Henderson spread the quilt across the bed, pulling it up to Mr. Henderson's chin. He rubbed several of the colorful plaid patches within his reach and then stretched the quilt to reach his nose. Now his strength was failing more rapidly, his energy depleting with each moment his heart weakened and his blood pressure fell. Slowly, struggling, he began pulling the quilt to the right until much of the quilt lay on the floor beside his bed, and only half of it still covered him.

Once again he stretched the quilt to his nose, inhaled deeply, and then said, "I want your half over me, Ruthie."

Mrs. Henderson sat back down in the wicker chair next to the bed and laid her head on his chest. His daughter kissed his forehead, then went back out into the hallway. I sat silently on the empty bed in the room, already missing the softspoken farmer dying beside me.

Born into a farming family, he had finished only the sixth grade. When he was sixteen, his father had died and he had taken over the dairy farm. At eighteen he had married Ruth Lankston, the county vet's daughter. They had three children: a son who had moved away, a son who had died from tuberculosis, and a daughter who had married poorly, divorced, and now lived with her parents. He didn't smoke, drink, or talk about religion. All this and more he had told me during his last three weeks in the hospital. We had discussed my divorce and my children living in Atlanta. Why an interest in me? Because of sons he never talked to? Advice he never got to give? Perhaps. And always he ended our conversations with a smile and a wink, saying, "One day I'll tell you the secret to a happy marriage."

I looked at Mr. Henderson lying pale on the bed next to me, breathing shallowly now, eyes closed, no movement anywhere. Then I noticed his right hand lying by his side, no longer touching Mrs. Henderson's arm. It was the moment I knew he had died. I knew it more surely than if I had seen a straight line on the EKG monitor or heard no blood pressure with my stethoscope. He had said good-bye.

I led Mrs. Henderson out of the room and down the hall to the dayroom. Her daughter poured us a cup of coffee, sat down next to her mother, and put her arm around her. But Mrs. Henderson was smiling, and comforted her daughter who was crying now.

"We had a wonderful life together, dear," she said to her daughter. "Our love will keep us together while we're apart."

"I'll miss him so much, Mother."

"I will, too. But he left us with so many wonderful memories. Just think about those."

"Mrs. Henderson," I said quietly. "May I ask you a personal question?"

"Yes. What is it?"

"Mr. Henderson used to say that one day he would tell me the secret to a happy marriage. He never told me. Could you tell me what he would have said?"

"I don't know for sure," Mrs. Henderson said. "But I know he lived his love every day, and he was never afraid to show me his emotions."

"I see," I said, standing to leave.

"And I'll tell you something else," Mrs. Henderson said to

296

me, motioning me to sit back down. "I don't think Charlie would mind if I told you."

I sat down at the table and sipped my coffee as Mrs. Henderson looked down, collecting her thoughts.

"Most nights I went to bed before Charlie," she said. "I rubbed my hands with lotion before he came to bed so my hands would be softer and fresher when he touched them. He would shower and put on fresh pajamas before he crawled under the sheets. When he turned back the covers, I always put my book down, turned off the light, and held his hand until he fell asleep. He always hugged me and held me for a few minutes, no matter how tired he was. And every night after he kissed me good night, he whispered in my ear, 'Ruthie, this is the best part of my day.' "

The first four operations of the day proceeded uneventfully. Two of the patients had ruptured discs in their backs requiring surgery, one patient had a broken neck requiring a bone graft fusion, and the fourth patient had a malignant brain tumor which I decompressed, ensuring him one more year of life. At 5 P.M. I stretched out on the sofa in the surgeons' lounge to rest my throbbing feet. I wasn't in any hurry to go home. Thirty minutes to rest and unwind after nine hours in the operating room was more important to me than a date or a dinner out.

An hour later I got up, showered, changed clothes, then made ward rounds to check on each of the postoperative patients. When I was sure each patient was alert, with stable blood pressure and no excessive bleeding on the dressings, I left to go home.

At seven o'clock the summer evening was warm, with an

hour of daylight left. I picked up the newspaper in the front yard and retrieved several bills, a *Time* magazine, and a letter from the mailbox. I looked at the letter first, recognizing the scrawling handwriting of my seven-year-old daughter, Laura. As always, her letter was addressed to Daddy Rainer, Auburn, Alabama.

The postman had never missed delivering her letters, even though the address was incomplete. There were only two Rainers in Auburn: my brother and me. The postman knew the letter was for me—my brother's son didn't write letters to his father. He lived with him.

I sat down on the front steps and opened Laura's letter slowly, savoring each letter, each word, even the way the paper was folded.

"Dear Daddy," the letter began, "I miss you. When will you come see me? I went swimming today. I can jump off the high board now. Please come soon. I love you, Laura."

Inside the house I rummaged through the kitchen until I found a napkin to wipe my eyes. I fixed a cup of coffee and sat down at my desk, pushing bills and books to one side. I leaned back in my chair thinking about Laura, and wondering, too, what John was doing. He never said much about his activities when I visited, and he was too young to write. A friend and his father had taken John trout fishing, and he had camped one weekend. I knew he was very proud of the baseball glove, fly rod, and tool box friends had given him. But he never asked me for anything, except to stay longer when I came to Atlanta to see him.

And Laura—I see her two days each month. She sleeps in my house one night a month. I talk to her on the phone for a few minutes each Sunday morning. I send her a card on holidays, occasionally a letter. I've got to let her know how much I love her; I've got to live my love like Mr. Henderson did. I've got to show her how often I think of her, how much I miss her.

"My dearest Laura," I began my letter, but I was interrupted by the phone ringing.

"Dr. Rainer?"

"Yes."

"This is Jan, the nurse in the emergency room. We have a patient who was just brought in by ambulance from Tuskegee. He's been shot in the head—a hunting accident. The emergency room doctor needs you quickly."

"I'll be right there."

I grabbed my coat to go back to the hospital, then paused beside my desk, looking at the letter I had just begun. Tomorrow, I thought. I'll write Laura and John tomorrow.

ABOUT THE AUTHOR

J. Kenyon Rainer, M.D., is a neurosurgeon in private practice in Auburn, Alabama. He is Chief of Surgery at the East Alabama Medical Center. Dr. Rainer is certified by the American Board of Neurological Surgery. He is a Fellow of the American College of Surgeons and the International College of Surgeons. His daughter, Laura, is eight years old and his son, John, seven.